CHILDREN AS ENGINEERS

Meeting the diverse aspects of the science, and design and technology curricula can be challenging for many teachers. *Children as Engineers* addresses this problem, offering both new and experienced teachers an accessible resource to apply within the classroom and to their own professional development, while also supporting their students in developing as STEM thinkers. With an explicit focus on sustainability, each aspect of the curriculum is explored through a series of engineering challenges that present pupils with an everyday problem to be solved practically.

Filled with practical strategies to use in the classroom, topics covered include the following:

- The engineering design process
- Plants, animals and humans
- Everyday materials
- Living things and habitats
- Forces, light and sound
- States of matter
- Electricity

This essential classroom resource will support primary teachers in embedding opportunities for contextualised STEM experiences into their lessons, so that all children can develop as current and future learners of STEM.

Fay Lewis was a primary teacher for 15 years. She is currently a Senior Lecturer and Programme Leader within the School of Education and Childhood at UWE, Bristol where she teaches the STEM course for the primary Initial Teacher Education programme and provides continued professional development to a range of education professionals through her work on the M.A. Education.

Juliet Edmonds is a Programme Leader for the international PGCE at UWE, Bristol and teaches the Primary Science modules on Primary Education courses. For many years, she taught in London primary schools as a science specialist, before becoming an advisory teacher for Science and Assessment at Hammersmith and Fulham. Additionally, she has contributed to the Primary Committee for the ASE and advised Friends of the Earth on their educational materials and strategy.

CHILDREN AS ENGINEERS

Teaching Science, Design Technology and Sustainability through Engineering in the Primary Classroom

Fay Lewis and Juliet Edmonds

LONDON AND NEW YORK

Designed cover image: © Getty Images

First published 2024
by Routledge
4 Park Square, Milton Park, Abingdon, Oxon OX14 4RN

and by Routledge
605 Third Avenue, New York, NY 10158

Routledge is an imprint of the Taylor & Francis Group, an informa business

© 2024 Fay Lewis and Juliet Edmonds

The right of Fay Lewis and Juliet Edmonds to be identified as authors of this work has been asserted in accordance with sections 77 and 78 of the Copyright, Designs and Patents Act 1988.

All rights reserved. The purchase of this copyright material confers the right on the purchasing institution to photocopy pages which bear the photocopy icon and copyright line at the bottom of the page. No other parts of this book may be reprinted or reproduced or utilised in any form or by any electronic, mechanical, or other means, now known or hereafter invented, including photocopying and recording, or in any information storage or retrieval system, without permission in writing from the publishers.

Trademark notice: Product or corporate names may be trademarks or registered trademarks, and are used only for identification and explanation without intent to infringe.

British Library Cataloguing-in-Publication Data
A catalogue record for this book is available from the British Library

ISBN: 978-1-032-35209-1 (hbk)
ISBN: 978-1-032-35210-7 (pbk)
ISBN: 978-1-003-32582-6 (ebk)

DOI: 10.4324/9781003325826

Typeset in Interstate
by MPS Limited, Dehradun

CONTENTS

1 Science and design and technology through engineering?   1

2 The engineering design process   20

3 Plants/states of matter   41

4 Animal and humans   57

5 Everyday materials, their uses and properties   73

6 Living things and habitats   88

7 Forces   108

8 Light and sound   125

9 States of matter   145

10 Science focus: Electricity   164

11 Summary and key thoughts   182

Appendix   188
Index   195

1 Science and design and technology through engineering?

Introduction

This book serves as a teachers' resource that sets out the research, rationale, model, and resources for teaching science and design and technology through engineering in primary and elementary schools. This approach is not about asking teachers to teach an extra subject in an already crowded curriculum, but instead, introduces a different approach to teaching science and design and technology with real-world contexts and applications.

Engineering is the application of science and technology to solve problems. To represent this activity, each chapter presents a series of engineering challenges based on 'real-life' environmentally focussed problems. The challenges introduce children to a fictional character who is experiencing a 'real-life' problem and asks them to design, make, and evaluate a product to help to solve this problem. Children are supported in finding the best possible solution to these challenges through the embedding and application of their knowledge of science and design and technology.

Rather than requiring children to make a predetermined product and providing a set of instructions of how to make this, here, the product to be made as a solution to the challenges set is left more open ended. Children use the Engineering Design Process (EDP) to research, investigate, design, and make their own suitable solutions. This enables them to apply their scientific knowledge in depth, exploring concepts, and growing their understanding as their product is being developed. In this way, children and teachers explore and experience an enquiry-based approach and a true reflection of how these subjects interact and intertwine in the real world, the true multidisciplinary approach to STEM (science, technology, engineering, and maths) subjects as advocated by English et al. (2016), Banks and Barlex (2014), and Gomez and Albrecht (2013).

A full explanation and exploration of the Engineering Design Process and how this works in the primary/ elementary classroom is provided in Chapter 2.

So, if science is the exploration of our natural and physical world and technology is the application of science why is such a multidisciplinary approach necessary; why not do separate subjects? Multidisciplinary STEM approaches provide opportunities for teachers to encompass real-world, problem-based learning into their lessons (STEM Task force report, 2014) and offer children realistic examples of how STEM subjects are encountered beyond

DOI: 10.4324/9781003325826-1

the classroom. Engineering has the potential to provide a cohesive link across the disciplines (Bryan et al., 2015; Lucas et al., 2014; NGSS, 2013; The National Academies, 2014; Barnes, 2018) and yet, despite this, the integration of the 'E' element of multidisciplinary STEM approaches is almost non-existent at the primary or elementary level internationally (Cunningham, 2009; Hoachlander, 2015; English et al., 2016). This book fills this gap by providing a resource for teachers that frames teaching and learning within science and design and technology through a series of engineering challenges.

This book therefore aims to deliver an alternative, long-term approach to the way that STEM subjects are taught.

A sustainable focus

STEM-focussed engineering challenges could be drawn from many sources (literature, topics covered across the curriculum, current affairs etc.). However, the engineering challenges presented in this book arise from issues surrounding climate change and sustainable development. The consequences of climate change are becoming part of our world, impacting the everyday lives of young people and children. As a result, the Sustainable Development Goals (SDGs) have been developed as part of The 2030 Agenda for Sustainable Development, adopted by all United Nations Member States (UN, 2015). These call for urgent actions to address poverty, education, health, and other inequalities all whilst tackling climate change. A recent report showed that most young people are willing to support such key habits in reducing climate change and called for further opportunities to develop pedagogies and practices in all schools to support young people in learning about and mitigating this (Jones, 2021). The materials presented in this book sit within these sustainable development goals to capture this interest and to provide practical resources and support for teachers and children.

> **Our Mission**
>
> This book aims to provide teachers with the background subject knowledge, ideas, and resources needed to be able to adopt a multidisciplinary approach to teaching science and design and technology through engineering whilst also working towards developing understanding of the UN Sustainable Development Goals.

Grounding STEM learning within a 'real-world' inquiry-based context

Having a clear context in which to embed new knowledge and understanding has been advocated as an effective strategy to enhance children's learning within any subject. The cognitive theorist Ausubel (1961) argued that new concepts form by building on existing ideas or knowledge. Grounding new knowledge and understanding within a familiar real-world context may therefore help children to make sense of new material presented to them, impacting on the nature and depth of their understanding, as supported by recent research in educational neuroscience (Goswami, 2020). It would therefore be remiss to learn STEM concepts without a clear link to the world around the child and a consideration of how they link to the child's life.

The process of taking an abstract STEM concept, using it, and testing it in real life can support the development and consolidation of that concept in the child's mind. Children form their ideas of the world and the science that governs this through their senses from their first days on Earth (Gopnik, 2012) but even at the primary/elementary school age, most children still need concrete experiences to help them form their ideas in STEM subjects. This can happen through the manipulation and observation of materials and living things as well as practical experiences, ensuring that ideas are linked to what has been observed (Abrahams and Millar, 2008). Contextualising STEM learning in this way not only builds on the concepts that children have already established about the world around them and extends their understanding, but it is also when misconceptions become evident. Through such work, teachers are therefore able to identify, assess, and meet learning needs more thoughtfully.

The approach presented here is at the intersection of discussions about what 'inquiry' teaching means in STEM and the embedding of enriched and deep understanding into science lessons. Before children can engage in critical thinking and problem solving, it is desirable to first teach the necessary foundational content knowledge. There will be fundamental aspects of understanding that the children will either require to be able to engage with the challenge itself or to successfully create a product to solve the challenge posed to them. The activities and resources presented here are therefore grounded in different areas of scientific and design and technology concepts and skills so that these aspects of the curriculum are covered and can be applied in a meaningful manner.

Case Study: Building a vacuum cleaner

Contextualised problem: Can you make a vacuum cleaner to clear up the paper streamers left over after a classroom party?

In carrying out an activity with 11-year-olds, to build a vacuum cleaner with propellers (Figure 1.1) the children all drew and cut out two-dimensional flower petal-shapes out of cardboard. When these were tested, the children were surprised that they were no good at scooping up the air. The design and technology focus the lesson that was on evaluation skills. However, it became obvious that the children did not have any hands-on experience or understanding of propellers and so were unable to suggest ways to improve their products, as application of their knowledge revealed a deficit in an understanding of the basic science around air resistance and thrust. In response to this, the teacher then took a couple of steps backwards to explore propellers and watermills to help the children's understanding of the science.[1]

4 Science and design and technology through engineering?

Figure 1.1 Building a vacuum cleaner

The process of taking STEM knowledge and applying it to a real-life context can also give children an appreciation of the role that STEM subjects play in our society. Although dated now, Murphy and Beggs (2003) found attitudes to science were impacted by the perceived relevance of the science being learnt. The less children could see the relevance of the science that they were being taught the less they liked the subject. The OECD (2006) even argue that an 'awareness of how science and technology shape our material, intellectual and cultural environment' is an essential part of scientific literacy that every adult should have.

Why use engineering as a context for STEM learning?

Engineers are vital to the way we live. Their work pervades our everyday experiences and activities making everything we do in our everyday lives possible. Without engineers, the world would be a very different place.

Activity

Look around you: What has been engineered?

Chances are you will see a building from a civil engineer, chairs and tables from design engineers, and vehicles from mechanical engineers. But what about the clothes you are wearing, the food you ate today, and even yourself?

Would any of these be here without engineers working on medical, transport, and manufacturing innovations over many, many years?

In fact, without engineers, you may be standing in an uncultivated patch of land and naked! You may not even be here at all. At some point in your ancestral history, medical interventions made possible by engineers are likely to have occurred to keep you and your family members alive and well.

When we consider how much of the everyday world that children interact with has been engineered it seems strange that such little attention is paid to the human-made world and the STEM understanding that underpins this in early education. With this in mind, it seems odd that engineering is almost non-existent at the primary/elementary level internationally (Cunningham, 2009; Hoachlander, 2015; English et al., 2016) (except the United States, who have integrated engineering into the National Science Standards (NRC, 2014) despite it being an ideal opportunity to ground wider STEM learning within everyday and familiar contexts.

The resources presented in this book offer teachers an opportunity to bridge this gap, linking the science and design and technology curricula learning objectives with real-life experiences of engineering and the engineering design process.

Case Study: Making a floating platform (Engineer, 2015)

Contextualised problem: Can you make something to carry personal items whilst swimming so that they do not get wet?

To design and make a solution to this problem the children had to explore and develop their knowledge of floating, density of materials, and displacement. At first, many children were observed trying to evaluate the weight of the various materials and much effort was put into only using materials that were deemed light enough. This revealed misconceptions around density, buoyancy, and forces as the children thought that floating platforms made from heavy materials would sink. The teacher challenged these misconceptions by showing the children pictures of large cargo ships and asked the children if they thought that these were light or heavy. The children then tested a variety of materials of differing densities to explore how well they floated or if they sank. Following this, the children were then able to adapt their ideas about using materials such as plastic piping and bottles in their platforms as they had developed a better understanding of the role of the air inside the bottle or pipe. This learning was more relevant to the children than it may have been in a stand-alone lesson as the children had an immediate use for it and it was introduced on a need-to-know basis (Figure 1.2).

6 *Science and design and technology through engineering?*

Figure 1.2 Building a floating platform

Learning science and design and technology through engineering is also interesting and fun; it has a practical focus and allows the children to work collaboratively (see Figure 1.3 as an illustration). The use of practical problem-solving tasks in engineering has been found to increase children's positive attitudes to science and engineering and most of the children reported that they wanted to do more activities such as these (Fogg-Rogers *et al.*, 2015).

Science and design and technology through engineering? 7

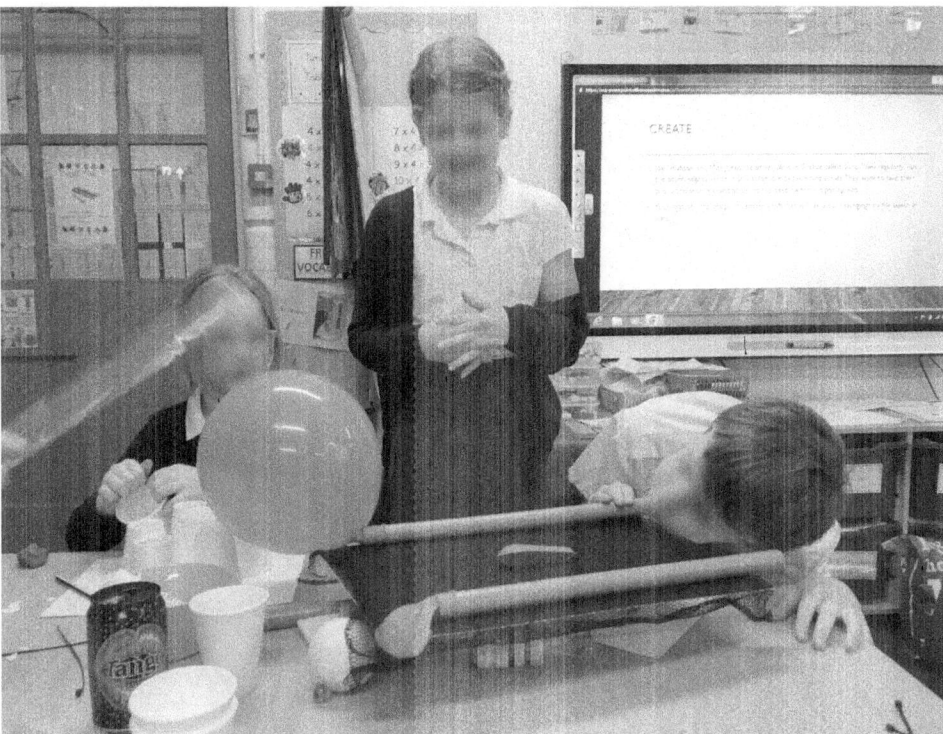

Figure 1.3 Having fun with engineering

Whilst it is good to know that children enjoy the learning activities they undertake, enjoyment has also been found to enhance learning (Harlen, 2018); the more fun the children have, the more they learn.

Learning science through engineering activities allows for context-rich learning, problem solving drawing on scientific knowledge, and skills as well as enjoyment.

Having presented the case for teaching science and design and technology through engineering, we will now look at what engineering is and explore the ideas children have about engineering.

What is engineering?

If you heard someone say the words 'engineer' or 'engineering,' which images would spring to mind? You may think of wooden cogs, heavy machinery, or people working with oily rags, or you may associate these terms with people fixing things such as washing machines and cars. If you were asked to describe engineering, you may use terms such as 'noisy' or 'dirty.' Often, young people only come to value and understand the possibilities that engineering offers when they are well past the primary/elementary phase of their education when they may have already made choices or developed preferences about subjects which would make it difficult for them to enter the engineering profession (Royal Academy of

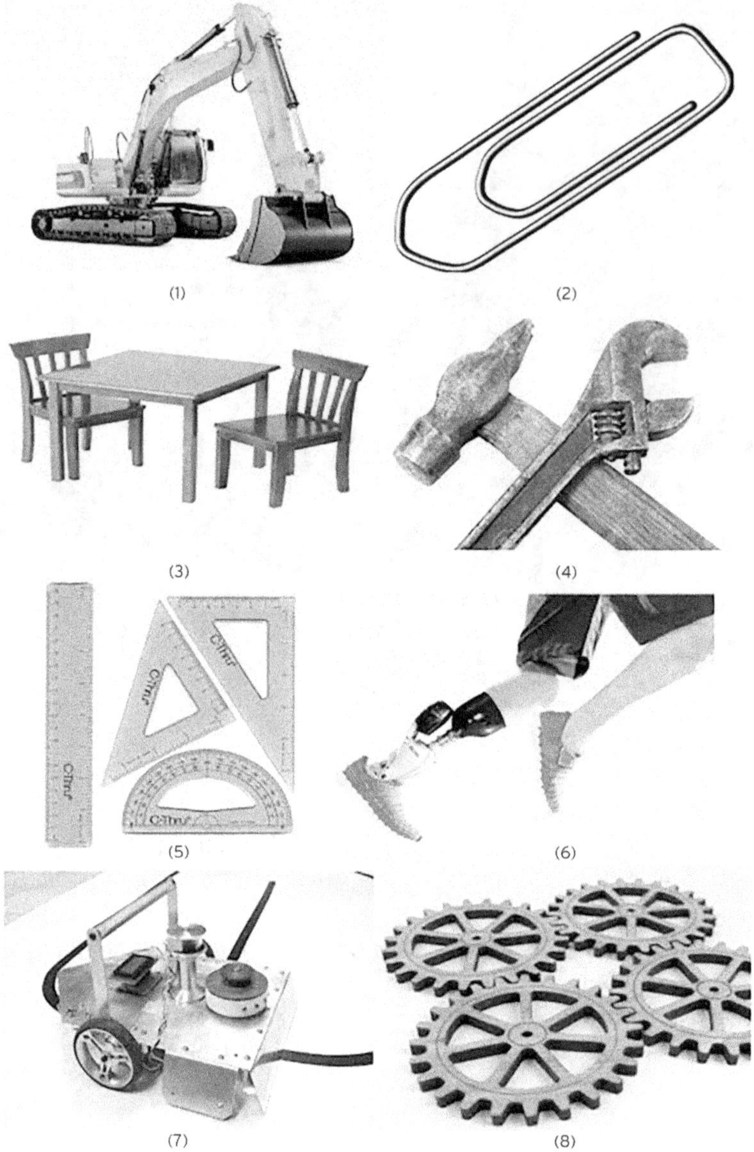

8 *Science and design and technology through engineering?*

Figure 1.4 Engineered objects?

Engineering, 2018). This approach therefore aims to change common perceptions of engineers and engineering for both teachers and children and to introduce the wonderful world of engineering into the primary and elementary classrooms.

So, what does engineering look like? Look at the pictures in Figure 1.4. Which depicts the process or products of engineering and why?

What does your selection of pictures tell you about your perception of engineering and engineers?

If you picked pictures 7 and/or 8, you may associate engineering with mechanical things. You would have been correct as this is certainly an aspect of some form of engineering.

If you picked picture 5, you may associate engineering with maths. Again, you were correct, engineering involves using and applying mathematical knowledge and skills as well as science understanding and concepts as we will see later.

If you picked pictures 1 and/or 4, you may have thought about heavy industry, dirty or oily work that may be manual and may involve fixing things. Although this is a common perception this only relates to a small aspect of engineering.

If you picked pictures 2 and/or 3, you associate engineering with everyday life. This is true!

Lastly, if you picked picture 6, you may associate engineering with problem solving and with making the world a better place. Again, this is true. Engineers look at issues surrounding us and try to find solutions to problems.

In fact, all these pictures could be associated with engineering; it pervades our lives on a routine basis. Ninety-five percent of our everyday environment is human made!

Activity: Thinking like an engineer. Engineering a cup of tea

Everything made by humans has been engineered in some way. You may have had a cup of tea this morning. Let us think about the tea bag you used. During the engineering process of a tea bag someone has had to consider if ...

- The string is long enough to fit over the edge of the cup without being pulled back in by the weight of the tea bag
- The paper is strong enough to hold the weight of the wet tea but light enough and thin enough to let the flavour out
- The perforations in the tea bag are big enough to let the flavour out but small enough to hold the tea leaves in
- The tea bag is big enough so that it contains enough tea for one cup and that the leaves can swell but that it is not too big so that it does not fit into a standard cup
- The tea bag uses glue that does not dissolve in hot water or influence the taste of the tea.

Even a humble tea bag has had a great deal of thought put into it!

Try it yourself

Have a look at a paper clip. What has been considered to make it work in just the right way? Think about the materials, size, shape, etc.

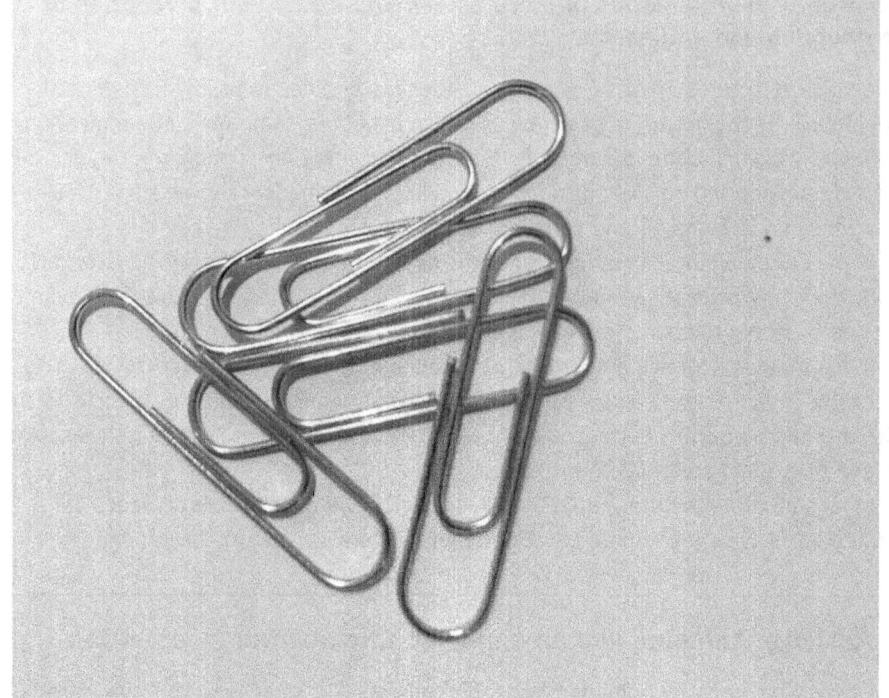

Figure 1.5 Paper clips

Class activity: Thinking like an engineer

Provide your class with a simple, everyday object (such as the tea bag or paper clip examples used above). Ask them to consider what has been thought about to make it work in just the right way. Think about the materials, size, shape, etc.

Public and children's perceptions of engineering

Despite the obvious importance of engineers and engineering, the public often perceive engineers as white men who wear hard hats and carry plans around with them or white men who do oily, noisy, or dirty jobs working with machinery. Many resort to the "conventional" stereotype of engineers as train operators or car mechanics (Knight and Cunningham 2004; Bartholomew, 2021) (Figure 1.6).

Like adults, children perceive engineers as men who design, make, and build things (Ata-Aktürkto and Demircan, 2022) (see Figure 1.5 for example). When Fralick *et al.* (2009) asked children to draw an engineer, the majority drew a man. Many children also drew surrounding objects; 32% of these were vehicles, 16% building tools, and 16% civil structures,

Figure 1.6 A child's depiction of engineers

with only 1.7% related to maths, 0.5% books, and 0.1% diplomas or qualifications. Actions inferred in the drawings strongly indicated that children perceive engineers as do-ers, engaged in lower-level mental processes and physical actions rather than thinkers. Fifty-two percent of the drawings inferred activities such as making, operating, and designing whilst only 6% inferred experimenting, observing, and explaining.

Although these activities are undeniably part of some engineering activities, these stereotypes can potentially dissuade children from pursuing careers in engineering and related fields.

> **Activity: Perceptions of engineers**
>
> Conduct a simple internet image search for the term 'engineer.' Chances are that the results will fit the stereotypes discussed above. Whilst many images for the term 'engineer' these days show women in this role, the images that you are likely to find will be predominantly of white men dressed in safety gear such as hard hats and high-vis jackets.
>
> It becomes clear why children may hold the perceptions that they do.

> **Class activity: Draw an engineer**
>
> Ask your class to draw an engineer. What do their pictures show? Do they focus on one gender or ethnicity? What do the objects held by, or surrounding, the engineers in their pictures indicate about their perception of engineers? You could use these drawings as a basis to challenge these preconceptions and discuss the roles that engineers play in society.

Having a positive interaction or encounter with an engineer or an engineering activity can change the stereotypical perceptions of engineers and engineering discussed above. Fogg-Rogers et al. (2015) reported that before an engineering outreach activity with 9-11-year-olds, the children reported that they thought engineers ...'*fix cars, build bridges, always get very oily and use spanners.*' Whilst after the activity they stated that engineers ... . '*Solve problems, design, and make things we need, make things better and keep improving things.*' Changing the perceptions of and attitudes towards engineers and engineering could potentially help to keep children engaged with STEM subjects throughout their education and further into their careers.

The importance of engineering

We know that pupils' interest in STEM subjects wanes as they reach the end of primary school (Murphy et al., 2005). De Witt et al. (2014) report, even if their interest is retained, their interest in science-based careers is not. Girls in particular make early value judgements (before age 11) on the suitability of STEM as a future career choice (Engineering UK, 2015; Jarvis and Pell, 2005; De Witt et al., 2014). But why should this matter?

Engineering as a career and industry is a key contributor to the a nation's aims for innovative knowledge and skills as well as the overall economy (Perkins, 2013). STEM graduates are crucial to the the economy, with research suggesting that STEM jobs were predicted to grow at double the rate of other occupations, creating 142,000 jobs before 2023 (Giddings, 2019). Despite this, we are facing a shortage of engineers. For example, according to the Royal Academy of Engineering (2012), in the United Kingdom there is a well-documented engineering skills crisis. An ageing workforce means that hundreds of thousands of skilled technicians and professional engineering roles will need replacing over the next ten years. Alongside the sheer number of engineers needed to be recruited into the profession, diversity is also a major issue. Only 7% of UK engineers are female, while only 6% are from Black and minority ethnic backgrounds (EngineeringUK, 2015).

These figures have led to multiple public relations and education programmes being launched to change the perception of engineering (EngineeringUK, 2015). Parents and teachers are identified as two key sources who may influence children to consider engineering as a career, and so are also key audiences with whom to engage (Perkins, 2013; Edmonds et al. 2020).

> **Activity: Importance of STEM subjects**
>
> Ask the children in your class what they want to be when they grow up. Some may say engineer or scientist, and that is great, but what about others who can see no relevance of STEM subjects to what they want to do or how they live their lives? It is easy to see why these children may dismiss STEM subjects. Spend time with the children that you teach talking to them about the relevance of STEM subjects to the things that they enjoy doing and their ideas about what they may want to do in the future.
>
> **Case Study:** Let us use Dylan as a case study to examine how we help children to make these connections.
>
> Dylan came from a family of horse breeders and wanted to be a horse rider when he grew up. He could see no relevance to science at all. His teacher helped him to realise that there were many relevant STEM aspects.
>
> **Science** - health and nutrition, animal care and medical needs, inheritance of favoured attributes, materials for blankets, and general care.
>
> **Technology** - measuring instruments, recording of a performance.
>
> **Engineering** - best fence and jump design and construction, prosthetics, splint leg supports.
>
> **Maths** - speed and distance measurements, course-plotting, angles, and shapes within dressage.

Even for those children who will not eventually end up working within the STEM market, STEM skills and knowledge are important across different career paths and other aspects of life (Hoyles et al., 2011; Dare et al., 2021). Whilst STEM employment grew three times faster than non-STEM employment between 2010-2012, there is a serious and looming skills mismatch for science- and engineering-based industries, with two-thirds of businesses who employ people with STEM skills reporting difficulties recruiting such employees (EU Commission, 2019).

Providing positive experiences within these subject areas can help to keep the doors open for STEM-based career choices for children and develop wider, transferrable skills. It would therefore appear to be important that children can access these positive experiences of STEM whilst still at primary school. Such experiences can produce a future workforce able to boost innovation, provide an economic return, as well as enhancing the educational and career prospects for the individual.

The Royal Academy of Engineering (2016) has identified the following factors could all potentially help to address this shortfall:

- improving the understanding of, and attitudes towards engineering among young people, their influencers, and the public.
- increasing support for teachers of STEM subjects.
- providing greater STEM support in primary schools.

Through exploring science through engineering, we can hope to contribute to these identified factors without overburdening primary teachers and the primary classroom timetable.

The possible impact of teaching science through engineering in the primary school

Having made the case for developing positive attitudes towards science and engineering we now turn our attention to the impact that teaching science and design and technology through engineering can have on your class of children. Is it worth doing and how can we make it more effective?

In the United States, at the Museum of Science, Boston, a programme called 'Engineering is Elementary' was developed to teach science through engineering to elementary school children aged 7-11 years (Lachapelle et al., 2013). The units have a real-life context and address areas of the science curriculum. An example of one of their units is a medical engineering topic on developing a knee brace for a child who has damaged their knee ligaments. The children explore the role of knee ligaments in stabilising the knee joint and the effect of a damaged knee joint using a model constructed by the children. They carry out testing of materials to ascertain which materials would be best to make a removable knee support and test it. This covers biological sciences and material sciences as well as a range of science skills and processes. These units are used in many states in the United States and have been the subject of a great deal of research on their effectiveness in learning science, especially to unrepresented groups, as well as understanding of the nature of the range engineering and its processes. Their results indicate that the children doing the 'Engineering is elementary' units made greater progress in science learning than those doing traditional science curricula (Lachapelle et al., 2010). It was also found that the experience improved the attitudes to science and engineering in all children but especially amongst girls (Cunningham et al., 2012). The units appeared to raise the children's interest in science and engineering and their understanding of the range of engineering fields (Lachapelle et al., 2010).

Using a similar model, but new content, the EU Engineer project (https://www.ecsite.eu/activities-and-services/projects/engineer) developed and trialled ten units across ten countries. The project found that there was a greater enthusiasm for science and engineering in the children who experienced the units, with the girls interested in how engineering and science could improve our way of life. These children were also more positive about careers in science and engineering and had a greater awareness of the field of engineering (Harnett et al., 2014). Whether this interest stays with them through their later education will remain to be seen.

Learning science and design and technology through engineering can also provide opportunities for more effective teaching and learning strategies such as problem solving. An engineering task without drawing on science can become a craft exercise (Davies, 2011). However, when children explore and draw on their science knowledge to solve a task, it can take the child to a deeper level of thinking and engagement. In a time where we are concerned with mastery in maths, surely the application of STEM knowledge and skills to real-life problems is a form of STEM mastery.

Such an approach will support teachers in having a clear intent and implementation for STEM teaching. It will allow teachers to present subject matter clearly, promote appropriate discussion about the subject matter they are teaching, and to address children's misconceptions.

Working with real-life engineers

Having an 'expert' engineer in the room (for example, in the form of an engineering undergraduate or apprentice) can increase the impact of engineering activities on children's aspirations, understandings, and attitudes further than when the materials are delivered by a class teacher alone (Fogg-Rogers et al., 2015). There are suggestions of why this could occur in the research of the Aspires project from King's College London (De Witt and Archer, 2015), which looked at the attitudes that children aged between 10 and 14 years had to STEM subjects and their aspirations in choosing a STEM career. They found that although children had positive attitudes to STEM subjects, they did not aspire to work or study in these areas. They suggest that the 'science capital,' the knowledge, value, social contact, and qualifications of a child's family, was one of the main influences on their aspirations. Social contact with a professional engineer may influence children's thinking about the STEM roles and engineering more widely.

This suggests that, if you can, having an engineer from industry involved in your science and engineering project, even just to visit, could be beneficial to the children's attitudes and aspirations. The Aspires 2 research (Archer et al., 2020) could also indicate that the use of some of these activities with children and parents during an open evening may also raise the profile of STEM within the family for the child. Further contacts and suggestions are listed in Chapter 11.

Activity: Working with engineers

As you work through the materials in this book, think about which type of engineering these relate to and which aspects of science they contain. You could consider inviting STEM specialists into the class to support the children with the challenges they have been set. These could be parents or carers who have an interest or work in a related

16 *Science and design and technology through engineering?*

> sector or staff and students from local universities, colleges, or secondary schools. Local engineering industries often have outreach activities and ambassadors who can support work at the primary level.

Issues with STEM in the primary classroom

With such evident benefits of doing engineering in the primary/elementary classroom, why is this not happening in all schools regularly? It can be difficult to incorporate innovative, purposeful, and engaging STEM activities without teachers going to a lot of expense and effort. This, coupled with the fact that STEM subjects are not taught widely enough in primary or elementary schools means that these subjects can be forgotten within a crowded primary/elementary curriculum.

The process of taking scientific knowledge and applying it to real-life problems is often when science misconceptions become evident. Children need the skills of a teacher to help them to understand the links between what they see and the ideas of science. However, there have long been concerns over the STEM subject knowledge of teachers of children of the primary/elementary age (The Royal Society, 2010; Murphy *et al.*, 2007; Sharp and Grace, 2003; Sorsby and Watson, 1993), particularly in the physical sciences (Royal Society, 2010; Murphy and Whitelegg, 2006). Furthermore, it can be difficult to incorporate innovative, purposeful, and engaging STEM activities for teachers who may not have subject expertise, potentially making the teaching of STEM subjects through a contextualised and inquiry-based multidisciplinary approach problematic. This book aims to help teachers to address these common difficulties by providing a clear and in-depth exploration of the scientific understanding required alongside each engineering challenge, for example by providing:

- an examination and explanation of the scientific knowledge and understanding underpinning each of the engineering challenges
- potential solution ideas
- resource ideas
- ideas for addressing common misconceptions often held by children
- design and technology and science links
- signposting to sources of further support for science knowledge development, and vocabulary.

Common problems in STEM education and how this book can help

- Crowded primary/elementary curriculum. The activities outlined in this book are truly cross-curricular. Their main aim is to teach science and design and technology through engineering, covering the learning objectives of these subjects in a meaningful and contextualised way.
- Health and safety concerns can mitigate against practical science and design and technology. Each activity comes with health and safety guidance. All the activities are

designed to be carried out with everyday materials and tools which are commonplace in the primary/elementary classroom.
- Lack of confidence to teach practical science among primary staff. Each activity comes with background scientific explanations and a knowledge summary for teachers. The activities are also designed to help children (and teachers) discover understanding for themselves. Teachers and children will be able to learn together.
- Lack of equipment/facilities to teach practical science and design and technology. As the activities are contextualised into an everyday problem, they will only need everyday materials and equipment.
- Extension/outreach work in primary schools is not always sustainable. This book aims to deliver a different, long-term approach to the way that STEM subjects and science in a particular approach. This is not a one-off activity approach.

In the next chapter, we take you through the structure of the book and how each of the engineering challenges will be presented. We will provide an explanation of the engineering design process and will show how the resources presented can be used for in-class activities.

References

Abrahams, I., and Millar, R. (2008) Does practical work really work? A study of the effectiveness of practical work as a teaching and learning method in school science. *International Journal of Science Education*, 30(14), 1945-1969.

Archer, L., Moote, J., MacLeod, E., Francis, B., and DeWitt, J. (2020) *ASPIRES 2: Young people's science and career aspirations, age 10-19*. London: UCL Institute of Education.

Ata-Aktürk, A., and Demircan, H. Ö. (2022) Engineers and engineering through the eyes of preschoolers: A phenomenographic study of children's drawings. *European Early Childhood Education Research Journal*, 30(4), 495-514.

Ausubel, D. P., and Fitzgerald, D. (1961) Chapter V: Meaningful learning and retention: Intrapersonal cognitive variables. *Review of Educational Research*, 31(5), 500-510.

Barnes, J. (2018) *Applying cross-curricular approaches creatively: The connecting curriculum*. Routledge: London.

Bartholomew, S., and Seymour, A. (2021) Influencing perceptions of STEM through the best STEM books list. *Science and Children*, 58(6), 68-72.

Banks, F., and Barlex, D. (2014) *Teaching STEM in the secondary school: Helping teachers meet the challenge*. London: Routledge.

Bryan, L. A., Moore, T. J., Johnson, C. C., and Roehrig, G. (2015) Integrated STEM education. In C. C. Johnson, E. E. Peters-Burton, and T. J. Moore (Eds.), *STEM roadmap: A framework for integration* (pp. 23-37). London: Taylor & Francis.

Cunningham, C. M. (2009) Engineering is elementary. *The Bridge*, 30(3), 11-17.

Cunningham, C. M., Lachapelle, C. P., and Hertel, J. (2012) *Research and evaluation results for the engineering is elementary project: An executive summary of the first eight years*. Boston, MA: Museum of Science.

Dare, E. A., Keratithamkul, K., Hiwatig, B. M., and Li, F. (2021) Beyond content: The role of STEM disciplines, real-world problems, 21st century skills, and STEM careers within science teachers' conceptions of integrated stem education. *Education Sciences*, 11(11), 737.

Davies, D. (2011) *Teaching science creatively*. London: Routledge.

DeWitt, J., Archer, L., and Osborne, J. (2014) Science-related aspirations across the primary-secondary divide: Evidence from two surveys in England. *International Journal of Science Education*, 36(10), 1609-1629.

DeWitt, J., and Archer, L. (2015) Who aspires to a science career? A comparison of survey responses from primary and secondary school students. *International Journal of Science Education*, 37(13), 2170-2192.

Edmonds, J., Lewis, F., and Fogg-Rogers, L. (2020) Primary pathways: Elementary pupils' aspiration to be engineers and STEM subject interest. *International Journal of Science Education, Part B*, 12(3).

EngineeringUK. (2015) The state of engineering. Available at: http://www.engineeringuk.com/EngineeringUK2015/EngUK_report_2015_Interactive.pdf

English, J., Haupt, T., and Smallwood, J. J. (2016) Women, construction and health and safety (H&S): South African and Tanzanian perspectives. Construction in Developing Countries International Symposium, Santiago, Chile.

EU Engineer Project. Available at: https://www.ecsite.eu/activities-and-services/projects/engineer

European Commission. (2019) Analysis of shortage and surplus occupations based on national and Eurostat labour force survey data shortages and surpluses. Available at: https://ec.europa.eu › social › BlobServlet

Fogg-Rogers, L. A., Edmonds, J., and Lewis, F. (2015) Children as engineers: Paired peer mentors in primary schools final report summary July 2015. Project Report. Engineering Professors' Council. Available at: http://eprints.uwe.ac.uk/26053

Fralick, B., Keam, J., Thompson, S., and Lyons, J. (2009) How middle schoolers draw engineers and scientists. *Journal of Science Education and Technology*, 18(1), 60-73.

Giddings, L. (2019) Who's studying STEM? The Breakdown of STEM Graduates in the UK. Accessed 31 July 2020. Available at: https://www.fenews.co.uk/fevoices/27852-whos-studying-stem-the-breakdown-of-stem-graduates-in-the-uk

Goswami, U. C. (2020) *Cognitive development and cognitive neuroscience: The learning brain*, 2nd edn. London: Routledge.

Gomez, A., and Albrecht, B. (2013) True STEM education. *Technology and Engineering Teacher*, 73(4), 8.

Gopnik, A. (2012) Scientific thinking in Young children: Theoretical advances, empirical research, and policy implications. *Science (American Association for the Advancement of Science)*, 337(6102), 1623-1627.

Harlen, W., and Qualter, A. (2018) *The teaching of science in primary schools*, 7th edn. London: Routledge.

Harnett, P., Edmonds, J., and Last, K. (2014) Engineer project. Evaluation and analysis of project Impact. Available at: https://uwe-repository.worktribe.com/output/810589

Hoachlander, G. (2015) Integrating SET&M. *Educational Leadership* (December 2014/January 2015), 74-78.

Hoyles, C., Reiss, M., and Tough, S. (2011) *Supporting STEM in schools and colleges in England. The role of research. A report for Universities UK*. Institute of Education, University of London.

Jarvis, T., and Pell, A. (2005) Factors influencing elementary school children's attitudes toward science before, during, and after a visit to the UK National Space Centre. *Journal of Research in Science Teaching*, 42(1), 53-83.

Jones, V. (2021) *Young people and climate change: Hear our voice*. Global Goals Centre.

Knight, M., and Cunningham, C. (2004) Draw and engineer test (DAET): Development of a tool to investigate students' ideas about engineers and engineering. *Proceedings of American Society for Engineering Education Annual Conference Exposition (Vol. 111)*. Salt Lake City, UT: ASEE.

Lachapelle, C. P., Cunningham, C. M., Lee-St. John, T. J., Cannady, M., and Keenan, K. (2010) An investigation of how two engineering is elementary curriculum units support student learning. Presented at the P-12 Engineering and Design Education Research Summit, Seaside.

Lachapelle, C. P., Hertel, J. D., Phadnis, P., and Cunningham, C. M. (2013) *Evaluating the impact of engineering is elementary: Year 2 of implementation in Minneapolis and Hopkins Public Schools*. Boston, MA: Museum of Science. Available at: http://www.eie.org/sites/default/files/downloads/EiE/ResearchPublications/lachapelle_et_al_2013_minneapolis2.pdf

Lucas, B., Claxton, G., and Hanson, J. (2014) *Thinking like an engineer: Implications for the education system*. Royal Academy of Engineers.

Murphy, C., and Beggs, J. (2003) Children's perceptions of school science. *School Science Review [online]*, 84(308), 109-116.

Murphy, C., Beggs, J., Russell, H., and Melton, L. (2005) *Primary horizons: Starting out in science*. London: Wellcome Trust.

Murphy, P., and Whitelegg, E. (2006) *Girls in the physics classroom: A review of the research on the participation of girls in physics*. London, UK. Available at: http://oro.open.ac.uk/6499/1/girls_and_physics

Murphy, C., Neil, P., and Beggs, J. (2007) Primary science teacher confidence revisited: Ten years on. *Educational Research*, 49(4), 415–430.

National Research Council. (2014) *STEM integration in K-12 education: Status, prospects, and an agenda for research*. Washington, DC: National Academies Press.

NGSS Lead States. (2013) *Next Generation Science Standards: For states, by states*. Washington, DC: The National Academies Press.

OECD. (2006) *Assessing scientific, reading, and mathematical literacy: A framework for PISA 2006*. Paris: OECD.

Perkins, J. (2013) *Review of engineering skills*. DBI accessed at https://www.raeng.org.uk/publications/other/perkins-review-of-engineering-skills

Royal Academy of Engineering. (2012) *Jobs and growth: The imporance of engineering skills to the economy*. Available at: http://www.raeng.org.uk/publications/reports/jobs-and-growth

Royal Academy of Engineering. (2016) *The UK STEM education landscape*. Available at: https://www.raeng.org.uk/publications/reports/uk-stem-education-landscape

Royal Academy of Engineering. (2018) *Engineering the future: Training today's teachers to develop tomorrow's engineers*. Available at: https://www.raeng.org.uk/publications/reports/engineering-the-future-training-today-s-teachers-t

Royal Society. (2010) *The scientific century: Securing our future prosperity*. London, UK.

Sharp, J., and Grace, M. (2003) Anecdote, opinion and whim: Lessons in curriculum development from primary science education in England and Wales. *Research Papers in Education*, 19(3), 293–321.

Sorsby, B., and Watson, E. (1993) Students' and teachers' confidence about their own science knowledge and SMKills in relation to the sciences national curriculum. *Journal of In-Service Education*, 19(3), 43–49

The National Academies (NRC). (2014) *Next generation science standards: For states, by states*. Washington: National Academy of Sciences.

United Nations. (2015) *The 2030 agenda for sustainable development*. United Nations. Available at: https://sdgs.un.org/2030agenda

2 The engineering design process

Introduction

Engineering always starts with a need, something that is required to address a problem, to meet the demands of a challenge or a set of customer requirements. Engineers respond to this need by creating a new product or process, but this does not happen in an ad hoc manner. In fact, engineers follow a systematic design process, the Engineering Design Process (the EDP) and apply this whether they are creating a simple paper clip or a more complicated solar panel.

In this chapter, we will explore the EDP and will look at how this can be adapted for the primary or elementary classroom. To illustrate how this works we have used an imaginary engineering challenge that presents a need as below:

> **Illustrative Engineering Challenge: A cold drink on a hot day**
>
> Cery's plans to visit the beach on a hot summer's day. She would like to take her drink with her but only has a disposable plastic bottle that will not keep her drink cold for very long. Can you design something reusable that will keep her drink cold for her?

The engineering design process: How real engineers work?

Examining the initial need presented by the engineering challenge usually produces a loose set of generic requirements to begin with, e.g., here, keeping a drink cold when sitting on the beach. This then needs to be translated into more specific engineering requirements that become something more tangible that can be measured or quantified. For our example of a drink on the beach, this would be considerations such as how long the drink needs to be cold for, how big the drink is, and if the product is for an adult or a child, etc. These more quantifiable conditions then make up the design specification, which turns the initial need into a set of more focussed engineering targets. This design specification captures everything that is needed for the product (Figure 2.1).

DOI: 10.4324/9781003325826-2

The engineering design process 21

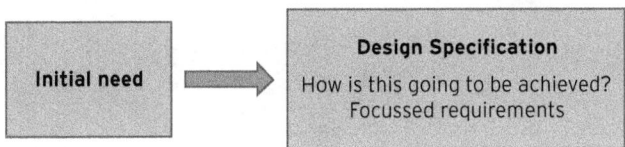

Figure 2.1 The initial stages of the EDP

To ensure that this design specification is a thorough examination of the requirements, engineers consider a range of aspects at this stage. These include factors such as:

- what materials will be used
- what is the context and environment that the product will be used in
- what are the anthropometric considerations (optimising the interaction of the human body with the product or environment)
- what forces or loads will the product be subjected to
- what are the costs and associated selling prices
- health, safety, and potential hazards
- reliability
- efficiency
- legal requirements

The design specification therefore sets out the intent as well as the constraints and limitations that need to be adhered to so that design decisions can be made. For our beach drink, this may be thoughts about the insulating properties of the materials used, the overall weight of these so that the final product is not too heavy, the cost of these materials so that the product is not too expensive, etc. As engineers work through their product designs and production, the design specification may evolve. It may be added to or refined as understanding of the product grows and matures.

Once the design specification has been decided upon, engineers start to look for ideas to inspire their designs to meet these needs and specifications. Engineers very rarely start their work from scratch. They almost always use the work of others as a starting point. This stage is known as ideation and is the process of producing things which inspire the design. These ideas could come from several sources, such as sharing ideas with fellow engineers, examining real designs and products or components to build on what has been done previously, potentially resulting in a similar product or design with a variation in functionality (Figure 2.2).

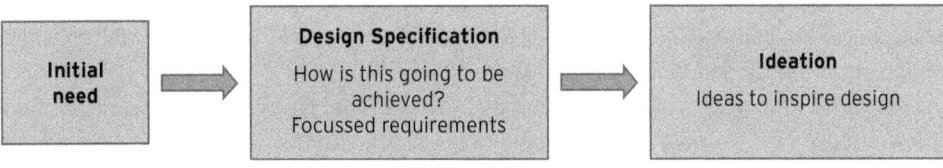

Figure 2.2 Incorporating ideation into the EDP

22 *The engineering design process*

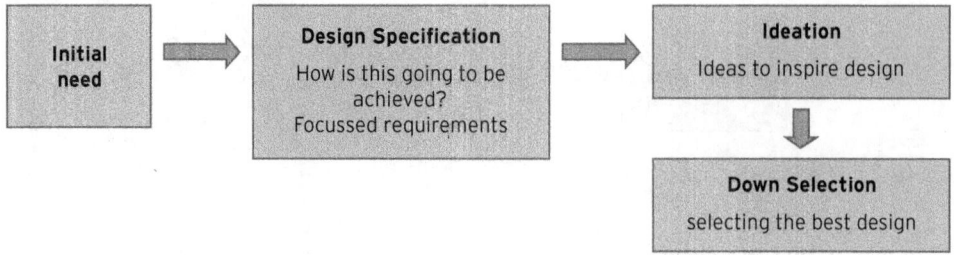

Figure 2.3 Down selection: selecting the best design

Let us consider the design of our beach drink. This is made up of a variety of different components, each with their own requirements for functionality (e.g., the inner casing to keep the drink cold, the outer casing for the customer to hold, the mechanism that the customer will use to drink and the attachment/detachment of the lid for filling). Each of these sub-functions may be created in diverse ways using different ideas and the ideas which inspire this may come from a variety of sources. With all these solutions for each function or component, an engineer will be able to produce many potential designs for the final product. Here, the job of an engineer is to decide and evaluate which of these designs is the best. This process is known as down selection.

During the down selection stage, an engineer goes back to the initial design specification and matches the designs against the specification criteria. So, for our beach drink, the engineer would consider the cost of the materials, the reliability of any mechanisms involved, the longevity of the materials in the hot and damp conditions on the beach, etc. Not all the initial designs will be weighted the same in response to evaluation against these specifications and so in this way the engineer is able to select the best design (Figure 2.3).

Once this decision has been made, the engineer can then start to consider how the product will be constructed and will create engineering drawings for the components, assembly mechanisms and the final product. This enables a prototype product to be made, the performance of which can be tested against the criteria in the design specification to measure the functionality, budget, and reliability, etc. of the product. For our beach cup, this would test if the cup would keep the drink cold enough for long enough, if it would be of a suitable size and weight for the customer, if it would be robust enough to survive the environmental conditions on the beach and would not be too expensive to buy. Some of this evaluation may even be carried out by user groups who may provide further feedback on wider aspects, such as aesthetic qualities. We can see this process in action by visiting a very well-known Scandinavian furniture store where we can see a replication of the forces and loads that a kitchen drawer would be subject to in its lifetime. This shows the product's overall performance and where the weaknesses are.

During this process, engineers may find that their product breaks, does not work, or is not fit for purpose in some way. This information feeds back into the design plans and drawings and changes are made. There may be a second, third, or even fourth version of the product

The engineering design process 23

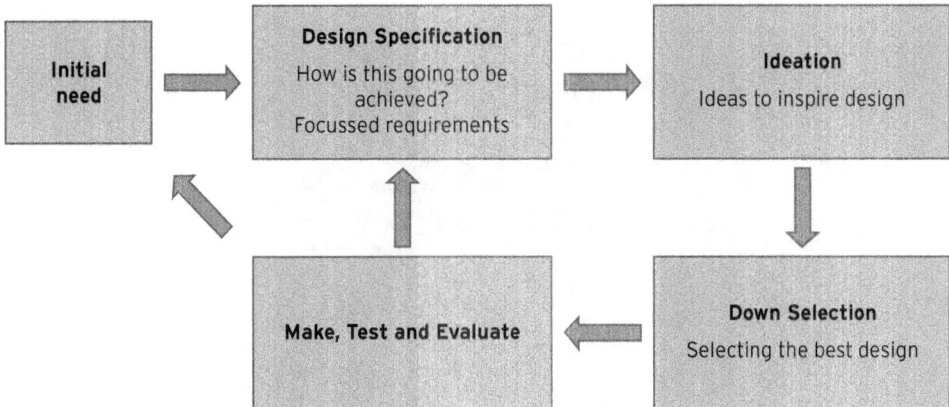

Figure 2.4 The engineering design process

as this process is repeated until the engineer finally has a product which is optimised and does what it is supposed to do against the design brief and specification. Engineers then consider how this could be scaled up for mass production and volume of number (Figure 2.4).

Engineering habits of mind (EHoM)

Throughout the processes above, engineers are making use of distinctive habits of mind that facilitate the engineering design process. These habits of mind can be seen as engineering thinking practices that are capable of change and development (Lucas and Hanson, 2016); however, they are also thinking practices that can benefit children across the curriculum and in everyday life (Figure 2.5).

The U.S. guidance on the primary/elementary curriculum suggests that engineering habits of mind should be developed as part of the standard curriculum as part of the U.S. Next Generation Science Standards (NGSS Lead States, 2013). The EHoM are often distilled down to six aspects:

Systems thinking: Bringing designs, ideas, and knowledge together, identifying patterns.

Problem Finding: Identifying the issue/need and the context of the issue or need, researching and identifying current solutions.

Visualisation: Being able to draw, describe, or model abstract ideas of a future solution or design or process.

Improving: Constantly taking your design and identifying ways in which it can be made better through drawing, experimenting, and making prototypes.

Creative Problem Solving: Identifying solutions with others, drawing on the ideas of others, and aspects from different disciplines.

Adaption: Analysing, re-thinking, and changing designs or processes.

Each of these habits of mind can be developed through the engineering design process.

24 *The engineering design process*

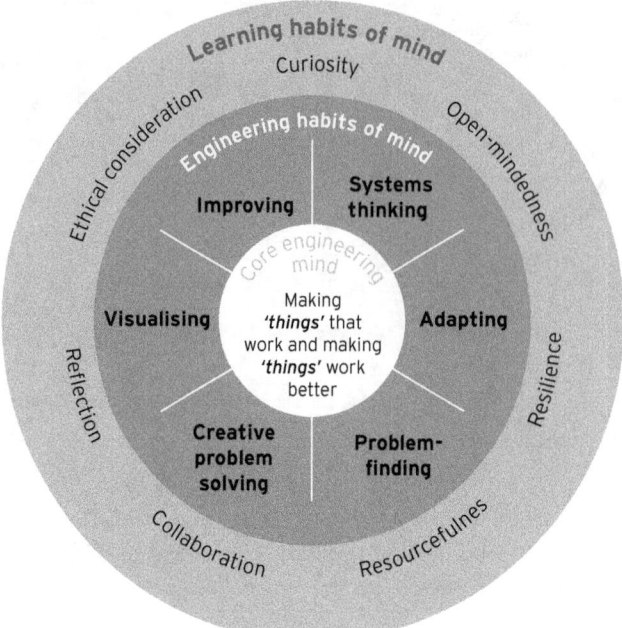

Figure 2.5 Engineering habits of mind (Diagram used with permission from the Royal Academy of Engineering. First published in 'Thinking like an engineer: Implications for the education system', 2014.)

How can we foster these habits in children?

These Engineering Habits of Mind need to be exemplified to children, modelled, and broken down into easy-to-understand chunks, as well as being communicated in a language that they can understand. To help children understand the ways we want them to be thinking the teacher needs to demonstrate themselves thinking, for example, talking about how they are looking at one of the glider designs the children have produced and identifying the positive features of the design and the areas that could be improved to give it more lift (Lucas et al., 2017).

The teacher can tell personal stories about times where they were given a problem and how they used EHoM to solve the problem. You could use published stories to give examples of types of thinking (e.g., Rosie Revere, Engineer) (Beaty, 2013).

Case Study: Engineering Habits of Mind

Mrs Singh, a year 2 teacher, did not have the right packaging to send a lightbulb to her son at his university. She knew the size of the lightbulb and that it was likely to break if unprotected. She had seen padded envelopes and the cardboard boxes in which bulbs are sold in shops (problem finding). The teacher could imagine a solution with a cardboard tube and some bubble wrap (visualisation). However, when she made the tube, the bulb kept falling out of the ends of the tube. She thought hard about this and then decided to try putting tissue paper down the ends of the tube as she knew many shops used tissue paper to protect items being sold (adaption). She was explaining this to her daughter when her daughter suggested she might also want to put some tape over the ends of the tube (creative problem solving, improving). She tried this and then tested it to make sure the bulb was protected enough to send in an envelope. When she was happy with her design, she sent it through the post. Her son received the lightbulb intact! She realised she used the engineering design cycle and drew on knowledge from her life experience to achieve her solution.

Other ways of explaining EHoMs might be to ask the children to identify examples of when they have used these thinking patterns in their everyday lives. You could use a poster of the Royal Academy of Engineering's EHoM Lucas et. al., 2014) to refer to and to help the children identify the thinking patterns, available at https://www.raeng.org.uk/publications/other/ehom-poster-royal-academy-of-engineering

Positive reinforcement of examples of EHoM during practical sessions and raised again at the end of the lesson can also be an effective way of explaining what you want from the children, e.g., 'I was impressed with the group on the back table as they carefully explained their design ideas to one another and drew pictures to support their explanation. They were able to build on each other's ideas. They were visualising their solution and identifying solutions together' (Lucas et al., 2017).

We recognise that some of the EHoMs require children to recognise failure and learn from it and to be able to objectively evaluate their own products or solutions. Some children find this difficult as they can equate the product with their own competencies and self-worth. Evaluating products as a class or as a group can alleviate this for individuals and modelling the teacher accepting and learning from their own failures can also be helpful. Being part of the activity, working alongside the children can be an effective way of modelling the habits of mind. Teacher messages about the importance of design failure are useful for all children at this point (Lottero-Perdue and Parry, 2017).

Another habit we have found to be tricky is the adaptation and improving EHoM. When the teacher points out feature of more successful designs or solutions in the class, other children are reluctant to use the ideas or learn from them as that is copying! Understanding that engineers research other engineers' solutions (ideation, see above) and then build on them is an important part of the process. Engineering activities in the classroom are an effective way of challenging and changing some of these mindsets for children and allow them to see benefits in both failure and collaborative.

The engineering design process provides the context and opportunities to develop these engineering habits of mind. This chapter explains how this works and how it can be part of classroom practice.

The engineering design process for the primary classroom

Despite resulting in a multitude of products ranging from something as simple as a cup to something as complex as a helicopter, the design and make process used by engineers

26 The engineering design process

remains consistent and is straightforward in its process. We are therefore able to adopt this in a simplified form for the primary or elementary classroom. In this next section, we set out the model of the engineering design process used throughout this book, and explain the purpose, thought processes, and activities encountered at each stage.

 ### Igniting ideas

Just like the EDP used by engineers, the child's version of the EDP starts with a need. As we discovered at the start of this chapter, engineers work in response to an issue or problem that they need to find a solution for. It is the job of an engineer to work out what needs to be done in response to this problem and to provide workable solutions. Giving children a problem to solve is the spark to set them thinking, to ignite their ideas.

Similarly, the engineering challenges in this book are all based on problems that children will need to design and make a product to find a solution for. These problems are set within a story context using everyday situations that the children in your class would be familiar with. These challenges are set by fictional characters of the same age as children at the primary or elementary stage of their education to make them more relatable for the children and to help the children to empathise with the needs of the characters involved. However, just as in the real EDP, the needs and requirements that are set out at this stage are generic and open ended.

Igniting Ideas	
Intention	During this stage of the EDP, the problem or challenge to be solved is presented to the children. This may be in the form of a letter or email or in another format that sets out the context for the problem, who is involved, and exactly what their need is.
Purpose	At this stage of the EDP, it is important that children have a firm understanding of the problem that they are being asked to solve.
Thought processes/ EHoM	Understand, empathise, connect. Problem finding
Activities involved	• Shared reading or presentation of the challenge set • Discussions to clarify the needs of the children involved. What is their situation? What is their problem? What do they need or want to happen? • Discussions around similar experiences, contexts, or problems that the children themselves have encountered.

 *Exploring ideas*

During this stage of the EDP, we encourage children to translate the initial need of the characters in the challenge story into a set of engineering requirements, in a comparable way to engineers turning their challenges into a design specification. In the classroom, this is done by helping the children to pose questions about the conditions, needs, and purpose of the challenge so that a set of more tangible and quantifiable criteria can be met.

In our beach cup problem, the children may need to know the answers to the following questions to be able to design and make a suitable product.

- How much drink does the cup need to hold?
- Who is the cup for?
- How long does the cup need to keep the drink cold for?
- Will the cup be reused?
- How much money do you have to spend on the cup?
- What materials and tools/equipment are available?

Through asking questions such as these, the children then develop their understanding of a more focussed set of requirements, and therefore capture everything that is needed for the product.

As you start to work with the EDP in your classroom, the children may require support to formulate suitable questions at first and so a set of potential questions that they could ask is provided in each chapter. However, with more practice, the children will become familiar with exactly what it is they need to find out at this stage of the EDP and so will become more adept at asking appropriate questions.

	Exploring Ideas
Intention	The stage of the EDP turns the needs set by the characters in the challenge into a more focussed and quantifiable set of requirements.
Purpose	The children will need to compile a list of requirements and constraints that they will need to work within when designing and making their product.
Thought processes/EHoM	Question, refine, focus, apply logic and systems thinking. Creative problem solving.
Activities involved	• Discussions about what the children need to know to provide a solution to the problem set. • Children composing and asking questions to obtain more purposeful information. This stage of the EDP revolves around talk. These discussions should involve a significant element of whole class discussion so that all children are aware of the conditions set. This also shares good practice and builds understanding around posing questions.

Developing ideas

As we learnt previously, engineering is a creative subject where thinkers who can look at problems from different angles and those who can produce imaginative solutions are welcome. Just like real engineers, during this stage of the engineering process, children are encouraged to use their imaginations and consider a variety of potential solutions where anything is possible. For example, for our beach cup problem, the children may consider designing a hat holding a drink bottle and straws, fluid ice boxes, or even a drink transporting drone to transport a cold drink straight from the fridge at the café to them! It is only through considering the wild and whacky ideas that new and novel solutions will be arrived upon.

Once the children have let their imaginations run wild, it is time to also look elsewhere for inspiration. Just as real engineers ideate, here we encourage children to undertake simple research about what is already available, which could provide potential ideas and inspirations for the design and product that they will produce. Children sometimes struggle with this stage (discussed above), as they may think that it is cheating or copying. To respond to this, children should be helped to understand that this is in fact how real engineers work: no one designs a bridge from scratch!

During this stage, the children may also need to do some initial investigations. For our beach cup example, this may involve testing the thermal insulation or waterproofing properties of potential materials.

Developing Ideas	
Intention	At this stage, the children will start to think about which product they will make.
Purpose	Here, the children will gather a range of ideas and information that will feed into their ideas and plans.
Thought processes/EHoM	Apply, research, investigate, analyse, compare, evaluate. Visualisation, creative problem solving.
Activities involved	• Brainstorming imagination sessions • Discussions about things that they have seen before or ideas that that may provide an answer • Internet or literature-based research about designs or products that could provide ideas. Investigating factors such as the properties of materials • Sharing of ideas discovered or imagined.

 **Designing ideas**

Again, like real engineers during this stage, the children will create their engineering drawings (designs or plans) for the final product using information gathered from the 'developing ideas' stage. Ideas in the designs should include:

- Dimensions and sizes
- Views of the sides, top and bottom of the product
- Materials to be used
- Separate drawings of any fixtures or components
- Mechanisms for fixtures and joins

Children should be encouraged to produce around three main ideas or plans. Using these three ideas, we can then mimic the work that engineers do in the down selection (i.e., evaluating) which of these designs is the best. This is done by looking back at the original need set out at the ignite stage and the set of criteria developed during the explore stage and evaluating which of their ideas best fits these necessities. It is vital that teachers remind children of the initial problem during this stage. Have they met what is required of them in terms of solving the initial problem? Is what they have planned realistic and will be achievable within the constraints set?

Designing Ideas	
Intention	Here, the children will produce a set of detailed plans for the final product, the component parts, and the assembly mechanisms or fixings that they will use.
Purpose	It is important that the children can evaluate their ideas about potential solutions and analyse and reason they have decided which solution would be best.
Thought processes/EHoM	Analyse, compare, evaluate. Visualisation, Adaption.
Activities involved	• Identify three main ideas • Evaluate and assess which of these ideas best meets the requirements set out in the ignite and explore stages of the EDP • Explain product choice to others in the class and share reasoning about why this product has been chosen.

 **Making, testing, and improving ideas**

Making

This is the hands-on bit where the children get to make their product. During this stage, children may need to be taught specific skills, such as how to use tools correctly; even something as simple as a pair of scissors for younger children. It is important that children are taught to use the right tool for the job correctly. Imagine trying to cut a raw carrot with an everyday butter knife; it would be both dangerous and tricky! It would be safer and easier to teach children how to hold and safely use a shaper knife, so take the time to teach the children that you work with how to use the tools that they will need correctly and safely. Throughout this book, health and safety ideas and tips are presented alongside each engineering challenge.

Testing

Engineers do not simply present their finished product and then walk away. They evaluate, test, and improve, sometimes going back to the drawing board and starting all over again! However, children may tend to make their product and very much see this as the final and completed version. It is important to challenge this idea and encourage children to evaluate and improve their work, just as a real engineer would with a prototype. One way to do this is to set up scenarios that test the products made. For example, can the beach cup made withstand being on damp sand for 10 minutes? How cold is the drink it contains after 10 minutes when under heat? It is through testing processes that faults as areas for improvement can be illuminated.

Improving

Some children may see finding faults in their products as criticism and give up if their product is not perfect immediately, whilst others may struggle to suggest ways in which their product could be improved. A great way to help with this is to encourage the sharing of ideas, but children can view this as copying. Teachers need to reiterate that engineers do not work on their own; they continually share ideas and develop ideas together. Try to actively encourage this through the following activities:

- Ask groups of children to display their product or holding a product carousel where children are free to examine the work of other groups.
- Ask children to share with the class a problem, issue, or triumph that they are having with their product (e.g., how to get a lid to fit onto a drink bottle). The rest of the class can then share how they overcame the same issue or use the developed knowledge themselves.
- During this stage, children may encounter common difficulties such as a product not being stable or strong enough to support a designated weight. This provides a great opportunity to go back to research other products to consider how they have been made more stable or stronger, etc.

Once the products have been tested, evaluated, and improved, the EDP suggests that the children go back to the very first stage of the process, the initial problem. Have they provided a viable solution?

	Making, Testing and Improving Ideas
Intention	This is the hands-on stage where children will work towards making their final product, going through many review and test stages.
Purpose	Here, it is important that the children can evaluate their products rather than simply accepting their first attempt. Can they identify elements that do not work so well? Can they find ways to improve on these?
Thought processes/EHoM	Analyse, compare, evaluate. Improving
Activities involved	• Explicit teaching of how to use specific tools • Health and safety briefings • Making activities • Testing against specific criteria • Self-appraisal of products • Researching solutions to common problems • Sharing of common issues and solutions • Sharing of common solutions or ideas • Examining the products and ideas of others • Evaluating product against the initial need and set of requirements

These stages then come together to form the children's version of the EDP, as shown in Figure 2.6.

A photocopiable Childrens' Engineering Challenge Sheet can be found in Appendix.

How does this fit with science curricula?

The EDP provides real-life situations for using science to inform designs. Engineering draws on science to provide knowledge about the natural and physical world. It also draws on the scientific method to test products or materials to evaluate their use. Science skills are used throughout the design process and, at specific points, science knowledge and the scientific method are particularly relevant.

Raising scientific questions:
- Raising questions that can be researched or investigated is an important skill at primary/elementary schools. It is an even better skill if it arises from an observation

32   *The engineering design process*

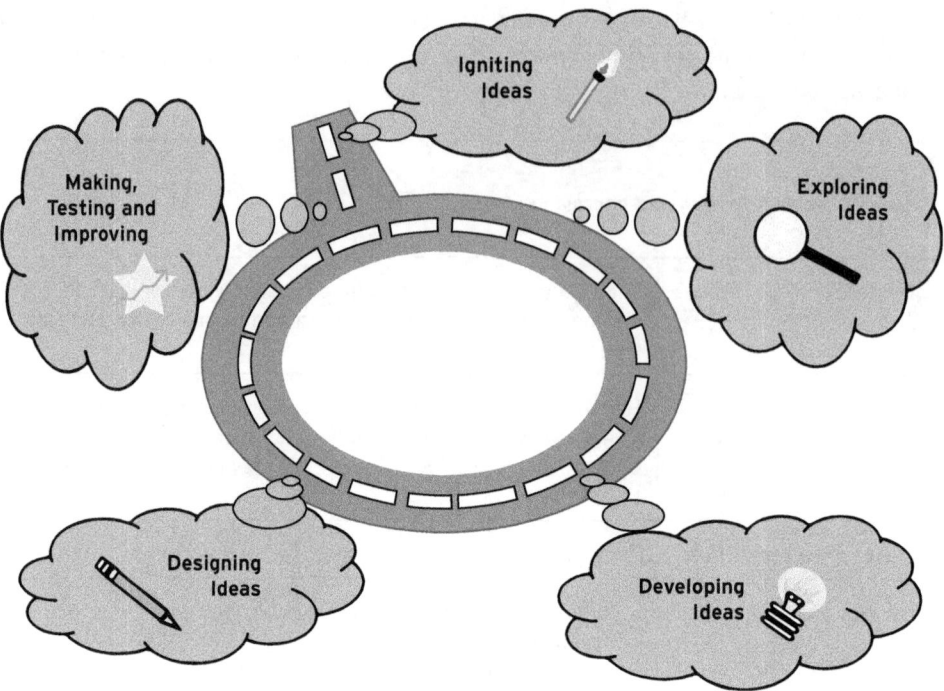

Figure 2.6 The engineering design process

building on prior knowledge. This is a similar science skill to the questions raised in the igniting ideas and exploring ideas phases of the EDP. Adults tend to think that children are full of questions but, interestingly, this rarely is exhibited in a school environment. Children think it is the teacher's role to ask questions, not the children's (Tizard and Hughes, 2002). One teacher we came across employs children in her class to act as 'question detectives', spotting other children raising key questions throughout the science activity. This raised the status and skills level of the questioning in the class.

Measurement:
- Measurement is a complex skill. Children need to know what to measure, how to measure, and why we measure in science. The EDP can provide a context for the measurement of length, weight, volume, force, and time using a range of units and different equipment. Basic skills work, where children practice taking measurements with a new piece of equipment, may be necessary (e.g., measuring the temperature of a cold drink with a thermometer).

Planning and carrying out investigations:
- To test a design or a material to be used in a design may require the children to design a fair test or comparative test. This happens in the making, testing, and improving phases of the EDP. Additional ideas for linked scientific investigations are provided in each chapter.

Recording and evaluating results

These skills are also a part of the making, evaluating, and improving phases of the EDP. Recording and evaluating results can be an area that overlaps with data analysis in maths. Children need to learn to record their findings in tables or charts and then describe what it means. What is the story of the data? What is it telling us? This can inform the improvement stage by comparing the data with that of other groups' designs or to inform the choice of design features.

Each of the challenges relates to some recognisable science content knowledge from primary/elementary school science. For example, the activity in Chapter 3 relates to science knowledge on plants needing water to grow and the functions of the roots and stem.

However, children do not just learn science as it is presented to them in the classroom. The research on children's learning in science points to the fact that children often have ideas about science, developed from birth, that are counter to the science that is currently accepted by the science community. Research states that children's ideas could be that evaporation is caused by the earth sucking up puddles or that the moon and the sun change places in the sky at night or that our bodies are empty cavities to be filled with food and drink (Watt and Russell, 1990).

As children hold these alternative viewpoints or misconceptions, it is important to find out what they really think before embarking on science. Luckily, there has been much research on common children's ideas on science that can help teachers understand the nature of children's ideas and build and question them. However, much of the research found that children's ideas were resistant to change in the primary school. Sometimes we need to just make them start to question what they believe (Watt and Russell, 1990; Allen, 2019).

Ways of finding out about children's ideas in science could be:

- Asking the children to draw their ideas, such as, 'draw how we can see to read a book in a window.'
- Using other published children's ideas to help children question their own ideas (e.g., concept cartoons)
- Questioning what children mean when they use words like 'evaporation.'
- Open-ended questioning of children.
- Children constructing concept maps.
- Use published research on children's ideas to find the common trends.

There are some excellent books outlining the main misconceptions that children hold in science that you can refer to (Allen, 2019). This allows you to be ready for the misconceptions before they arise in the classroom and allow you to think about how you can help the children to challenge them (see bibliography at end of chapter).

Helping children form ideas in science and engineering

Children's ideas and misconceptions on scientific concepts are difficult to change as they are children's only ways of explaining their physical world. However, in school, we can go some way in offering them alternate scientific theories, challenge their thinking, and provide evidence that is counter to their current beliefs.

One way to help children form scientific understanding is to make the links explicit between the practical science activities and the theories. Abrahams and Reiss (2012) found that children enjoyed the practical work but that they often were not clear about how that related to the scientific ideas being studied. For example, if you think back to your secondary/high school science, it may be memories of bad smells you made in the chemistry labs or dissecting a cow's heart and your classmates being dramatic about it; but think about the science behind the activity and it is more difficult to remember.

Some strategies that can support with children thinking:

- Discussion and making posters to describe the science ideas.
- Providing models and analogies to provide concrete experiences for the children to relate to the practical work. Two analogies or models works better than one as children can get fixated on features of the models or analogies (Chiu and Lin, 2005). Refer to the models and analogies during practical work and also when drawing conclusions.
- Acting out the science (e.g., being air particles moving away from the source of sound, passing on the energy by bumping into other air particles (Edmonds, 2022)).
- Watching cartoon representations of the scientific concepts.
- Questioning children's ideas in discussion, following up questioning with further questions to help children really think through what they are saying.
- Comparing children's ideas with those of scientist (e.g., 'you might say it like that, but scientists think it goes like this … . your suggestion about the water disappearing is like the scientists as it is in exceedingly small parts that you cannot see. Where you differ is that scientists say the water is still there.').
- Having a thinking frame structure to move brainstorming of ideas to theories.

Vocabulary in science and engineering

The use and understanding of scientific or engineering vocabulary is also tightly related to children's understanding of the concepts. I once had a child in my class who knew that jelly set but then could not relate that to what he thought was happening on the horizon when the sun set! Children like collecting and using novel words but sometimes their understanding does not match their confidence in using the words. It is always an idea to ask children what they think they mean when using words like 'evaporation,' 'force,' 'resistance,' etc.

Other strategies can include

- Pre-teaching vocabulary.
- Using word mats with relevant vocabulary.
- Making displays with key vocabulary and definitions.

The engineering design process 35

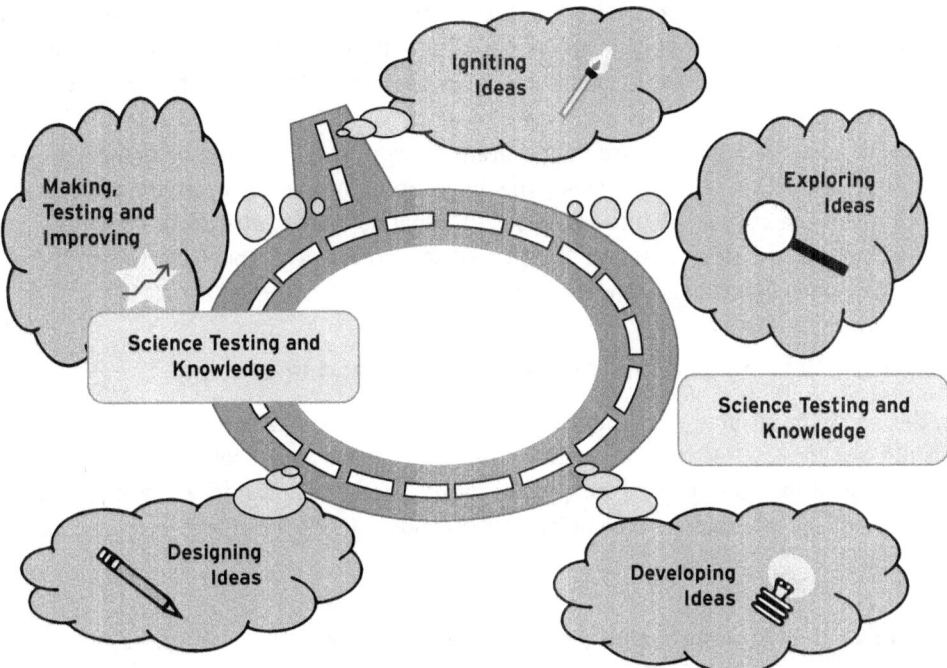

Figure 2.7 The engineering design process with opportunities for science

- Say as I say. 'You might say the car is pushed by the wind. I call that the force of the wind.'
- Making a class dictionary or glossary of vocabulary to be used.

Specific points for science in the EDP

In the EDP, there are two places where we believe science is particularly important (Figure 2.7).

Scientific testing and knowledge in exploring ideas

One opportunity for science in the EDP is when the children are exploring their ideas. This point could initiate a teacher-led investigation or a teacher demonstration. The purpose of this phase is to provide the children with scientific knowledge that will help them inform the decisions they make about their future designs. For example, when solving the problem of the rabbit hutch door that keeps being left open, the children needed to understand how to make simple electrical circuits and how buzzers work in a circuit in order to install a simple alarm system. The teacher could do some drama modelling with a loop of string in a circuit and a child acting like a buzzer when the rope passed through her hands, followed by some exploration of putting buzzers into circuits and exploring breaks in a circuit and switches with silver foil and cardboard. The teacher then can demonstrate a selection of switches, such as a paper clip switch, a tilt switch with a ball of silver foil completing a circuit when inverted connecting two wires, a push button switch, etc. The children then will have enough knowledge and a mental model of the circuit to be able to form their own designs.

This can also be a point where the children carry out research from secondary sources using the internet or reference books. This might focus on previously existing designs or answer questions such as what to add to soil to help it hold water, what stops bananas going brown, etc. Having clear questions to answer can prevent the children's research from wandering when interrogating the internet.

Scientific testing and knowledge in testing and improving

At this point, the children will either have a prototype design or an adapted design that they wish to test for its effectiveness. Scientific testing methods allow them to evaluate the effectiveness of their design. For example, the weight that a table can take, the length of the flight of a glider, the length of time before the fruit goes off. The data can help them evaluate their design.

How does this fit with design and technology curricula?

Most curricula at the primary/elementary age include some design and technology knowledge and skills. These curricula include a focus on creative, practical, and technical knowledge and skills such as understanding how mechanisms such as levers and axles work and the ability to select and use appropriate tools and materials. These are the elements of the design and technology curricula that are done well; it is common to see children in classrooms making things and using tools.

However, many design and technology curricula go beyond these elements, and in many classrooms these additional elements are often missing. Rather than just a focus on the making stage, the design and technology curricula also require children to be taught about a variety of other elements.

Solve real-life problems in a variety of contexts

This links directly to the 'igniting ideas' stage of the EDP presented here. Through this, children will develop an understanding of the purposes and importance of engineering, design, and technology.

Critique and evaluate their own products and those of others

Often, the evaluation and improvement stage are missed in lessons; children finish making their product and do not evaluate it. In the 'making, testing and improving ideas' stage, children are supported in this continual evaluation and improvement cycle. The 'developing ideas' stage encourages children to explore the ideas of others and evaluate them in terms of the engineering need that they are trying to meet.

Explore products against a set of criteria

There are several points where children are encouraged and supported in doing this through the EDP. The first is in investigating products that are already available against the needs in each engineering challenge. Children are encouraged to select which of their plans is the most appropriate by considering them in light of the requirements and criteria set during the 'exploring ideas' stage. Finally, the EDP requires children to evaluate and test their products against the criteria and make improvements when these factors are not met.

Understand and use the iterative process of designing and making

The EDP remains the same for each engineering challenge set. The more the children use it, the deeper they will understand the purpose of each section.

Improve technical knowledge of how to make products stronger, more stable, etc.

This process occurs through the 'making, testing, and improving ideas' stage. If children did not evaluate their products, they may, for example, simply accept a wobbly cup or a cup which collapses under the weight of its contents. The 'making, testing, and improving ideas' stage encourages children to find solutions to these issues either through researching everyday products or through collaborating with their peers.

Within each chapter, specific design and technology skills and understanding are covered in more detail. However, through use of the EDP, teachers can be assured that they are covering many of the more design and technology skills, understanding and purposes.

How do I fit this into a packed school curriculum?

All teachers are aware of how difficult it is to fit anything extra into the school curriculum, where even statutory subjects are at risk of getting reduced or omitted. This is not an extra subject but a meaningful approach to teaching science and design technology. However, it is always useful to know how other teachers organise their curricula. Here are some examples of the ways schools have organised teaching engineering:

- Having an off-curriculum day with an invited STEM ambassador from local industry. A local school looked at designing a knee brace for a person with damaged ligament by making knee models to understand the injury, testing materials for breathability, flexibility, and support, and designing removable knee supports. This was using the U.S. Engineering is Elementary Curriculum materials. They had contacted a local industry that made prosthetic knees to support the activity during the afternoon and to help the class evaluate their products.
- Fit engineering design challenges into your science lessons over a term. One school we worked with was covering sound and incorporated designing ear defenders, the best

way to muffle a ticking clock, and making instruments while exploring vibration, sound travelling, and hearing.
- Doing an activity during a science week across the school. Each class had distinctive design challenges related to their current science topic, culminating in a whole school assembly with parents and a local engineer talking about her job and life.
- Splitting the parts of the engineering design task into parts. One school used a design technology lesson to set the task of making a burglar alarm and to explore the ideas the children produced. They then carried out a science investigation in a science lesson, exploring breaks in circuits, and measuring sound when using different batteries producing numerical data to inform the children's understanding, wrote instructional texts about their task in English, used the data from the science investigation make a scattergram, and to carry out some data analysis in maths.
- Run a science and engineering club outside of school hours.
- Have a display board for collecting ideas/pictures of engineering problems. Have worksheets/posters taking the children through some of the EDP stages and a 'tinkering' station with materials for them to try out and test some of their ideas when they have finished their work.

How to use this book?

This book is intended as a teacher's guide to support you running your own engineering sessions in your own classroom. We would not expect all the science and design technology taught in your classroom to be covered through engineering or for engineering to be happening every week. Instead, you may want to consider teaching one science or design technology topic through engineering in a year or use the engineering challenges to accompany a topic. They could be used as an introduction to a topic or even as a summing up and application exercise. The choice is yours!

In Chapters 3 to 10, you will find a series of engineering challenges, each accompanied by a set of support materials. Some of these materials are resources to support you as a teacher, as below.

1. The engineering challenge setting out the problem to be solved.
   - this will be in the form of a message or email etc. from a fictional primary/elementary-aged child asking for help in solving a problem linked to the sustainable development goals
   - guidance on the aims and purpose of the challenge set
2. An outline of the science, design technology concepts and skills, and the sustainability goals covered by each engineering challenge.
3. An explanation and exploration of the science subject knowledge involved.
   - Teacher's notes setting out the background subject knowledge required to engage with the challenge set fully.
4. Guidance about how and where the science and design technology subject content knowledge could be covered during the EDP.
   - This includes a consideration not only of where this could be integrated, but also how this could be explored and experienced.

5 Teachers' instructions
   - Lesson plans formatted around the structure of the EDP with suggested timings
   - Teacher's notes for each section of the EDP (e.g., prompts and key questions for each stage of the EDP)
   - Specific ideas for activities to enable children to evaluate their designs and products effectively.
6 A list of potential solutions (for children who may need additional support)
7 Links to the sustainable development goals and further information/resources about the environmental issues discussed.
8 Ideas for addressing common misconceptions often held by children.
   - Suggestions about common misconceptions held by children related to the science knowledge and skills content will be presented alongside ideas and activities designed to address these.
   - Key vocabulary, definitions, and usage
9 Health and safety considerations (and steps to take to advert these)
10 Lists of potential resources needed.
   - These resource lists will only contain every day and common classroom resources and equipment. As the activities are contextualised into an everyday problem, each will only need everyday materials and equipment.
11 Links to wider resources for both teachers and children.
   - Signposting to sources of further support for science knowledge development, and vocabulary.
   - Lists of resources and activities related to the underlying science subject knowledge are provided alongside each of the challenges.

A photocopiable Childrens' Engineering Challenge Sheet for use by the children in your class can be found in the Appendix. These are as follows:

1 A photocopiable children's engineering page containing the following:
   - The engineering challenge in child-friendly form (igniting ideas)
   - A notepad area for factors arising in the 'developing ideas' stage (three questions that you need answering; factors that you will have to remember when designing your product)
   - Imagined ideas and ideas we have researched (developing ideas)
   - A space for three plans (with prompts to consider the pros and cons of each plan)
   - The selected plan. Justifying why the final plan has been selected (measured against the original challenge set)
2 A photocopiable sheet to aid children in testing and improving their products with prompts, including:
   - What went well
   - What parts of your design did not work so well
   - What innovative ideas other people produced
   - Further research/findings

- What you would tell someone else who was trying to solve the challenge problem
3   Where appropriate, there may also be a science investigation sheet, too.

We hope that you and the children that you work with enjoy using these challenges. Once you have become accustomed to this way of working, you may produce some engineering challenges of you own, or the children may notice issues in their everyday lives that you could engineer a solution for. We hope that the more that you and your children engage with these activities, the more you will want to do!

Bibliography

Abrahams, I., and Reiss, M. (2012) Practical work: Its effectiveness in primary and secondary schools in England. *Journal of Research in Science Teaching*, vol. 49, no. 8, pp. 1035-1055.
Beaty, A. (2013) *Rosie Revere, Engineer*. New York: Abrams Books.
Chiu, M., and Lin, J. (2005) Promoting fourth graders' conceptual change of their understanding of electric current via multiple analogies. *Journal of Research in Science Teaching*, vol. 42, no. 4, pp. 429-464.
Lucas, B., and Hanson, J. (2016) Thinking like an engineer: Using engineering habits of mind and signature pedagogies to redesign engineering education. *International Journal of Engineering Pedagogy*, vol. 6, no. 2, p. 4.
Lucas, B., Hanson, J., Bianchi, L., and Chippindall, J. (2017) Learning to be an engineer. *Implications for Schools. Royal Academy of Engineering*. Available at https://www.stem.org.uk/system/files/elibrary-resources/2018/01/learning-to-be-an-engineer.pdf
Lucas, B., Hanson, J., and Claxton, G. (2014) Thinking like an engineer: Implications for the education system. *Royal Academy of Engineering*. Retrieved from: www.raeng.org.uk/thinkinglikeanengineer
Lottero-Perdue, P.S., and Parry, E.A. (2017) Elementary teachers' reflections on design failures and use of fail words after teaching engineering for two years. *Journal of Pre-College Engineering Education Research (J-PEER)*, vol. 7, no. 1, pp. 1-24.
NGSS Lead States. (2013) *Next Generation Science Standards: For States, by States*. Washington, DC: The National Academies Press. https://www.nextgenscience.org/. Accessed 1 February 2021.
Royal Academy of Engineering Standing Committee for Education and Training. (2014) *Thinking like an Engineer*. Available at https://raeng.org.uk/media/brjjknt3/thinking-like-an-engineer-full-report.pdf
Tizard, B., and Hughes, M. (2002) *Young Children Learning*, 2nd ed. Malden, Mass: Blackwell.
Watt D., and Russell, T. (1990) *Primary SPACE Project Reports*. Liverpool: Liverpool University Press.

Resources on children's misconceptions in science

Allen, M. (2019) *Misconceptions in Primary Science*. London: OUP.

3 Plants/states of matter

Design and technology focus: Evaluating existing products and solutions

The Engineering Challenge

Mrs. Parker has made an announcement to the school:

The school lunchtime gardening club has planted some peas, but they need a lot of water. Is there a way that the children in the club could collect rainwater to use for watering? (rainwater collection and/or irrigation system) She mentioned that peas need a lot of water; roughly 397 litres of water for a kilogram of peas! (Poore and Nemecek, 2018).

Aim of the challenge

The aim of this challenge is an agricultural engineering task to design and test a water collection system for growing crops. The activities will look at evaporation of water and allow thinking on how evaporation could be reduced.

Agricultural engineering is a field that is practised across the world. Solving problems in food production is an ancient activity; it might be a farmer trying to maximise their crops in difficult climatic situations or large companies finding technological solutions to growing and producing food.

A photocopiable Childrens' Engineering Challenge Sheet can be found in Appendix.

Sustainable development goals

This design challenge connects to the UN sustainable development goals (2013) of:

Goal 3: Zero Hunger: End hunger, achieve food security, and improved nutrition and promote sustainable agriculture

Goal 12: Ensure sustainable consumption and production patterns.

DOI: 10.4324/9781003325826-3

Part of Goal 2 has an emphasis on sustainable food production, avoiding waste and increasing yields of crops through sustainable means.

The International Food Policy Institute (2015) published a report that indicated that, although rates were falling, 829 million people globally are undernourished. Undernourished means that people are not getting the right number of calories a day and their intake of nutrients, essential for growth and repair, is lacking.

They cite the main causes of undernutrition to be conflict and weather-related issues. Climate change has the effect of increasing rainfall in some areas of the world but also decreasing rainfall in other areas. This lack of rainfall can lead to farmers needing to irrigate their crops, often diverting water away from other settlements, possibly causing agricultural issues elsewhere.

In Kenya, 350 million tonnes of food and flowers are grown and exported to the European markets while parts of Kenya experience hunger and undernutrition. The process of producing the beans, peas, and other vegetables deplete water, which is a scarce resource in Kenya. However, on the other hand, the agricultural activity in Kenya provides employment for many workers.

See the YouTube video reported by George Aligiyah. Kenyan beans

While it is possible to grow peas and beans in more temperate countries like the United Kingdom, because of the climate, the produce would only be available in the summer. In many countries, the population has grown used to having year-around produce through the growing and shipping of produce in warmer climates, like Kenya. Not only does this cause environmental issues in the countries where the produce is grown, but it also relies on air transportation creating a greater carbon footprint. This in turn contributes to climate change. One could argue that this is not sustainable production and consumption of vegetables. For further information on food miles, see https://www.bbc.co.uk/bitesize/topics/zjr8mp3/articles/zjnxwnb.

Growing our own vegetables is achievable in the summer. Even flats and houses with small outdoor areas can grow some vegetables for the kitchen. For some advice on growing plants in small areas, see https://www.rhs.org.uk/garden-design/roof-gardens-balconies.

Potential solutions

The children could suggest we just put out a bucket and hope for rain, but the water may get spilt, dirty, or evaporate before we get to use it.

Houses have a system where the rain is collected from the roof into water butts via guttering; this is from a large area of the roof.

Around the world, people have designed ways of collecting water. Here are some to get you thinking.

For example, a woman may use a sari to increase the area from which she collects water and funnels it into a container. Alternatively, some people may use nets to collect the fog in the air which then runs down into a container. Other systems used by the Romans collected water from the mountains and channelled it through many kilometres to take the water to the farmland on the lower slopes. You could construct a slope to increase the area to collect the rainfall and then use guttering to channel the water.

In each of these systems, there may be evaporation from the surface of the water. The children could design a system with an impermeable lid or cover to prevent water loss.

Science content

The science content for this challenge lies in subject knowledge on plants and how plants make food and the movement of water in plants as well as states of matter in particular evaporation.

Children aged 5-7 years

Naming and understanding the functions of basic parts of a plant (e.g., leaves, stem, root, flowers, and roots).
   That plants need light, water, and warmth to grow.
   Becoming aware of weather (e.g., when it rains and how much it rains).

Children aged 7-11 years

Understand what soils are made from.
   Understand what happens to the rate of evaporation with temperature, sunlight, wind speed, and surface area.
   Recognise that water can change state when evaporating and condensing.

Vocabulary

- Liquid/gas/solid
- Soil/soil particle, humus
- Evaporation/condensation/water vapour, liquid, gas, solid
- Surface area, wind speed, temperature, and heat
- Impermeable/porous/waterproof. Whether materials will let water in its gas form move through them.

The science explained

Water as a solid, liquid, or gas and evaporation.
   Water is made up of two elements of hydrogen and one of oxygen combined. In water, ice and steam in these combined elements act together as one part, a water molecule. These molecules vibrate according to how much heat energy they have (e.g., a cold solid will vibrate less than a warmer solid). In a solid, these molecules are arranged tightly together in a rigid structure, with very little vibration.
   In a liquid, water, the water molecules are moving faster, as it is warmer, and have enough energy to break some of the bonds between them. They are still attracted to each other so stay as one entity. When water is heated further, some of the water molecules will have the energy to break away from the surface of the water and move off into the air. This is how water evaporates. If they cool a bit in the air, they may clump together with other water molecules as steam or tiny droplets of water.

There are numerous molecules of water in the air at any point. If they cool or hit a cooler surface, they lose the energy to be free of each other, are attracted to each other, and form small droplets of water that we call condensation.

Plants and water

Plant matter is made up of 95% water. Water is responsible for many essential functions in plants, such as making food, transport, rigidity, and cooling, and is an essential part of photosynthesis in plants (the way a plant makes food).

The plant uses the energy of the sun to combine carbon dioxide from the air and the hydrogen from water to make starches, which form food for the plant. Plants use water to dissolve and transport this food around the leaves, stem, roots, and leaves to feed and grow the whole plant. The roots also take up water with dissolved micronutrients from the soil.

Water exits the plant through small holes in the leaves called stoma. The evaporation from the leaves causes a pulling effect on the water travelling around the plant helping the roots take up more water. The evaporation of the water from the leaves also cools the plant when it is hot. It is the water in the plant that makes the plant rigid and upright. If you have seen a floppy plant that is lacking water, you can see what a lack of water can do!

Soil is a mixture of water, small particles of rock, and decaying matter. Soils hold different amounts of water according to their type. Gravel soils can contain as little as 15-20% water, whereas clay or silty soil can contain as much as 50-80% water. If the soil has a lot of organic matter added, the water content can reach 500%. The water in soil usually sits between the soil particles but is also attracted by and sticks to the particles. These attractive forces become much stronger when less water is available making it harder for plants to access. The water in soil can be tested by weighing and comparing two samples of the same amount of soil, one having been baked in an oven to remove all the water.

Water loss from soil can be reduced through adding organic matter to soils and mulching (putting material on the surface of the soil that reduces water loss). Reducing the air temperature can also reduce evaporation, as can increasing the humidity.

Some farmers add water to the soil through irrigation. Another technique is to plant the plant in a hollow, so water does not run away when it rains or to space out plants, so they have better access to the water in the soil.

Design and technology content

Age	Skills	Example product for this challenge
Ages 3-6	For young children, the skills required should be kept as simple as possible. This could involve selecting and trying out various containers for collecting rainwater and verbally evaluating their effectiveness.	Identifying a suitable container for collecting rain

Ages 6-8	Older children start to design solutions for collecting larger amounts of water (e.g., increasing the area for collection).
	    Cutting and exploring fixings of materials to each other to collect water.
	    The children can build structures and work out how to make them stronger/more effective.
		Design and make a collection area for water and a way of feeding the water into a vessel for collection.

Ages 8-11	At this stage, the children could explore ways to collect larger amount of water through using a larger surface area and explore how we can store the water to prevent evaporation. Cutting and exploring fixings, understanding about the use of gravity for transporting water. They will learn about strengthening and reinforcing structures.	Design and make a lid that prevents evaporation or siting the storage to reduce water loss. The children could think of solutions for transporting the water from the collection area to the storage.

Teacher's guidance (lesson and activity plans)

The tables below set out how the science and design and technology content could fit within the EDP. This is not an exhaustive list, and you may well be able to think of alternatives or different ways of organising the content for your own class.

These tables also give example activities to do at each stage of the EDP and key questions to ask. Again, these are ideas for you to use, adapt, and add to for your own classes.

EDP stage: Ignite

Learning Objectives: To be able to identify a presented need or requirement. To be able to articulate what is needed as an outcome of the challenge set.		
Thought Processes/Engineering Habits of Mind (EHOM) Understand, empathise, connect. Problem Finding		
Key Questions	Vocabulary	Resources
What is the problem that that the gardening club is having?	• Requirements/parameters/constraints • Absorbent, waterproof, permeable, porous, impervious • Evaporation, condensation, water vapour, liquid, gas, solid • Soil, soil particle, humus	Copies of the children's engineering challenge page

46 *Plants/states of matter*

Activities
Describing the challenge
- Share the challenge with the children
- Discussions to clarify the need presented in the challenge

Assessment
The children should be able to define the challenge that has been set for them, showing that they understand the need presented and what they are required to do to provide a solution.

 **EDP stage: Exploring Ideas**

In this stage, we help the children understand about the conditions in which water evaporates.

Exploring Evaporation in Wate
Science Content Learning Objectives: - Recognise that water can changes state when evaporating and condensing. - Explore some of the conditions that speed up and slow down evaporation. - Understand what the movement of water in plants and what might affect the speed of movement (e.g., light water and temperature).
Design and Technology Learning Objectives: - To be able to discuss the potential solutions to the problem of capturing rainwater. - To be able to ask questions about the conditions, needs, and purpose of the challenge set. - To be able to identify requirements and constraints of the set challenge.
Thought Processes/Engineering Habits of Mind (EHoM) Question, refine, focus, apply logic and systems thinking. Creative problem solving

Key Questions	Vocabulary	Resources
- How much water do we need? - How much water is in the soil already? - How can we collect a large amount of water? - How can we keep the water clean? - How can we stop the water evaporating? - What materials do we have to carry out the problem?	- Evaporation, condensation, water vapour, liquid, gas, solid - Temperature, heat - Air speed - Water particles	Each group needs 3 of the same saucers Food colouring, measuring cylinder or measuring jug, felt pen Activity 1 need thermometer Activity 2 may need cling-film

- How can we prevent it being knocked over?
- How can we keep it so we can transport it to the peas?
- Where do you think the water goes?
- What do you think speeds up puddles drying?
- How could we test the conditions in which water evaporates slowest?
- How can we make it a fair test?
- Do you think the shape of the container will make a difference?

Identifying the requirements and constraints of the set challenge
- Discussions about what the children need to know to provide a solution to the challenge set (see suggested questions above)
- In groups, each group composes three questions to ask about the parameters of the challenge set
- Children writing lists of challenge constraints and requirements
- Children complete 'exploring ideas' section on their EDP worksheet
- Examine the range of materials and tools available to use
- Teachers may need to prompt and guide children on any missed information (e.g., time allowance, conditions that the product will be used in, materials available, etc.)

Thinking about evaporation and condensation
- Teacher to demonstrate evaporation with a pan of boiling water or kettle; in small groups discuss what the children think is happening to the water and where it is going. Ask the children to draw what is happening.
- Hold a cold plate above the water vapour and ask the children to observe what is happening.
- Do some drama in the playground with the children acting as water molecules, clustered together in a liquid and then speeding up and slowing down with varying amounts of heat energy (hot, moving faster and cold, moving slower). The fastest children could break away from the liquid into the air as a gas.
- Model heat's effect on water molecules with ping-pong balls in a box. Jiggle them to indicate the movement of molecules in a liquid and shake the box to let some out as a gas.

See science investigations in the table below for other ways to develop the children's thinking on evaporation and movement of water in plants.

Assessment Indicator
Children should understand that evaporation is water becoming a gas and moving away from the surface of the liquid. They should understand that evaporation can be speeded up by changing the conditions of the liquid (e.g., temperature).

Children should understand the function of the roots in plants and the movement of water throughout the plant.

48 Plants/states of matter

 EDP stage: Developing ideas

Science Content Learning Objectives:
- Investigate the properties of materials used in similar products.
- To be able to discuss why these materials have been chosen.
- To investigate the properties of materials (could also be covered during the Designing Ideas stage or the Making, Testing and Improving Ideas stage).

Design and Technology Learning Objectives:
- To investigate how similar products have been made. (How have the materials been joined together?
- To use information from a variety of sources to generate ideas for potential solutions.

Key Questions	Vocabulary	Resources
• What is the item made from? Why do you think that this material was chosen? • How have the parts of the item been joined together? • What have you seen or used before that may help you to develop ideas? • What can we find out about what other, similar products are made of? • What have you found out from your research/looking at other products which could help you with your own designs?	• Absorbent, water-proof, permeable, porous, impervious • Evaporation, condensation, water vapour, liquid, gas, solid • Soil, soil particle, humus	• Children's engineering worksheet • If possible, have a range of similar items made from different materials. • Access to laptops or tablets, etc. for research into a range of products related to the challenge (e.g., mist nets, rainwater capture).

Activities
- Brainstorm imagination activities in small groups to produce wild and whacky solutions.
- Sharing of ideas discovered or imagined.
- Complete the 'developing ideas' section of the photocopiable children's engineering page.

Examine similar products/discuss why these systems and materials have been chosen
- Ask the children to examine what they have at home or what they have seen before that might be used to collect water. What are these items made from?
- Internet or literature-based research about designs or products that could provide ideas.
- Using real items or internet searches investigate the range of materials used to made similar items. Which material would be best for the product and why?
- Explore watering systems that only deliver small amount of water to a plant at a time. How do they work?

To use information from a variety of sources to generate ideas for potential solutions
- How could the product be improved?
- Which ideas could you take to use in your own product?

Assessment Indicators
Children are able to identify at least one product/system which could be used to solve the challenge set.
   Children are able to explain how this product/system works and why it has been chosen.
   Children are able to identify features of a researched product or system for use in their own designs.

EDP stage: Designing idea

Science Content Learning Objectives:
- To draw on knowledge of plants and evaporation to design a solution to the challenge, being aware of ways to reduce water loss.

Design and Technology Learning Objectives:
- To be able to draw and design a set of plans relating to an intended product.
- To be able to draw on wider research to inform a product design.
- To be able to analyse and evaluate plans and potential products for their suitability in meeting the requirements of the challenge set.
- To be able to evaluate methods of joining and reinforcement (testing of various tapes and staples) to decide which ones work best with the materials, which are the strongest or most suitable for the job).

Thought Processes/Engineering Habits of Mind (EHoM)
Analyse, compare, evaluate, visualise, adapt

Key Questions	Vocabulary	Resources
• Why have you decided on your final product design? • What makes this one better than your other options? • How does your design meet the challenge and the constraints/requirements set out in the Explore stage? • Do you anticipate any problems or issues when making your product? • How have you used what you have learnt from your research in your design?	• Analyse, compare, evaluate, visualise, adapt • Prototype • Product • Research, investigate • Joint/fixing • Collection, storage • Evaporation	• Children's engineering worksheet

Activities
Designing
- Identify and design three main ideas for water collection systems to be made.
- Draw up plans for three potential systems, including some that deliver water to roots of plant.

50 Plants/states of matter

- Evaluate and assess which of these ideas best meets the requirements set out in the Ignite and explore stages of the EDP.
- Explain product choice to others in the class and share reasoning about why this product has been chosen.
- Share with the class how the knowledge gained through investigating other products and systems has been used in this design.
- Identify how the separate parts of the product will be joined together or how any attachments will be added on.
- Complete the 'designing ideas' section on the children's engineering worksheet.

Testing
- Testing joints between materials and parts of system (e.g., the joint between the collection and the transport to the storage system). Testing out sticky tape and duct tape, staples, and other fixings with materials and observing what happens when the fixings are wet or moved a great deal by pouring the same volume of water on each fixing.

Assessment Indicators
Children can select on design from a range and articulate why this is the most suitable choice.
Children can explain how they will join the separate components of their product together and explain why they have chosen this method.

 **EDP stage: Making, testing, and improving ideas**

Science Content Learning Objectives:
- To investigate the properties of materials (could also be covered during the Developing Ideas stage or the Designing Ideas stage).
- To be able to apply scientific understanding within a 'real-world' context.

Design and Technology Learning Objectives:
- To develop explicit skills (e.g., using a hot glue gun, cutting with a craft knife on a cutting mat).
- To be aware of a variety of health and safety considerations.
- To be able to turn a design for a solution to a set problem into a product.
- To be able to test a product against a set of pre-determined criteria (from the 'exploring ideas' stage).
- To be able to share ideas and use and adapt the ideas of others.

Thought Processes/Engineering Habits of Mind (EHoM)
Analyse, compare, evaluate, improve

Key Questions	Vocabulary	Resources
- Does your water collection system help the gardening club's problem?	- Test, improve, evaluate, improve, appraise - product - research, investigate	- Children's engineering worksheet - Black plastic bin bags - Sheets of card

• Does your product meet all the specifications set out in the 'exploring ideas' stage? • Did you encounter any problems when making your product? • What solutions to these problems did you find? • Did other groups encounter similar problems? What solutions did they produce? • Did you choose the most appropriate material to make your product out of? Why/why not?	• Requirements/parameters/constraints • Absorbent, waterproof, permeable, porous, impervious • Flexible, rigid, strength, malleable, ductile, floppy, elastic, stretchy, supple, bendy, pliable, firm, dense, bendable, soft, spongy	• Duct tape • Glue guns • Elastic bands • Plastic shopping bags • Measuring jugs • Sheets of corflute • Guttering (if available) • Plastic buckets or bowls • Containers, various • Measuring cylinders • General making equipment such as scissors, rulers, etc.

Activities

Explicit Skills Teaching
- Demonstrations of how to use various tools, such as scissors, glue guns, or craft knives safely.

Health and Safety
- Children could make safety posters or warning signs for the various tools to be used.
- Teachers will need to decide which pieces of equipment are suitable for the children in their classes based on the age and skills level of the children.

Making Activities
- Time for children to make their designed product. Children may need help to use the angle of a pipe or channel to move water from the collector to the plant or storage. They may also not realise how heavy water can be and need help to reinforce or support structures.

See also the linked scientific investigations below.
- Investigate the evaporation and water travelling in plants (could also be covered during the 'developing ideas' stage or the 'designing ideas' stage). See additional section below.

Testing and Appraising Ideas
- The different water systems can be constructed and put into place. They can be tested by having the same amount of water in a watering can with a sprinkler to simulate the rain. The water that reaches the storage system can be measured. The water can then be left in the storage system for a couple of days to observe the loss of water through evaporation. The water should be weighed again to calculate the loss.
- Use the children's engineering worksheet to evaluate what went well, which parts of the design did not work so well, and what needs to be improved.
- Refer back to the original challenge set. Have the children designed and made a product that solves the issue presented?

Improving Ideas
- Often, during this stage the children encounter problems with their product. This provides an opportunity to revisit the science involved to help them to solve these issues.
- Again, when encountering issues, this would be a good opportunity for children to go back to do some further research (e.g., what materials are used to make water pipes? Why are these chosen?).

- Children display their part or fully completed products alongside their designs. All children move around the classroom to examine the work of others. Encourage the children to note down good ideas that they could use in their own designs and products.
- Ask each child/group of children to share an issue or triumph that they have had with their design and product. The rest of the class can either use the idea that worked or offer a solution to the issue experienced.
- Children then return to their own designs and products and adapt, considering this new information.

Assessment Indicators

Children can identify features of each other's designs that work well and consider how they could be used in their own design.

Children are able to describe what they like and don't like about their product.

They are able to describe why their product is suitable for the conditions that it will be used in.

Children are able to describe how their product has been designed and made in order to performs its function.

They are able to evaluate if they have met the design brief and if they have solved the original challenge set.

They are able to offer solutions to various problems encountered by themselves and others.

Their product shows the application of the relevant scientific principles.

Linked Science Investigations	Investigating Evaporation
	There are three different activities the class could do here. The children could do each activity, or the four groups could each do the activity and report back to the class on their findings: 1 Explore the effect of temperature on evaporation. 2 Explore the impact of air movement on evaporation. 3 Explore the effect of surface area on evaporation. 4 Explore the impact of sun on evaporation. *Activity 1* Measure the same amount of water in the measuring jug, colour the water with food colouring. Decide on three separate places of differing temperature (e.g., radiator, fridge, classroom). Ask the children to predict which saucer will contain the least water after the test and why they think this. Pour water into saucer and mark the diameter of the water on the saucer with the felt pen. Leave the saucers for 1 day and see which diameter has the smallest circumference. *Activity 2* Measure the same amount of water in the measuring jug, colour the water with food colouring. Decide on three separate places of differing air movement (e.g., one with cling film, one by a fan, and one in the classroom). Ask the children to predict which saucer will contain the least water after the test and why. Pour water into saucer and mark the diameter of the water. Leave the saucers for 1 day and see which diameter has the smallest circumference.

Activity 3

Measure the same amount of water in the measuring jug, colour the water with food colouring. Decide on three different containers for the water, one on a saucer, one in a bottle and one spread on a dinner plate. Ask the children to predict which container will have the least water after the test and why. Pour water into the containers and weigh each container. Leave the saucers for 1 day and then weigh again to monitor water loss.

Activity 4

Measure the same amount of water in the measuring jug, colour the water with food colouring. Decide on three separate places of differing amounts of sunlight (e.g., in the classroom window, in a cupboard in the classroom, on the side not in the sun, in the classroom). Ask the children to predict which saucer will contain the least water after the test and why. Pour water into the containers and weigh each container. Leave the saucers for 1 day and then weigh again to monitor water loss.

Bring the children together and compare the results. What does this tell us about evaporation under different conditions? What will the class need to think about when trying to collect water for a watering system?

Plants and Water

Collect some house plants, water them, and place a plastic bag over the pot and seal around the stem from the bottom. Put the plant in the window of the classroom. Measure the weight of the pot, plant, and plot this on a graph over time. The weight will reduce as the water is taken up by the plant and is lost through the leaves.

Transpiration in Plants

Put a plastic bag on a branch of a pot plant (not one with waxy leaves) and seal with a tie. Water the plant and observe the plastic bag over a few days. The bag will fill up with condensation from the water coming out of the leaves on the plant.

Movement of Water in Plants

Cut up the middle of a stick of celery as though you were giving it legs. Cut the bottom of the legs off by about 1 cm. Get two beakers or jam jars. Fill them with water and different colours of food colouring. Place each leg of the celery in each of the jam jars. Leave for a few days and watch the celery change colour. If you cut a cross section of the celery you can see the coloured water in the vessels or Xylem of the plant transporting the water.

Different Roots in Plants

Collect a carrot and supermarket herb, and compare. Take the supermarket herb out of its pot and shake over a bin. Both are roots. Watch what happens if you leave both without water. (The carrot may take some time to become limp.)

Grow a broad bean in a jam jar from seed with a kitchen roll and water. Observe how the bean swells up with the water before it sends a shoot out.

54 *Plants/states of matter*

Resources for activities
- Black plastic bin bags
- Sheets of card
- Duct tape
- Glue guns
- Elastic bands
- Plastic shopping bags
- Measuring jugs
- Sheets of corflute
- Guttering (if available)
- Plastic buckets or bowls
- Various containers
- 3 of the same saucers
- Food colouring
- Measuring cylinder or measuring jug
- Felt pen
- Activity 1 need thermometer
- Activity 2 may need cling-film
- House plants
- Plastic bags
- Plastic bag ties
- Weighing scales
- Graphing paper
- Broad beans
- Glass beakers
- Kitchen roll
- Measuring cylinder

Health and safety

The materials and tools used for this challenge do not pose significant health and safety threats. Children should be taught how to use craft knives and cutting mats correctly and general classroom safety with these, such as not moving around the classroom with them in their hands and placing them into the centre of the table when not in use. With sharp tools such as scissors and knives it is good practice to count out how many you have made available at the start of the lesson and then to count them back in again.

Glue guns may be used by children, depending on their age, but try to use the cold glue gun versions and only have these available under close adult supervision. Make sure the cable is not in a position where it can catch on children or objects.

Plants/states of matter 55

Common misconception on evaporation and plants

Many children believe that a plant's food comes from the soil or from plant foot dissolved in water. Although the plant food does contain micronutrients essential for plant health, almost all a plant's food is made through photosynthesis. Water is an essential part of this process.

Evaporation

Children sometimes believe that water disappears when it evaporates. It is useful to show the children the condensation that forms on the bottom of the plate above a kettle to show the water is still there and can be seen when it clumps together again in water droplets.

The modelling activities in the activities will support their understanding in this area.

Some children also believe that changes of state from ice to water to water vapour are irreversible and you cannot change them back. The activities in the sessions will support their understanding that these are reversible changes.

Wider resources related to materials, their properties, and uses

For children aged 5-7-years, the BBC has some good materials for learning about parts of the plant. Https://www.bbc.co.uk/bitesize/topics/zpxnyrd/articles/z2vhxbk

Science and Plants for Schools (SAPS) has teaching materials for all primary ages on the function of parts of the plant at https://www.saps.org.uk/teaching-resources/resources/1373/primary-booklet-1-parts-of-a-plant-and-their-functions/

Stem learning has a selection of resources for plants at all primary age ranges
https://www.stem.org.uk/primary-science

For learning on states of matter see
https://www.stem.org.uk/resources/community/collection/12345/year-4-states-matter

The American Chemistry Society (ACS) has some fun activities to show how heat is molecules and atoms moving faster at
https://www.acs.org/content/acs/en/education/whatischemistry/adventures-in-chemistry/experiments/heat-energy-on-move.html

Other example activities for plants

- Georgie loves eating strawberries, but they only sell them in plastic tubs, and she wants to cut down on using plastics. She does not have a garden and so would like something that she can grow strawberries in on her windowsill. Design a window box that would allow for drainage but would keep the water, soil, and plants in.

- Aisha's mum like to grow tall poppies in her garden, but they flop over easily. Design a structure to keep the plants upright.
- See also Chapter 8 about growing plants in a greenhouse.

Bibliography

International Food Policy Research Institute. (2015). Global Nutrition Report 2015: Actions and Accountability to Advance Nutrition and Sustainable Development. Washington, DC.

Poore, J., and Nemecek, T. (2018). Reducing food's environmental impacts through producers and consumers. *Science*, 360(6392), 987–992.

UN. (2013). Sustainable Development Goals. Available at https://www.un.org/en/sustainable-development-goals

4 Animal and humans

Design and technology focus: Evaluation of a final product

The Engineering Challenge

Ben is concerned about his granny. She lives in an old house and does not want to put on the heating as it costs a lot, and she knows it is bad for the environment. She sits in her chair reading and gets very cold. Sometimes she wants a covering when she goes out in her wheelchair. Can you help with a solution that will keep granny warmer?

Aim of the challenge

The aim of this challenge is to produce a product that would keep Granny warmer without spending money on more heating. It could be a solution that insulates the room further or a very warm cover that she could wear when reading.

Energy-efficiency engineers work on solutions to reduce energy use and lower energy costs. They work on alternative energy solutions such as wave power, solar energy, and wind power.

A photocopiable Childrens' Engineering Challenge Sheet can be found in the Appendix.

Sustainable development goals

This design challenge connects to the UN sustainable development goals (2013) of:

> Goal 3: Ensure healthy lives and promote well-being for all at all ages. This task focuses on the target aiming to reduce non communicable disease, in this case, circulatory disease through cold conditions. Many people suffer from cardiovascular diseases through a range of factors. Cold conditions can exacerbate issues of high blood pressure.

> Goal 7: Ensure access to affordable and clean energy.

In Europe, most people use oil, gas, or electricity to heat their homes. We need to reduce this energy use by 95% if we are going to reach the goal of net zero (the balance between carbon emitted and carbon removed from the atmosphere) set by some governments (Energy Saving Trust, 2023). Heating systems such as these release carbon into the atmosphere in the form of carbon dioxide which is a greenhouse gas. These greenhouse gases absorb heat and scatter it in many directions including back down to Earth. This is important to keep the world's surface from freezing, but an excess of greenhouse gases mean the heat reflected to Earth is raising the temperature of the Earth's surface and disrupting the climate patterns.

Some of the ways of reaching net zero are to convert heating systems to ground source or air heat pump systems but these are expensive at present. We can make energy savings through loft insulation, draft proofing, and cavity wall insulation.

However, many people find it difficult to pay their heating bills. It is estimated that approximately 14.5% of the UK households will be in fuel poverty in 2023 (meaning more than 10% of their household income after housing cost is used on fuel) (Department of Energy Security and Net Zero, 2023). Current rises in energy prices due to world events may mean this percentage is even higher.

Potential solutions

The children could design a leg/foot warmer after researching circulation and materials. There are several commercially available foot warmers or blankets some with integral heating elements.

They could design a warm blanket with a pocket for a hot water bottle of a foot pad that also integrates a hot water bottle.

The children could make wheat bags or rice bags that can be put in the microwave and then will retain heat, see below. (Safety note: Please see safety instruction for making and using wheat or rice bags in microwave.)

Alternately, they could research and design a blanket with different layers of materials to keep in the heat, with some bubble wrap.

They could design a box that you put your feet in that contains materials that insulate heat.

However, they may get interested in designing slippers using a range of fabrics and materials. They might have to think about the soles and tops of the slippers and how they are going to fix them together.

> **Make a heated wheat or rice bag**
>
> The cover should be 100% cotton to prevent burning in the microwave. Use buckwheat, barley, or uncooked white rice; 3.5 cups of filling should be ideal for a bag measuring 18 x 28 cm. The edges should be sewn with cotton thread preferably on a sewing machine. When heating the warmer, place a cup of cold water in the microwave and try heating the bag for 1 minute and then increase by 30 seconds. **Do not reheat until cold. Do not use it in a bed** (Figure 4.1).

Animal and humans 59

Figure 4.1 Examples of heated wheat bags

Science content

The science content for this challenge lies in subject knowledge on human and human organ systems, especially circulation. There are also links to materials and their properties.

Children aged 5-7 years

Children should be able to group materials together based on their simple properties such as rough, smooth, bendy, rigid, etc. They should be able to describe and compare those properties. They should think about the suitability of a material for a particular purpose (e.g., something shiny for fluffy to keep something warm as it will trap the heat in).

Children should be starting to consider what animals and humans need for life (e.g., water, food, shelter, and warmth).

60 Animal and humans

Children aged 7-11 years

At this age, children should be able to compare and identify materials based on a wider range of properties (e.g., absorbency, rigidity, etc.).

The children should also be able to identify and name the main parts of the human circulatory system, and describe the functions of the heart, blood vessels and blood.

Vocabulary

- Heat/cold/freeze
- Circulation, blood vessels
- Pulse, pulse-rate
- Blood/muscle/lung
- Capillaries/heart
- Red blood cells, white blood cells, plasma
- Thermal insulator/conductor
- Skin
- Air pockets/heat reflection

The science explained

In humans, water, and nutrients are transported in the circulatory system. The blood is made of plasma, a straw-coloured liquid that transports liquids and nutrients and red blood cells (that carry oxygen). There are also white blood cells that attack unknown bacteria and viruses in the body. The blood also carries waste products from the organs to the liver and kidneys.

The blood travels around the body through arteries (vessels travelling away from the heart) and veins (blood travelling back to the heart). When blood reaches the skin and organs the blood divides down into tiny blood vessels called capillaries. This is where the blood moves its nutrients and liquid into the tissues surrounding the capillaries. The waste products move into the capillaries and are carried to organs where they can be processed and removed from the body. The heart pushes the blood to the lungs through one side where the blood takes up oxygen and then returns to the other side of the heart where it gives the blood a big push around the body. The different strengths of the different sides of the heart can be felt through the thickness of the heart muscle (see the linked science activities).

When parts of the body get cold, the brain responds in several ways to preserve the heat and make new heat. The capillaries and blood vessels narrow at the skin surface, reducing the amount of blood, and therefore heat loss, from the surface of the skin to deeper down in the body. This has the effect of making the blood thicker, which makes the body more prone to heart attacks. The hairs on the skin raise, trapping air to reduce heat loss in the same way that your duvet is full of fibres and trapped air. The skin can also shiver using muscles and producing warmth to the arms and legs.

See Chapter 5 for further explanation on thermal insulators and thermal conductors.

Design and technology content

The design and technology focus for this chapter is all about evaluation of a final product. An enhanced list of suggested activities for this focus is therefore provided in the 'Teacher's Guidance' section below under the 'making, testing, and improving' ideas section. These enhanced ideas can be lifted and used for any of the other chapters and challenges presented in this book.

Design and technology guidance for the practical elements of this challenge is provided below.

Age	Skills	Example product for this challenge
Ages 3-6	For young children, the skills required should be kept as simple as possible. This could involve selecting and trying out various choosing material for a blanket and verbally evaluating their effectiveness.	Making a warm blanket.
Ages 6-8	Older children start to design solutions for keeping warm while sitting. Cutting and exploring fixings of materials to each other to make coverings.	Making a warm covering for legs and feet Making rice or wheat bag.
Ages 8-11	At this stage, the children could design solution for keeping warm perhaps by incorporating a heat source. Some children might be interested to explore insulating homes solutions (e.g., detecting draughts, blocking drafts, etc.).	Making a covering or garment or slippers that incorporates a heat source such as a hot water bottle/rice or wheat bag. Designing a cushion for granny that contains a heat source. Creating a reflector that sits behind a radiator.

Also see Chapter 5 for guidance on activities involving textile work with children.

Teacher's guidance (lesson and activity plans)

Science and Design and Technology into the EDP (Engineering Design Process) for this Challenge – Teacher's Notes

The tables below set out how the science and design and technology content could fit within the EDP. This is not an exhaustive list, and you may well be able to think of alternatives or different ways of organising the content for your own class.

These tables also give example activities to do at each stage of the EDP and key questions to ask. Again, these are ideas for you to use, adapt, and add to your own classes.

62   Animal and humans

🔥 EDP stage: Ignite

Learning Objectives:
To be able to identify a presented need or requirement.
To be able to articulate what is needed as an outcome of the challenge set.

Thought Processes/Engineering Habits of Mind (EHoM)
Understand, empathise, connect. Problem finding

Key Questions	Vocabulary	Resources
• What problem does Ben's granny have? • What does Ben want us to do? • What might keep legs and feet warmest? • What is the temperature in the room? • What would be a safe form of heat? • What does granny like to wear on her legs and feet normally?	• Requirements/para-meters/ constraints • Insulating • Circulation • Degrees Celsius (Fahrenheit-USA) • Skin temperature • Heat source • Heat transfer • Conduction • Buck wheat	• Various fabrics • Silver foil • Cardboard • Fleece fabric • Fur fabric • Waterproof fabric • Bubble wrap • Handwarmers/hot water bottle • Wheat/rice bags • Cold glue gun

Activities
- Share the challenge with the children.
- Discussions to clarify the need presented in the challenge.
- Discussions about what the children use to keep warm at home.

Assessment Indicators
Children are able to define the challenge that has been set for them, showing that they understand the need presented and what they are required to do in order to provide a solution.

EDP stage: Exploring ideas

In this stage, we help the children understand about circulation and blood and keeping warm.

Science Content Learning Objectives:
- Explore skin temperature on parts of legs and feet and relate that to knowledge on circulation.
- Understand circulation, and the role of blood and the heart.
- Explore some heat sources and how heat loss occurs over time.

Design and Technology Learning Objectives:
- To be able to understand the areas of legs and feet than get the coldest and therefore need a design solution.
- To be able to ask questions about the conditions, needs and purpose of the challenge set.
- To be able to identify requirements and constraints of the set challenge.

Thought Processes/Engineering Habits of Mind (EHoM)
Question, refine, focus, apply logic and Systems thinking. Creative problem solving

Animal and humans

Key Questions	Vocabulary	Resources
Where do you think the skin is coldest on legs and feet? Why do you think this is? Are parts of the body furthest from the heart the coldest? How can we test the heat sources to find out which keeps warmest longest? How can we make it a fair test? What materials keep the warm in for longest? What materials do we have? Do layers of fabric mean the heat loss is less? Does granny need to get up often so have to remove covers? Does granny need to use it outside?	• Circulation • Skin temperature • Capillaries • Arteries • Heart • Lungs • Heat source • Heat loss • Insulation • Air pockets • Heat conduction	Each group needs: A Red and blue balloons or red and blue card or PE bands, cards with names of organs on them, chalk. B Temperature strips, table for recording results. C Wheat bag/rice bags/hot water bottles. D 5 drinks cans, elastic bands, stirring thermometers or digital thermometers, fabric, silver foil, bubble wrap, rulers, scissors. Table to record results.

Identifying the requirements and constraints of the set challenge
- Discussions about what the children need to know to provide a solution to the challenge set.
- In groups, each group composes three questions to ask about the parameters of the challenge set.
- Children writing lists of challenge constraints and requirements.
- Children complete 'exploring ideas' section on their EDP worksheet.
- Examine the range of materials and tools available to use.
- Teachers may need to prompt and guide children on any missed information (e.g., time allowance, conditions that the product will be used in, materials available, etc.)
- Explore skin temperature on parts of legs and feet and relate that to knowledge on circulation.
- Understand circulation, and the role of blood and the heart.

Understand circulation, and the role of blood and the heart.
- Children could do some drama/role-play acting as blood in the circulatory system in the playground. Choose children to act as organs or limbs. Other children can act as blood holding cards with a red and blue side or using red and blue balloons. Have a central heart area and arteries and veins drawn on the ground with chalk. The children, acting as red blood cells, move around the arteries and heart. They can speed up when passing through the heart and swop their red balloons for blue balloons when visiting organs. They will then need to travel to the lungs to swop their cards or balloons for red ones again.

https://www.bbc.co.uk/teach/class-clips-video/science-ks2-how-our-circulatory-system-keeps-us-alive/zhf76v4

Exploring skin temperature on parts of legs and feet and relate that to knowledge on circulation.
- Children in groups explore skin temperature using temperature strips of mid-thigh, knee, calf ankle, top of foot, and toes. Repeat the measurement on three or more children and record results on table. Is there a pattern? Where is the skin coldest, where is the skin warmest? What is the average temperature of the skin on the readings (some children may be sensitive about having their skin temperature measured on their feet as this involves removing socks. This should be a voluntary activity). Here is a chart of ready-prepared data in case this activity is not possible or desirable.

64 Animal and humans

Mid-Thigh	Calf	Ankle	Bottom of Foot	Toes
30.6°C	31.4°C	29.1°C	25°C	25°C

Exploring some heat sources and how heat loss occurs over time
- Activity 1 - Heat Sources
  Children could make wheat or rice bags, see above. The rice/wheat bags need to be heated in the microwave for 90 sec with a cup of water in the oven (see safety guidance above). The Teacher can fill the hot water bottle with off the boil water. Reusable handwarmers could be used as well if available. The heat sources need to be placed in the same location and their temperature monitored every 5 minutes with a digital thermometer and recorded. If these are not available the children could order the items in terms of hottest and coolest at each recording point.

Ask:
Which heat source cooled quickest? Which heat source is the warmest after 30 minutes/60 minutes/90 minutes? The items will all start at different temperatures. How can we tell which is best for keeping granny warm?

Activity 2 - Drinks can people
- The groups should cut out fabric to the same size, enough to cover the side of the drinks can. You could stick little faces on the top of the cans, so the children associate the cans with humans. The children can choose five fabrics, silver foil or bubble wrap to cover the drinks can and secure with an elastic band. The teacher should fill the drinks can with water with hot but not boiling or near boiling water (below 44°C if you want to be very safe). Cans should be placed on a tray so if the spill they do not splash on children. Children can then record and monitor the temperatures of the drinks can over time.
- Which materials kept the drinks can person warmest? Which of the drinks can people was the coldest? What do you think about the materials you used helped to keep the drinks can warm?

For each of these activities, discuss how what has been learnt could feed into their potential solutions for Ben's granny.

Assessment Indicator
Children should be able to explain how the circulatory system works and how this will affect the temperature of the limbs.
   Children should understand the function of the heart, lungs, arteries and veins in transporting food, water, and heat around the body.
   Children should be able to explain how heat is lost through the body.
   Children should have some ideas about what materials can prevent heat conduction from the body and which are less good.

 EDP stage: Developing ideas

Science Content Learning Objectives:
- To draw on knowledge of circulation and materials to design a solution to the challenge

Design and Technology Learning Objectives:
- To be able to draw and design a set of plans relating to an intended product.
- To be able to analyse and evaluate plans and potential products for their suitability in meeting the requirements of the challenge set.

	• To be able to evaluate methods of joining and fixings (testing of various sewing solutions and staples) to decide which ones work best with the materials, which are the strongest or most suitable for the job).

Thought Processes/Engineering Habits of Mind (EHoM)
Analyse, compare, evaluate, visualise, adapt

Key Questions	Vocabulary	Resources
• Why have you decided on your final product design? • What makes this one better than your other options? • How does your design meet the challenge and the constraints/ requirements set out in the Explore stage? • Do you anticipate any problems or issues when making your product?	• Analyse, compare, evaluate, visualise, and adapt • Prototype • Product • Research, investigate • Joint/fixing • Heat insulation • Heat conduction • Air pockets	• Children's engineer worksheet • Various fabrics • Silver foil • Cardboard • Fleece fabric • Fur fabric • Waterproof fabric • Bubble wrap • Handwarmers/hot water bottle • Wheat/rice bags • Cold glue gun • Sewing materials – needles, thread • Scissors • Rulers • Duct tape, Sellotape • Laptops or tablets and/or real life products to investigate

Activities
Investigate how similar products have been made.
- Ask the children to consider what they may have seen or used before that may help them to develop ideas.
- Either using real-life products or researching other products on the market consider, the following:
- Would this product help Ben's granny?
- What is the item made from? Why do you think that this material was chosen?
- How have the parts of the item been joined together?
- How has the product been made strong and stable?
- Would this product last in the conditions in the habitat that you identified?
- What size and shape or the products? Is this suitable for the organism that you will be helping or the space where your product will be used?
- Ask the children to consider which ideas from their research that they could use in their own product.

Initial ideas
- Brainstorm imagination activities in small groups to come up with wild and whacky solutions
- Identify and design three main ideas for keeping granny warm to be made.
- Draw up plans for three potential systems, including some that use heat sources.

66 Animal and humans

- Evaluate and assess which of these ideas best meets the requirements set out in the Ignite and explore stages of the EDP. Explain product choice to others in the class and share reasoning about why this product has been chosen.
- Complete the 'designing ideas' section on the children's engineering worksheet.

Joining components
- Identify how the separate parts of the product will be joined together or how any attachments will be added on.
- Test out fixings between materials and parts of system (e.g., fixings holding fabrics together). Testing out Sellotape and duct tape, staples, and other fixings with materials and observing what happens when the fixings moved.

Assessment Indicators
Children can select a design from a range and articulate why this is the most suitable choice.

Children can explain how they will join the separate components of their product together and explain why they have chosen this method.

Children are able to investigate similar products and identify features that they could incorporate into their own designs and products.

Children are able to articulate a range of ideas about potential products and solutions.

 EDP stage: Making, testing, and improving ideas

Science Content Learning Objectives:
- To be able to apply scientific understanding within a 'real-world' context.

Design and Technology Learning Objectives:
For support and guidance about textile-based activities with children, please see Chapter 5.
- To develop explicit skills (e.g., using a hot glue gun, cutting with a craft knife on a cutting mat, sewing).
- To be aware of a variety of health and safety considerations.
- To be able to turn a design for a solution to a set problem into a product.
- To be able to test a product against a set of pre-determined criteria (from the 'exploring ideas' stage).
- To be able to share ideas and use and adapt the ideas of others.

Thought Processes/Engineering Habits of Mind (EHoM)
Analyse, compare, evaluate, improve

Key Questions	Vocabulary	Resources
• Does your design keep a person warm when sitting in a chair? • Does your product meet all the specifications set out in the 'exploring ideas' stage? • Did you encounter any problems when making your product?	• Test, improve, evaluate, improve, appraise • Product	• Children's engineering worksheet • Various fabrics • Silver foil • Cardboard

• What solutions to these problems did you find? • Did other groups encounter similar problems? What solutions did they produce? • Did you choose the most appropriate material to make your product out of? Why/why not?	• Research, investigate • Requirements/ parameters/ constraints • Insulation/conduction • Circulation • Joint/fixing • Air pockets	• Fleece fabric • Fur fabric • Waterproof fabric • Bubble wrap • Handwarmers/hot water bottle • Wheat/rice bags • Cold glue gun • Sewing materials – needles, thread • Scissors • Rulers • Duct tape, Sellotape • Fabric glue • Needles of different thicknesses • Threads of different thicknesses • Thimbles • Hemming web • Iron (adult use only)

Activities

Explicit Skills Teaching

For further support and guidance about textile-based activities with children, please see Chapter 5.
- Children may need help sewing fabrics together. A simple running stitch could be good for prototypes, but a stronger back stitch would be better for a finished product.
- Children might choose to use a cold glue gun to fix fabrics together.
- Skills teaching for pattern making and cutting.
- Sewing skills, how to pin materials together, how to thread a needle, how to start and end a run of stitches.
- Teaching of different stitches
- Teaching of how to use the different tools (e.g., a thimble, tape measure, glue gun, etc.).

Health and Safety
- Demonstrations of how to use various tools such as scissors, glue guns or craft knives safely.
- Children could make safety posters or warning signs for the various tools to be used.
- Teachers will need to decide which pieces of equipment are suitable for the children in their classes based on the age and skills level of the children.

Making Activities
- Time for children to make their designed product.
- Use the Children's engineering worksheet to evaluate what went well, which parts of the design did not work so well, what needs to be improved.

Testing Ideas
- The different leg and foot warming solutions could be tested by children by recording the skin temperature of the child on the lower leg and foot before using the design solution and after.

Qualitative evidence about comfort and warmth could also be recorded. The ability to remove the warmer and put it on could be given a score.
- The products made could be placed around/over a cup of warm water. Regular temperature recordings of the water could be taken to record the heat loss. These readings could be compared to a cup of water at the same temperature which is left without a covering product.
- Ask the children to try the products out for themselves. Which feel the nicest, which do they feel keep them warm, which are the most comfortable, etc.?
- Demonstrate the products to a range of other people in school for feedback. What do they think of the functionality/design/comfort, etc.?

Evaluating Ideas

Evaluating a final product and process forms the main design and technology focus for this chapter. For this reason, a more extensive list of evaluation activities is provided here. These evaluation activities could be used and applied for any of the challenges presented in any of the chapters in this book.
- Use the Children's engineering worksheet to evaluate what went well, which parts of the design did not work so well, what needs to be improved.
- Often, during this stage the children encounter problems with their product. This provides an opportunity to revisit the science involved to help them to solve these issues. Again, when encountering issues this would be a good opportunity for children to go back to do some further research (e.g., what materials are used to in sleeping bags or blankets? Why are these chosen?).
- Share ideas, using and adapting the ideas of others.
- Children display their part or fully completed products alongside their designs. All children move around the classroom to examine the work of others. Encourage the children to note down good ideas that they could use in their own designs and products.
- Ask each child/group of children to share an issue or triumph that they have had with their design and product. The rest of the class can either use the idea that worked or offer a solution to the issue experienced.
- Children then return to their own designs and products and adapt in light of this new information.
- Evaluate and reflect on the process rather than the product.
- 3-2-1: Ask the children to write or talk about 3 things they learned, 2 things they still want to learn, and 1 question they have.
- Hold a Dragons' den type of interview and pitch.
- Write a letter or note to your past self saying how the product can be improved and what difficulties could be encountered.
- Produce an instructions sheet or an instructional video so that another person can make the product.
- Compile an evaluation blog throughout the process.
- Produce a 140-character evaluation wall where improvement ideas with speech bubble real quotes are added throughout the make, improve, and evaluate process.

Assessment

That the children can identify features of each other's designs that work well and consider how they could be used in their own design.

Linked Science Investigations	**Waterproofing the product** **Activity 1** If the children decide that their design needs to be able to be used outside, they could test the materials for their degree of waterproofing. Using beakers, droppers, and elastic bands, stretch the materials over the top of the beaker and fix across with an elastic band. Using a plastic dropper, drip water on the fabric and record how many drops it takes until the water leaks into the beaker. Alternately you can drip the same amount of water on all the samples and record how much water passes into the beaker. **Exploring the heart and circulation further** **Activity 2 Hearts** Get a lamb's heart from the butcher. Place in a tray. Show the children the heart and ask them which side they think pumps the blood to the nearby lungs and which side pumps blood around the body. Children can be invited to place a finger into the main vessels at the top of the heart. It is easy then to feel that one side of the heart has much thicker muscles than the other side of the heart. You could then cut down each side of the heart and show the four chambers. Children and teachers need to wash their hands after handling raw meat and to use disposable gloves if there are open cuts on hands. **Activity 3** **Model of the blood** Children can make a model of the blood using water retaining crystals for houseplants in red (also known as water beads), white dried beans (or ping pong balls), and small strips of red craft foam. The water crystals (red blood cells) can be soaked in water dyed slightly yellow with food dye (plasma), white blood cells are symbolised by either white beans or ping-pong balls, and platelets by the craft foam. **Activity 4** **Pulse rates and heat** Children should be taught how to take their own pulse rates with their fingers around their wrists (small pulse rate meters are available cheaply and robust and are a good school investment). They could also record the skin temperature on their forehead with a temperature strip. Record resting heart rate. Design some running and jumping activities in the playground and ask the children to record their pulse rates directly after the exercise and then every 2 minutes until the pulse returns to the resting heart rate as well as forehead temperature. This is a terrific opportunity to make line graphs as a recording of change over time. The children could repeat the story of the graph and if you compare you can see that each child will have different patterns of heart activity.

Resources for activities

- Children's engineering worksheet
- Various fabrics
- Silver foil

70 *Animal and humans*

- Cardboard
- Fleece fabric
- Fur fabric
- Waterproof fabric
- Bubble wrap
- Handwarmers/hot water bottle
- Wheat/rice bags
- Cold glue gun
- Sewing materials – needles, thread
- Scissors
- Rulers
- Duct tape, Sellotape
- Temperature strips
- Heart rate monitors
- Red and blue balloons or red and blue cards or PE bands, cards with names of organs on them, chalk
- Wheat bags/rice bags/hot water bottles
- Drinks cans
- Elastic bands
- Stirring thermometers or digital thermometers
- Beakers
- Droppers
- Trays
- Kettle

Health and safety

The materials and tools used for this challenge do not pose significant health and safety threats. Children should be taught how to use craft knives and cutting mats correctly and general classroom safety with these such as not moving around the classroom with them in their hands and placing them into the centre of the table when not in use. With sharp tools such as scissors and knives, it is good practice to count out how many you have made available at the start of the lesson and then to count them back in again.

If you use an iron (e.g., to attach iron on webbing) this should be done only by an adult. Glue guns may be used by children, depending on their age but try to use the cold glue gun versions and only have these available under close adult supervision. Make sure the cable is not in a position where it can catch on children or objects.

Warm water should be handled and supervised by the teacher. Boiling water should not be used.

The advice above on wheat and rice bags needs to be followed to reduce any small risk if fire or burning. Teachers need to carry out the use of the heating in the microwave and testing of the wheat/ rice warmer before allowing children to test.

Animal and humans   71

Common misconceptions

Children are aware of their own heart beating from an early age. However, when asked to draw a heart it is often depicted as a valentine's heart and placed on the left side of the body. Although the heart is slightly tilted to the left, it is mostly central in the body.

Young children may express the belief that blood is swishing around the empty cavity of the body. At 10-11, children are more aware of an arterial system of transport.

Children in primary schools are not often aware of the constituent part of blood or their function.

Wider resources related to circulation and the heart

For 5-7-year-olds, the BBC has materials about what is inside your body and their functions
https://www.bbc.co.uk/teach/class-clips-video/science-ks1-the-human-body/zf8jqp3

For 7-11-year-olds, they have videos on the circulatory system and the heart
https://www.bbc.co.uk/teach/class-clips-video/science-ks2-how-our-circulatory-system-keeps-us-alive/zhf76v4

There are downloadable resources on the circulatory system and the heart at
https://www.stem.org.uk/resources/elibrary/resource/35233/human-body-game#&gid=undefined&pid=7

Amazing facts about the heart and blood at
https://www.theschoolrun.com/homework-help/human-circulatory-system

Heart beaters from the Wellcome Trust. Set of lessons and activities on the heart, circulation, and activity.
https://www.stem.org.uk/elibrary/resource/34279

Other example activities for humans

Ralph's family want to cut down on eating meat. Their favourite pizza is pepperoni pizza. Can you design some pizza topping that are tasty but do not use meat products for his family?

Mumtaz would like to cut down on the number of plastic water bottles she buys but knows she does not drink enough water during the day. She does not like her water to be warm. Design a cover for a reusable bottle that will keep Mumtaz's drink cool.

There is a lot of litter floating in the stream near Liam's school. Liam thinks that this is bad for the animals living there and his mum thinks it might also contribute to flooding. Can you help Liam design something to clean up the stream so that the animals living in it can remain healthy?

Bibliography

Department of Energy Security and Net Zero. (2023) Annual Fuel Poverty Statistics Report: 2023. Available at https://www.gov.uk/government/statistics/annual-fuel-poverty-statistics-report-2023

Energy Saving Trust. (2023) Energy at Home. Available at https://energysavingtrust.org.uk/energy-at-home/

UN. (2013) Sustainable Development Goals. Available at https://www.un.org/en/sustainable-development-goals

5 Everyday materials, their uses and properties

Design and technology focus: Textiles

The engineering challenge

> **Rachel's Blog**
>
> So yesterday, my dad decided to clear out my wardrobe. He said that he had noticed that I had suddenly grown out of a lot of my clothes. It was time to get rid of some and work out what new clothes I needed. It took all day to do as my dad made me try on everything!
>
> We ended up with two piles of clothes. One pile is going to the charity shop, but dad says that the clothes in the other pile are not good enough to go to the charity shop as they have small holes or stains in them. He says that we should just throw them away, but I don't want to add them to the landfill. I'm going on holiday to a beach soon. Is there some way that I can use the material from these old clothes for something useful for my holiday?

Aim of the challenge

The aim of this engineering challenge is to help children consider new ways in which to use materials, to see how they can be repurposed rather than simply disposed of and replaced with something new. The challenge incorporates the idea of a holiday to extend thinking beyond making new clothes to encompass a range of potential products, encouraging children to consider the properties of the materials that they are working with. Through considering if the materials available would be suitable for making a sun hat, toiletries bag, or a splash-proof phone case, etc., children will need to consider properties of the materials such as waterproofing, flexibility and strength.

A photocopiable Childrens' Engineering Challenge Sheet can be found in the Appendix.

Sustainable development goals

This challenge sits within two of the UN's sustainable development goals (2013):

74 *Everyday materials, their uses and properties*

Goal 12: Ensure sustainable consumption and production patterns.
Goal 13: Take urgent action to combat climate change

According to the United Nations (https://sdgs.un.org/goals/goal12), the global material footprint (i.e., the amount of material consumed by the total population of the world) increased by 70% between 2010 and 2017. Simply disposing of unwanted items in landfill sites means that new resources need to be found to meet consumer demands. Not only is this unsustainable as the planet is stripped of its natural resources, but landfilling also poses a range of environmental threats.

Rubbish thrown into landfill sites can take many years to break down, meaning that we are passing on the problem of unwanted waste to future generations and producing long-term environmental damage. Waste disposed in landfill sites can break down to release toxins such as ammonia, lead, and arsenic, as well as a host of bacteria. When it rains, these toxins get flushed out and a foul-smelling liquid called leachate is produced. As the name implies, leachate leaches (or leaks) into the soil, groundwater, and waterways, contaminating the local environment, adding to costs for water treatment, and potentially damaging human health.

You can find out more about landfill sites and the dangers that they pose by looking on the Unisan website: https://www.unisanuk.com/what-is-a-landfill-why-are-landfills-bad-for-the-environment/.

One solution to this issue is to recycle materials. However, there is often a high energy usage associated with this, which again has a knock on environmental impact. We need to look at ways that we can reuse or repurpose items as this has little environmental impact, can save us money, uses less energy, and can be fun! You can find out more about other alternatives to disposal and recycling on the Greenpeace website: https://www.greenpeace.org.au/blog/beyond-reduce-reuse-recycle/ or through the One Green Planet website: https://www.onegreenplanet.org/lifestyle/why-reusing-and-repurposing-is-better-than-recycling/.

Potential solutions

Due to the open-ended nature of this challenge in asking the children to make a product for use on holiday, there are multiple possible solutions. Try to encourage the children to consider and explore a range of potential products as this will help them to engage more fully with the properties of the materials on offer.

Potential products to make could include blackout curtains for a caravan or holiday flat, a picnic blanket that is soft to sit on but does not let the damp through, a warm wrap to use after swimming, or a wrapper for an ice cream tub that will keep the ice cream cool but will stop your hand from getting cold. Encourage the children to engage with the properties of the materials and then find a use for them.

Science content

The scientific content for this challenge sits within the field of materials and their properties. This firstly involves being able to describe the properties of the materials.

Everyday materials, their uses and properties 75

Children aged 5-7 years

Younger children could use everyday terms such as:

- Rough/smooth
- Stretchy/stiff
- Bendy/not bendy
- Shiny/matt or dull

Children should be encouraged to describe these properties but also to group materials according to the properties described above. For this challenge, this could involve sorting the materials into two piles (e.g., those that would be good to make a towel out of and those that would not be good for this purpose). Children will also need to be able to explain why they have chosen a particular material for a purpose (or why they have rejected another one). Here, a child may explain that they have selected denim for a sun hat as it is thick and will keep the sun out, whereas a mesh would let the sun through the holes. This will also help them to see that different materials can be used for the same purpose.

Children aged 7-11 years

Older children will need to be able to use and apply a range of more technical terms, such as:

- Flexible/malleable/rigid
- Transparent/translucent/opaque
- Thermal insulation/conductivity
- Absorbent/waterproof

Again, older children will need to be able to describe and classify materials according to their properties and discuss potential uses for materials based on these properties, but they may also be expected to test these materials. For example, which materials keep a tub of ice cream the coolest for the longest? Which block the most sunlight out to create a blackout curtain?

Vocabulary

- **Absorbent/waterproof:** permeable, porous, impervious
- **Flexible/rigid/strength:** malleable, ductile, floppy, elastic, stretchy, supple, bendy, pliable, firm, dense, bendable, soft, spongy
- **Opaque/translucent/transparent:** clear, see-through, dense
- **Fabric/material:** 'fabric' refers to cloth used to make clothing or bedding, etc., whereas 'material' refers to any substance that an object is made from (this could be glass, brick, cotton, wood, plastic, etc.)

The science explained

Thermal insulation and conductivity

Thermal insulation or conductivity refers to the ability of a material to allow heat energy to pass through it. Materials that are less able to allow heat to pass through them are known as thermal insulators and those that allow heat to pass through them more easily are known as thermal conductors. A thermal insulator will therefore prevent or reduce the amount of heat which passes from one object to another. Gases make much better thermal insulators than solids or liquids as they are much less able to let heat pass through them. Materials that contain spaces or gaps, which will contain gas in the form of air (such as fibrous wool, sponge, or polystyrene) therefore tend to be good thermal insulators. This is why the sleeve on your coffee cup may contain ridges, to increase the amount of gas between your hand and the hot cup. When warm things are wrapped in a good thermal insulator, the heat is kept inside as it is unable to escape and so the contents stay warmer for longer. When cold things are contained within a good thermal insulator they stay colder for longer as the heat from outside cannot pass through the insulating material.

Absorbency/waterproofing

Similarly, with absorbency and waterproofing, we also need to look closely at the material to explain these properties. The more tightly packed together the fibres within a material, the more waterproof a material tends to be. Absorbent materials are those that contain more spaces between the fibres. Water (and other liquids) can be drawn into these holes and then spread out through the material using these holes. In fully waterproof materials, these holes are not big enough to allow water in.

Flexible/rigid

The rigidity or flexibility of a material is a result of the bonds (or joins) between the atoms in the material. If the atoms fit together tightly and can slide over each other easily, the material is flexible. If there are irregularities in the ways that the atoms are organised, it is less likely that the atoms will be able to move over each other and so the material may be more rigid. If the bonds between the atoms are strong, then the material may be hard to break.

Opaque/translucent/transparent

If a material is opaque, it does not let any light through; if it is translucent, it lets some through; and if it is transparent, it lets almost all light through. But why is this? What makes some materials opaque and some transparent? Light is a form of energy, when it hits the surface of an object it will either reflect off the surface of the object, be absorbed or pass through. When light hits an opaque material, the energy is absorbed or bounces off, whereas in transparent materials this energy can pass through without any dispersion, making the

Everyday materials, their uses and properties 79

• What might you use this material for? • Are all the materials that we have the same? How do they differ? • Can you describe what this material is like? What are its properties? How might this affect what we use it for?	• Absorbent, waterproof, permeable, porous, impervious • Flexible, rigid, strength, malleable, ductile, floppy, elastic, stretchy, supple, bendy, pliable, firm, dense, bendable, soft, spongy • Opaque, translucent, transparent, clear, see-through, dense • Fabric, material	range (e.g., denim, canvas or raincoat fabric, silk, cotton, wool, mesh, gauze, plastic, materials of assorted colours). • Scissors • Needles of different thicknesses • Threads of different thicknesses • Fabric glue/glue guns • Hemming web • Iron (adult use only) • Tape measures, rulers • Materials and objects for decoration such as sequins

Activities

Identifying the requirements and constraints of the set challenge:
- Discussions about what the children need to know to provide a solution to the challenge set.
- In groups, each group composes three questions to ask about the parameters of the challenge set.
- Children writing lists of challenge constraints and requirements.
- Children complete 'exploring ideas' section on their EDP worksheet.
- Examine the range of materials and tools available to use.
- Teachers may need to prompt and guide children on any missed information (e.g., time allowance, conditions that the product will be used in, materials available, etc.).

Describing the properties of materials
- Give the children cards with the vocabulary associated with the properties of materials and ask them to attach this to materials with those properties.
- Place a mystery material into a paper or cloth bag. Ask a child to put their hand into the bag and describe what they can feel to their classmates. The other children try to guess the material inside using these descriptions.

Sorting and grouping according to property
- Give the children a vocabulary card and ask them to gather all the materials matching this word and place in pile together.
- Use large hoops (or circles drawn on the playground) to sort materials by property. Children assign a property label to each group. For younger children, this could be using simple terms such as hard/bendy, etc.; for older children, this could be a Venn diagram with overlapping properties.

Identifying the potential uses of a range of materials based on their properties
- Examine a range of classroom objects, describe the properties of the materials that these have been made from. Discuss why these materials were selected. What is it about the properties of the materials that they have been made from that makes them fit the purpose?
- Name an object, ask the children to hold up an example of a material that would be good to make that object out of, and ask them to justify their choices by referring to the properties of the materials.
- Examine the materials available for the challenge. Can the children name three products that each material would be suitable for?
- Ask the children to think of nonsense ideas! For example, what would be the most ridiculous material to make a table out of and why? (e.g., using felt to make a table would be nonsense as felt

is not rigid). Other ideas could include what would be a nonsense material to make a window (metal, leather), saucepan (satin, chocolate), or a T-shirt (glass, plastic). Discuss what it is about the properties of these materials that makes them unsuitable.

Assessment
Children can identify the needs set by Rachel in her challenge and can describe a set of quantifiable requirements.

Children understand and can appropriately use a range of vocabulary associated with the properties of materials.

Children are able to describe why a material is a suitable choice for a specific use, drawing on the properties of materials to justify their choices.

 EDP stage: Developing ideas

Science Content Learning Objectives:
- Investigate the properties of materials used in similar products.
- To be able to discuss why these materials have been chosen.
- To investigate the properties of materials (could also be covered during the Designing Ideas stage or the making, testing, and improving Ideas stage).

Design and Technology Learning Objectives:
- To investigate how similar products have been made. (How have the materials been joined together? How have attachments been added on? Which stitches have been used and why?)
- To use information from a variety of sources to generate ideas for potential solutions.

Key Questions	*Vocabulary*	*Resources*
<ul><li>What is the item made from? Why do you think that this material was chosen?</li><li>How have the parts of the item been joined together?</li><li>What have you seen or used before that may help you to develop ideas?</li><li>What can we find out about what other, similar products are made of?</li><li>What have you found out from your research/ looking at other products which could help you with your own designs?</li></ul>	<ul><li>Fabric, material</li><li>Seam, hem, join</li><li>Stitch, Sew/Sewn</li><li>Running/Cross/Blanket stitch</li><li>Product</li><li>Research, investigate</li></ul>	<ul><li>Children's engineering worksheet</li><li>A range of products related to the challenge (e.g., sun hats, swimwear, luggage and bags, beach towels, blackout curtains, beach sarongs, etc.).</li><li>If possible, have a range of similar items made from different materials.</li><li>Access to laptops or tablets etc for research.</li></ul>

Activities
- Brainstorm imagination activities in small groups to produce wild and whacky solutions.
- Sharing of ideas discovered or imagined.
- Complete the 'developing ideas' section of the photocopiable children's engineering page.

Examine the properties of materials used in similar products/ discuss why these materials have been chosen.
- Ask the children to examine what they have at home or what they have seen before that they may take on holiday with them. What are these items made from?
- Have a selection of holiday items available for children to examine. What are they made from and why?
- Internet or literature-based research about designs or products that could provide ideas.
- Using real items or internet searches, investigate the range of materials used to made similar items. Which material would be best for the product and why (e.g., a shirt could be made from lightweight cotton, silk, denim, leather or even plastic).

Investigate how similar products have been made.
- Examining a range of beach/holiday items. How have the materials been joined together? How have attachments been added on? Which stitches have been used and why?

To use information from a variety of sources to generate ideas for potential solutions.
- Examining a range of beach/holiday items. Is the product fit for purpose? i.e., is the product strong enough/will it provide enough shade/is it waterproof enough?
- How could the product be improved?
- Which ideas could you take to use in your own product?

To investigate the properties of materials (could also be covered during the making, testing, and improving stage), see additional section below.

Assessment
Children can make a reasonable and relevant choice of product relating to the materials available to them and can justify this choice based on the properties of the material(s).

Children can investigate similar products and identify features that they could incorporate into their own designs and products.

Children are able to articulate a range of ideas about potential products and solutions.

EDP stage: Designing ideas

Science Content Learning Objectives:
- To investigate the properties of materials (could also be covered during the 'developing ideas' stage or the 'making, testing, and improving ideas' stage).

Design and Technology Learning Objectives:
- To be able to draw and design a set of plans relating to an intended product.
- To be able to analyse and evaluate plans and potential products for their suitability in meeting the requirements of the challenge set.
- To be able to evaluate methods of joining (testing of various stitches and glues to decide which ones work best with the materials, which are the strongest or most suitable for the job).

Everyday materials, their uses and properties

Thought Processes/Engineering Habits of Mind (EHOM)
Analyse, compare, evaluate, visualise, adapt

Key Questions	Vocabulary	Resources
• Why have you decided on your final product design? • What makes this one better than your other options? • How does your design meet the challenge and the constraints/ requirements set out in the 'explore' stage? • Do you anticipate any problems or issues when making your product?	• Analyse, compare, evaluate, visualise, adapt • Fabric, material • Seam, hem, join • Stitch, sew/sewn • Running/cross/ blanket stitch • Product • Research, investigate	• Children's engineering worksheet • A range of fabrics and materials • Scissors • Needles of different thicknesses • Threads of different thicknesses • Fabric glue/glue guns • Hemming web • Safety pins • Staples and stapler • Iron (adult use only) • Tape measures, rulers • Materials and objects for decoration such as sequins

Activities
Identify and design three main ideas for products to be made.
- Draw up plans for three potential products.
- Evaluate and assess which of these ideas best meets the requirements set out in the 'ignite' and 'explore' stages of the EDP.
- Explain product choice to others in the class and share reasoning about why this product has been chosen.
- Identify how the separate parts of the product will be joined together or how any attachments will be added on.
- Complete the 'designing ideas' section on the children's engineering worksheet.

Testing of various stitches and glues to decide which ones work best with the materials, which are the strongest or most suitable for the job.
- Join two separate pieces of the same material together using a variety of methods (different stitches, glue, hemming web, staples, safety pins, etc.). Hold one piece of the material and attach a Newton metre to the other piece. Pull the two pieces away from each other and, using the Newton metre, measure the force that the join can withstand, or the force required to break the join.
- Repeat the above with different materials. Is the same joining method the best for all materials?
- Repeat the above joining two different types of materials.

Investigate the properties of materials (could also be covered during the 'developing ideas' stage or the 'making, testing, and improving ideas' stage). See additional section below.

Assessment
Children can select a design from a range and articulate why this is the most suitable choice.
Children can explain how they will join the separate components of their product together and explain why they have chosen this method.

Everyday materials, their uses and properties 83

 **EDP stage: Making, testing, and improving ideas**

Science Content Learning Objectives:
• To investigate the properties of materials (could also be covered during the Developing Ideas stage or the Designing Ideas stage)
• To be able to apply scientific understanding within a 'real-world' context
Design and Technology Learning Objectives:
• To develop explicit skills (e.g., threading a needle, starting a run of stitches, etc.) (see activities section below for more details).
• To be aware of a variety of health and safety considerations.
• To be able to turn a design for a solution to a set problem into a product.
• To be able to test a product against a set of pre-determined criteria (from the 'exploring ideas' stage).
• To be able to share ideas and use and adapt the ideas of others.
Thought Processes/Engineering Habits of Mind (EHOM)
Analyse, compare, evaluate, improve

Key Questions	Vocabulary	Resources
• Does your product answer Rachel's problem? • Does your product meet all the specifications set out in the 'exploring ideas' stage? • Did you encounter any problems when making your product? • What solutions to these problems did you find? • Did other groups encounter similar problems? What solutions did they produce? • Did you choose the most appropriate material to make your product out of? Why/why not?	• Test, improve, evaluate, improve, appraise • Fabric, material • Seam, hem, join • Stitch, sew/sewn • Running/cross/blanket stitch • Product • Research, investigate • Requirements/parameters/constraints • Absorbent, waterproof, permeable, porous, impervious • Flexible, rigid, strength, malleable, ductile, floppy, elastic, stretchy, supple, bendy, pliable, firm, dense, bendable, soft, spongy • Opaque, translucent, transparent, clear, see-through, dense • Fabric, material	• Children's engineering worksheet • A range of fabrics and materials • Scissors • Needles of different thicknesses • Threads of different thicknesses • Fabric glue/glue guns • Hemming web • Safety pins • Staples and stapler • Iron (adult use only) • Tape measures, rulers • Materials and objects for decoration such as sequins

Activities

Explicit Skills Teaching
- Skills teaching pattern making and cutting.
- Sewing skills, how to pin materials together, how to thread a needle, how to start and end a run of stitches.
- Teaching of different stitches.
- Teaching of how to use the different tools (e.g., a thimble, tape measure, glue gun, etc.).

Health and Safety
- Demonstrations of how to use various tools such as scissors, glue guns, or needles safely.
- Children could make safety posters or warning signs for the various tools to be used.
- Teachers will need to decide which pieces of equipment are suitable for the children in their classes based on the age and skills level of the children.

Making Activities
- Time for children to make their designed product.

Testing and Appraising Ideas
- Testing of various stitches and glues to decide which ones work best with the materials, which are the strongest or most suitable for the job (see ideas presented in the activities section of the 'designing Ideas' stage).
- Sunhats and products designed to provide shade. Place the product under a light source or out in the heat (NB not under a direct heat source). Measure the temperature underneath using analogue or digital thermometers at different time intervals. Alternatively, use a digital monitor to measure the amount of light the product allows through or place an ice cube underneath and time how long it takes to melt. Compare this to an ice cube not under the shade of the product.
- Picnic blankets or products designed to keep out moisture. Place the product onto a wet surface and place some filter paper or sugar paper on top under a small weight. Time how long it takes for any dampness to seep through.
- Bags, pouches, etc. Hang the bag from a Newton meter and add weights of items to see how much it will hold. Is the product a suitable size and shape for the intended job?
- Beach wraps or products designed to keep in warmth. Wrap the product around a cup and fill this with warm water. Use an analogue or digital thermometer to measure the temperature over a period of time. Compare this to the water in a cup not protected by the product.
- Use the Children's engineering worksheet to evaluate. What went well, which parts of the design did not work so well, what needs to be improved?
- See also the linked scientific investigations below. Investigate the properties of materials (could also be covered during the 'developing ideas' stage or the 'designing ideas' stage). See additional section below.

Improving Ideas
- Often, during this stage, the children encounter problems with their product. This provides an opportunity to revisit the science involved to help them to solve these issues. For example, if making the rim of a hat the children may find that their chosen material is not flexible enough. Here, they could go back and re-examine the properties of the other materials available.
- Again, when encountering issues this would be a good opportunity for children to go back to do some further research (e.g., What materials are used to make the rims of hats? Why are these chosen?).

Sharing ideas, using, and adapting the ideas of others.
- Children display their part, or fully completed products alongside their designs. All children move around the classroom to examine the work of others. Encourage the children to note down good ideas that they could use in their own designs and products.

Everyday materials, their uses and properties

- Ask each child/group of children to share an issue or triumph that they have had with their design and product. The rest of the class can either use the idea that worked or offer a solution to the issue experienced.
- Children then return to their own designs and products and adapt considering this new information.

Assessment

Children are able to describe what they like and don't like about their product.

They have chosen a material that is suitable for the purpose of their product and can explain how the properties of this material make their choice plausible.

They are able to evaluate if they have met the design brief and if they have solved the original challenge set.

They are able to offer solutions to various problems encountered by themselves and others.

Linked Scientific Investigations	**Thermal Insulation:** Wrap ice cubes up in a variety of materials. Time how long they take to melt/weigh the ice cubes after a certain period of time. The better thermal insulation properties that the materials have, the more heat from outside will be kept away from the ice cube and so more of the ice cube will remain intact. **Waterproofing:** Cut out squares of tissue paper/kitchen towels. Weigh these out individually using a set of digital scales and note down the starting weight. Place each square of tissue paper under each material to be tested making sure that the entire surface of the tissue paper is covered. Pour a small amount of water (20 or 30 mL) onto each material to be tested. After a few minutes, carefully remove the material being tested and re-weigh each piece of tissue paper and calculate the difference between the starting weight and the new weight. This difference in weight is the weight of the water which has been absorbed. The greater the difference in weight, the more water has been absorbed by the tissue paper and so the less waterproof the material being tested is. **Absorption:** Add some water to a shallow dish and place the material to be tested in this. The amount of water absorbed can be measured by either calculating the change in weight in the material (any increase in weight will be absorbed water) or by calculating the change in weight of the dish and water (any change in weight will be the loss of water which has been absorbed). **Strength:** *To test the strength of a seam/fixing* Join two separate pieces of the same material together using a variety of methods (different stitches, glue, hemming web, staples, safety pins, etc.). Hold one piece of the material and attach a Newton metre to the other piece. Pull the two pieces away from each other and, using the Newton metre, measure the force that the join can withstand, or the force required to break the join. Repeat the above with different materials. Is the same joining method the best for all materials? Repeat the above, joining two different types of materials.

> *To test the strength of a material*
> Move two tables or chairs slightly apart so that you create a gap. Place the material to be tested over this gap, firmly weighing down the ends so that it does not slip through the gap. Tie a long piece of string or wool around the materials to create a loose loop. Hook weights of increasing sizes onto this loop to measure the weight that the material can hold, or the weight required to break the material. The more weight the material can hold the stronger it is. Keep children's feet away from the testing gap.
>
> **Flexibility:**
> On a large piece of paper mark out a series of angles in a circle from 0° to 360°. Place the material to be tested along the 0° line and bend it as far as possible. Note down the angle that you can bend the material to.
>
> **Opaqueness/Transparency:**
> Digital light readers or monitors would be a useful addition here. Shine a torch through a variety of materials and determine how much light can be seen on the other side. The darkness of the shadow cast could also be a way to determine the opaqueness of the materials used.

Resources

- A range of fabrics and materials. Try to make sure that a range of properties are represented by this range (e.g., denim, canvas or raincoat fabric, silk, cotton, wool, mesh, gauze, plastic, materials of different colours).
- Scissors
- Tracing paper/thin paper for patterns
- Needles of different thicknesses
- Threads of different thicknesses
- Fabric glue/glue guns
- Hemming web
- Iron (adult use only)
- Thimbles
- Tape measures, rulers
- Materials and objects for decoration such as sequins

Health and safety

The materials and tools used for this challenge do not pose significant health and safety threats. Children should be taught how to use scissors and needles correctly and general classroom safety with these such as not moving around the classroom with them in their hands and placing them into the centre of the table when not in use. With sharp tools such as scissors and needles it is good practice to count out how many you have made available at the start of the lesson and then to count these back in again.

Everyday materials, their uses and properties 87

If you use an iron (e.g., to attach iron on webbing) this should be done only by an adult. Glue guns may be used by children depending on their age but try to use the cold glue gun versions and only have these available under close adult supervision. Make sure the cable is not in a position where it can catch on children or objects.

Common misconceptions

Many children will associate the term 'material' with the cloth or the fabric that their clothes are made from. However, the term 'material' refers to any substance (including fabric, glass, metal, concrete, etc.). Try to ensure that children are clear about the distinction between fabric (a cloth or other material produced by weaving or knitting fibres) and the more general term 'material'.

Children can also often be confused when working with cold objects and thermal insulators. In their everyday experiences, thermal insulators such as coats or duvets are used to keep heat in, to keep you warm. Therefore, many children also assume that when a cold item is wrapped in a thermal insulator it will warm up, this is what they have experienced themselves. In fact, the thermal insulator will keep the cold object cool as it will prevent heat from outside getting to the cold object as heat is less able to pass through a thermal insulator. A tub of ice cream wrapped inside a material that is a good thermal insulator such as wool will therefore stay frozen for longer.

Wider resources related to materials, their properties and uses

There are many excellent sources of support and resources for the topic of materials, their properties and uses.

- The Institute of Engineering technology has a range of educational resources. The resource called 'Materials and their Properties' encourages children to consider the suitability of materials for various products: https://education.theiet.org/primary/teaching-resources/materials-and-their-properties/
- STEM learning also has a range of resources and links for this topic. For children aged 5–6, try exploring: https://www.stem.org.uk/resources/community/collection/12725/year-1-everyday-materials
- For those aged 6, 7, or 8 try: https://www.stem.org.uk/resources/community/collection/12724/year-2-uses-everyday-materials
- The Hamilton Trust has a range of interesting investigations related to materials and their properties for your children to try out: https://www.hamilton-trust.org.uk/science/year-5-science/properties-materials-music-festival-materials/

Other example activities for everyday materials, their uses and properties

- When Maiesha brings her banana in for packed lunch it gets damaged and goes brown, so she often throws it away. She would like you to design and make something for her that will keep her banana unbruised.

6 Living things and habitats

Design and technology focus: Woodwork

> **The Engineering Challenge**
>
> Charlie was telling his friends about his visit to his grandpa's house. He said that his grandpa had told him that when he was Charlie's age, his school playground was full of all sorts of wildlife. He used to love looking at all the minibeasts, birds, butterflies, and even animals like hedgehogs, rabbits, and newts! Charlie thinks that we should do more to encourage wildlife into our school grounds. Can you help him?

Aim of the challenge

The aim of this challenge is to encourage children to explore the needs of plants and animals in their habitats. Children will need to understand what the ideal conditions are for various species and what they need to survive.

The challenge requires children to build a structure from wood, which re-creates these ideal habitat conditions or supports wildlife within the school environment. To achieve this, children will need to consider how the wood used could be cut, shaped, joined, and finished and which would be the suitable tools to use for these purposes. The structures will need to be strong and stable and so the children will need to explore methods and mechanisms for achieving this.

A photocopiable Childrens' Engineering Challenge Sheet can be found in the Appendix.

Sustainable development goals

This challenge sits within Goal 15 of the UN's sustainable development goals:

> Life on Land: Protect, restore, and promote sustainable use of terrestrial ecosystems, sustainably manage forests, combat desertification, and halt and reverse land degradation and halt biodiversity loss.

According to UNICEF, biodiversity is declining faster than it has at any other time in human history. Species have always evolved and become extinct over time, but the rate of the extinction is now happening up to 1,000 times more quickly than normal levels (Natural History Museum). This means that roughly 40,000 species are at risk of extinction within the next decade (UN SDGs), with nearly a third of all monitored species being currently endangered due to human activities (BBC). More than 41% of amphibians, 27% of mammals, and 36% of coral reefs are currently on the ICUN's red list of endangered species. There are therefore concerns that the targets to reverse the decline of biodiversity by 2030 set at the 2022 UN Global Summit on biodiversity may be missed without urgent action (UN Biodiversity goals).

Animals and plants provide humans with everything that is essential for our survival, including oxygen, fresh water, food, medicines, and building materials, etc. We are an intrinsic part of the Earth's biodiversity; we are inseparable from it and fully dependent on it.

Much biodiversity loss is due to human activity. How we grow our food, source our energy, get rid of waste, and use natural resources all have an impact and so we need to act at a global level. However, the way that we live our everyday lives and interact with our local habitats is also vitally important. Everyday decisions such as how we travel, what we eat and buy, and even where we invest our money can have an impact on biodiversity. Understanding biodiversity loss and its impact on our health and wellbeing is therefore important in encouraging and supporting people to adopt more sustainable lifestyles.

Potential solutions

There are multiple possible solutions to this challenge.

Potential products to make could include

- a sprinkler/spreader for sowing seeds (to provide habitats for other species such as bees)
- a bee/bug hotel (to support minibeast populations)
- a composter (minibeasts help the decaying process and are a food source for other animals).
- a mini pond (e.g., even small container with a lining can provide a suitable habitat).
- a hedgehog home (important as numbers are declining)
- a container to grow wildlife friendly plants (e.g., raised beds, vertical gardens, planters, containers; these will attract pollinators like bees and butterflies)
- a bird feeder

Science content

The scientific content for this challenge develops understanding of the places where plants and animals live, why, and how they live there.

Children aged 5-7 years

Younger children should be able to identify a range of different habitats/microhabitats and name a variety of organisms living in these habitats. They could describe the conditions in

90 *Living things and habitats*

different habitats and find out how the conditions affect the number and type(s) of organisms that live there.

Children should understand how most organisms live in habitats to which they are suited and describe how these different habitats provide for the basic needs of these organisms. They should begin to understand how organisms within a habitat depend on each other (e.g., plants serving as a source of food and shelter for animals).

Children aged 7-11 years

In addition to the above, older children should also recognise that environments can change and that this can sometimes pose dangers to living things. They should therefore study and raise questions about their local habitats throughout the year, observing life cycle changes and changes in the numbers and types of species. Children should explore examples of positive human impact on environments (e.g., garden ponds) and the negative (e.g., litter or deforestation).

Children may also benefit from exploring how living things are grouped and classified (including broad groupings such as flowering and non-flowering plants, microorganisms, and animals as well as the subdivisions of these groupings such as invertebrates (such as insects, spiders, snails, worms) and vertebrates (fish, amphibians, reptiles, birds, and mammals).

Vocabulary

- *Parts of plants:* seed, fruit, shoot, petals, leaves, roots, branch, stem, trunk
- *Parts of animals*: fur, feathers, legs, beak, coat, head, body, eyes, mouth, nose, ears, skin, tail, feet
- *Classifying*: group, similarities, differences, variety (variation), features, plants, animals, birds, fish, minibeast
- *Processes (plants):* grow, germinate
- *Processes (general):* reproduce, living, non-living, life cycle
- *Habitats*: dark, cold, shaded, light, warm, cold, dry, moist, wet, position vocabulary (e.g., under, below, beside, etc.)

Older children (as for younger children and in addition)

- *Classifying*: keys, organism, classify, identify, observe
- *Processes (general)*: nutrition, reproduce, life processes
- *Habitats:* Habitat, environment, conditions, consumers, producer, predator, prey, food chain, overcrowding, adapted (adaptation), suited, diet, food pyramid

The science explained

Habitats

The word 'habitat' comes from a Latin word meaning 'to dwell' and is used today to describe the natural home or environment of an organism. A habitat meets all the environmental conditions an organism needs to survive. This includes all the living (such as food, a mate, etc.) and non-living factors (such as shelter) or conditions.

A microhabitat is a small area that differs somehow from the surrounding habitat. Its unique conditions may be home to unique species that may not be found in the larger region. For example, woodlice may live in a dark and damp microhabitat provided by a fallen log within a larger garden habitat.

Biodiversity

Biodiversity means the variety of life on Earth or in each habitat. It refers to living things and the complex ways in which they are connected. Each organism may play a different role, but all (and the balance between them) are equally important.

The part that animals play in supporting our health and wellbeing may be more obvious, but plants and microorganisms also have vital functions, too. For example, plants improve the physical environment: cleaning the air, limiting rising temperatures, and providing protection against climate change by absorbing carbon dioxide and removing pollutants from the air. Microorganisms also play a vital role in maintaining ecosystems through decomposing materials and recycling nutrients.

In relation to the engineering challenge set here, there are a few key aspects of biodiversity to consider. The first is the role of biodiversity in food production. This goes beyond the crops and the animals that eat, as it also encompasses aspects such as soil fertilisation and nutrient recycling (e.g., the composting suggested solution) as well as crop pollination (e.g., the bug hotel and wildflower seed suggested solutions). A loss of biodiversity destabilises ecosystems; any factor that alters the population of one species within an ecosystem will impact on all other species within that ecosystem. This is why it is important to consider the needs of all organisms within an ecosystem, even if they are not of direct use to us (e.g., the bird feeder suggested solution).

Food chains, webs, and pyramids

All living things within a habitat are interdependent on one another for food and energy. These relationships are often depicted in food chains or webs that show the flow of energy from one living thing to another. A food chain shows a simple linear representation of the feeding relationships between certain organisms (e.g., grass, rabbit, eagle whereas a food web shows how all the food chains within a habitat interact) (Figure 6.1).

Within food chains, trophic levels show which stage of energy transfer each organism exists at. All food chains start with a producer (a green plant or algae), which produces the energy within the food chain/web. Energy is not created anywhere else within the food chain/web. At the next trophic level are the primary consumers (organisms which eat the producers). Primary consumers are eaten by the secondary consumers, followed by tertiary consumers, etc. The final consumer is called a top (or apex) predator and is not eaten by anything else (Figure 6.1).

A food pyramid depicts energy transfer within a habitat by showing the number of organisms at each trophic level in a food chain (Figure 6.2). Some show the biomass at each

92 Living things and habitats

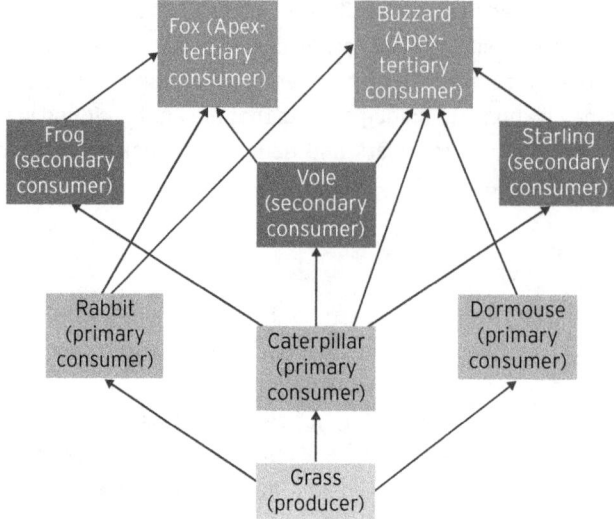

Figure 6.1 A food web

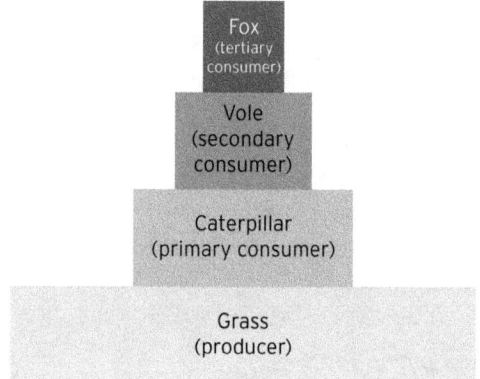

Figure 6.2 A food pyramid

level (the total mass of organisms at each level) rather than number of organisms. Food pyramids are often shown with smooth sides but should be represented as stepped pyramids as each level represents a distinct number. Energy is lost at each level of the food pyramid due to heat loss and movement, etc., so there are fewer animals/lower biomass at each level of the food pyramid (Figure 6.2).

Adaptation

Animals and plants that are best suited to the conditions of a habitat are the ones that will survive and thrive there. Where organisms are not ideally suited to these conditions, they may adapt unique features to help them to survive.

When reproducing, a spontaneous mutation can cause a change in the characteristics of an organism. Often these are detrimental, and the offspring does not survive. However, sometimes this results in a beneficial change (e.g., thicker fur on a polar bear or longer roots on a cactus). This means that this offspring has an advantage and is more likely to survive to adulthood and reproduce. Here, these advantageous genes are passed down.

Interdependence

All organisms depend upon each other for survival, known as interdependence. A good example of this is bees searching for nectar in flowers, spreading the pollen between flowers. This means that when the population of one species changes, this has an impact on the populations of others. For example, if the number of voles in the above food web declines, the numbers of foxes will also decline due to reduced food availability. However, the number of caterpillars may increase as fewer would be eaten.

Microorganisms and decomposition

Microorganisms are tiny organisms, mostly made up of only one cell. They include bacteria, some fungi (e.g., yeasts), and viruses. Whilst many cause disease (known as pathogens), there are also many examples that are beneficial to us, such as those that play a vital role in decomposition.

Decomposition is the process of rotting where dead matter (leaves, animal remains, etc.) are broken down. This process is crucial in maintaining health and balance within habitats as it recycles nutrients from one living organism to another. The stored nutrients in the dead matter are broken down by microorganisms, meaning that these elements can once again be used. Decomposition is therefore important in improving the quality of soil. One key element is nitrogen, which is needed by plants to make proteins for them to grow and repair themselves. Plants cannot absorb nitrogen gas, and therefore need to obtain it elsewhere. Microorganisms release this element back into the soil through breaking down proteins and urea.

Classification

All living things are grouped and classed according to their structures and characteristics. The different levels of classification are hierarchical in nature.

The broadest, and first level, is the five kingdoms, as below.

- plants
- animals
- fungi (moulds, mushrooms, yeast)
- protists (Amoeba, Chlorella, and Plasmodium)
- prokaryotes (bacteria, blue-green algae)

Below this is a series of other divisions (phylum, class, order, family, genus, species), again heirarchical in structure. When working with children, it is the 'class' division that they will be most familiar with as this contains the mammals, birds, amphibians, fish, and reptiles. It is the last two divisions of this classification system that give us the binomial (Latin) names of living things. Each name has two parts: the genus and the species. For example, human beings belong to the genus *Homo* and our species is *sapiens,* so the scientific name is *Homo sapiens.*

Design and technology content

For this challenge, children will need to be able to select from and use a range of tools and equipment to perform practical tasks (cutting, shaping, joining, and finishing) using wood as a resistant material. As they design and build their structures, they will also need to explore how they can be made stronger, stiffer, and more stable to ensure that they are fit for purpose.

Woodwork can be a low-risk activity if some basic safety measures are put in place. It is important that appropriate tools are used and that children are taught how to use these safely. Take time to discuss and demonstrate safe tool use and draw attention to hazards. It is only when the wrong tool is in untrained hands that there is a real danger of injury. If we teach children how to protect themselves, they will learn to make safe decisions.

With young children, you may want to start initially with a softer material so that children can master skills and techniques and gain confidence. This could include Balsa wood or even a material such as corrugated plastic or thick, layered cardboard.

Woodwork can be done indoors or outdoors, but wherever it takes place, you should consider the following:

- How many children are at each workbench
- How many active workbenches you have at any one time
- The availability of tools
- The staff/child ratio depending on age of the children, experience with the tools, and type of activity being done

Skill	*Techniques/resources*	*Safety considerations*
Measuring	Measure twice, cut once! Accurate measuring can reduce waste from mistakes. *Younger Children* You could provide pre-cut wood or card of a set length for use as a template. Children will need to be taught to line up the template to the edge of their wood and how to mark this off before cutting. *Older Children* Older children will be able to decide upon the desired length of wood needed for themselves and may have the skills to do this accurately using a ruler. These include:	Use of shatterproof rulers

	• Stating at the zero mark, rather than at 1 or the end of the ruler. • Understanding what the increments stand for. • Using the correct scale. • Understanding the relationship between different units of measurement (e.g., cm and mm).	
Joining with nails, screws, and glue	25 mm nails should be suitable for this challenge (depending on the thickness of the wood). Smaller nails are easier to hammer in than larger nails and therefore require less force, reducing injury risk. There is also less risk of splitting the wood. Start hammering with gentle taps at first to embed the nail; more forceful strokes can then be used. Short, stubby hammers make hammering much easier. For screws, a Philipps head (those with a cross rather than a slot) are easier for children. Whichever type of screw/screwdriver is used, make sure that these match. Wood glue can be used either on its own (depending on the weight and size of the wood being used) or in conjunction with other joining methods. Make sure that you use wood glue rather than more general glue.	Safety goggles in case of nail rebound. Hold the nail halfway down the shaft rather then by, or near, the head. All wood being hammered or screwed should be securely clamped to a stable table to minimise risk of slippage. Children should recognise nails and screws and flat head screwdrivers as sharp objects and be taught to treat these accordingly (i.e., not held in hands as moving around the classroom, passed carefully and not held near faces and eyes). Make sure that all nails and screws lie flat to or are sunk into the wood.
Cutting (sawing)	Small pull saws (which are held with both hands) are easier and safer for children. Begin by drawing the saw backwards along the line to be cut a few times to make a small groove. When using saws, children should use smooth, light strokes. They may instinctively press hard, thinking that this will make the cutting quicker or easier. However, this is likely to make the saw catch and get stuck.	Use close adult supervision when sawing. Safety glasses should be worn. Consider having a dedicated sawing area to prevent the need to move saws around and to minimise the movement of children. The wood being cut should always be clamped tightly in a vice that is securely attached to a table.

Living things and habitats

		Sand rough edges after sawing to minimise the risk of splinters. Tools such as saws should be counted out at the start of the activity and back in again at the end to ensure that all have been returned. After use, saws should be stored out of reach.
Strengthening structures	Right angle joins can be made more stable through the addition of a cross member, which is an additional piece of wood that sits diagonally across the corner, or use a corner brace, which is a triangle of wood that sits on top of the corner. Metal brackets are L-shaped pieces of metal bent at a right angle with holes in them for screws. These sit on the inside of a joint and are screwed into the wood to strengthen a join. Joins and joints can doubly secure using a combination of glue and nails or screws.	

Teacher's guidance (lesson and activity plans)

The tables below set out how the science and design and technology content could fit within the EDP. This is not an exhaustive list, and you may well be able to think of alternatives or different ways of organising the content for your own class.

These tables also give example activities to do at each stage of the EDP and key questions to ask. Again, these are ideas for you to use, adapt, and add to for your own classes.

EDP stage: Igniting ideas

Learning Objectives To be able to identify a presented need or requirement. To be able to articulate what is needed as an outcome of the challenge set.		
Key Questions	*Vocabulary*	*Resources*
• What is the problem that Charlie has identified? • What does Charlie want us to do?	• Animal/plant names • Habitat • Environment • Population • Identify • Observe	• Copies of the children's engineering challenge page

Living things and habitats 97

| • What animals and plants have you seen around our school?
• What would you like to see more of? | • Product/solution | |

Activities
- Share the challenge with the children.
- Discussions to clarify the need presented in the challenge.

Assessment
Children can define the challenge, showing that they understand the need presented and what they are required to do to provide a solution.

 **EDP stage: Exploring ideas**

Science Content Learning Objectives:
- To identify habitats and the animals and plants that live in a chosen habitat.
- To describe the conditions within a habitat and how animals and plants are adapted to these.
- To explore the needs and requirements of the plants and animals within habitats.
- To explore how changes to a habitat may impact on organisms living there.
- To understand inter-relationships between organisms in a habitat.

Key Questions	Vocabulary	Resources
• Can you describe what this habitat is like? • What is the name of the animal/plant that you have identified? • Which classification group does it belong to and how do you know? • What does your animal eat? What eats your plant or animal? • Is your plant/animal suited to live in this habitat? Why/why not? • What might happen to you organism if X or Y changed in this habitat? • What does your plant/animal need to survive?	• *Parts of a plants*: seed, fruit, shoot, petals, leaves, roots, branch, stem, trunk • *Parts of animals*: fur, feathers, legs, beak, coat, head, body, eyes, mouth, nose, ears, skin, tail, feet • *Classifying*: group, similarities, differences, variety (variation), features, plants, animals, birds, fish, minibeast, keys, organism, classify, identify, observe • *Processes (plants)*: grow, germinate • *Processes (general)*: reproduce, living, non-living, life cycle, nutrition, reproduce, life processes • *Habitats*: dark, cold, shaded, light, warm, cold, dry, moist, wet, position vocabulary (e.g., under, below, beside, etc.), habitat, environment,	• Magnifying glasses • Pond dipping equipment • Equipment for working with mini beasts (trays, pooters, tweezers, etc.) • Measuring equipment • Counting equipment • Drawing equipment • Identification keys (age and location appropriate) • Identification pictures for younger children • Access to books/internet

	conditions, consumers, producer, predator, prey, food chain, over-crowding, adapted (adaptation), suited, diet, food pyramid	

Activities

Identifying requirements and constraints of the challenge
- Identify a habitat, an organism within this habitat, and discuss its needs for survival.
- Compose three questions to ask about the parameters of the challenge. Teachers may need to prompt and guide children on any missed information (e.g., time allowance, conditions that the product will be used in, materials available, etc.).

Identifying and describing habitats
- Identify three habitats (or microhabitats) around the school grounds.
- Describe the conditions within each of these habitats. Are there any obvious issues presented within the habitats (e.g., no shade, a flooded area, etc.)?
- Ask the children which plants and animals they think would and would NOT be suited to live here and why.

Identifying plants and animals within habitats
- For each of the habitats, investigate the plants and animals that live there, using appropriate equipment.
- Encourage the children to make drawings of what they see and to take notes about the numbers of different organisms, where they were found, size, etc.
- Demonstrate how to use an identification key to name organisms found. These will be specific to your country/region but are available online (use simplified keys or picture cards for younger children).
- Conduct secondary research using books/internet searches to explore organisms typically found in similar habitats.
- Ask children to identify one plant or animal that they would like to work with in more detail.

Identifying and describing the needs of the plants/animals
- For the selected organism, observe the specific location that this is found in (plant: shaded, loose soil, etc.) or its behaviours (gravitates towards shaded or secluded areas, etc.) to identify preferences.
- Discuss how changes to this habitat might impact the selected organism.
- Identify other plants and animals within the habitat which may be in the same food chain as the selected organism. Draw food chains, webs, or even food pyramids.
- Use secondary research to find out more to explore about the selected organism, with specific reference to difficulties they may face and what could be done to support them (e.g., more wildflowers for bees, sheltered spots for bugs, greater availability of food for birds).
- Ask each group to report their findings back to the whole class.

Addressing the requirements of Charlie's engineering challenge
- Children write a note back to Charlie to explain that they have identified an organism with a need and describe what this need is.
- Children complete the 'exploring ideas' section on their EDP worksheet.
- Examine the range of materials and tools available to use.

Assessment

Children can identify a specific organism within a habitat and define its place within the ecosystem of this habitat.

Children can describe the requirements for survival for their specific organism and can identify the threats to this.

Children can identify one way in which the organism can be supported.

EDP stage: Developing ideas

Design and Technology Learning Objectives:
- To investigate similar solutions to the need identified.
- To investigate how similar products have been made.
- To use information from a variety of sources to generate ideas for potential solutions.

Key Questions	Vocabulary	Resources
• What have you seen before that may help you to develop ideas? • Would this product meet the need that you identified for your organism? • Is there more than one type of product/solution that would meet this need? • Which product or solution do you prefer and why? • What is the item made from? Why? • How have the parts been joined together? • How has the product been made strong and stable? • Would this product last in the conditions in the habitat that you identified? • What size and shape are the products? Is this suitable for your organism or the habitat where your product will be used? • What have you found out from your research/looking at other products that could help you with your own designs?	• Materials: wood (and potentially the name of the specific wood used), plastic, card, • Joining techniques screw, nail, glue, dovetail, moulded	• Children's engineer worksheet • Any real-life products such as bug hotels, bird feeders, etc. available • Access to laptops or tablets and books, etc. for research

Activities

Initial ideas
- Brainstorm imagination activities in small groups to produce wild and whacky solutions and share ideas.
- Complete the 'developing ideas' section of the photocopiable children's engineering page.

Investigate how similar products have been made
- Ask what the children may have seen before that may help them to develop ideas.
- Either using real-life products or researching other products, consider the following:
    - Would this product meet the needs of your organism?
    - What is the item made from? Why?
    - How have the parts been joined together?

- How has the product been made strong and stable?
- Would this product last in the conditions in the habitat that you identified?
- What size and shape is the product? Is this suitable for your organism or the space where your product will be used?

Summarising findings
- Share findings from research/examinations of other products which could help with their own designs. Is there more than one type of product/solution that would meet this need?
- How could the products investigated/researched could be improved?
- Which product or solution do they prefer and why?
- Which ideas could they use in their own product?

Assessment

Children can make a reasonable choice of product and materials and can justify this choice based on the identified needs of their organism.

Children can investigate similar products and identify features that they could incorporate into their own designs and products.

Children can articulate a range of ideas about potential products and solutions.

EDP stage: Designing ideas

Science Content Learning Objectives:
- To be able to apply scientific understanding within a 'real-world' context.

Design and Technology Learning Objectives:
- To design a set of plans relating to an intended product.
- To analyse and evaluate plans and potential products for their suitability in meeting the requirements of the selected organism within their specific habitat.
- To evaluate methods of joining, strengthening, and stabilising.

Thought Processes/Engineering Habits of Mind (EHOM)
Analyse, compare, evaluate, visualise, adapt

Key Questions	Vocabulary	Resources
• Why have you decided on your final product design? • What makes this one better than your other options? • How does your design meet the needs of your selected organisms? • Will your design and choice of materials be suitable for the habitat where your product will be used? • Do you anticipate any problems or issues when making your product?	• *Analysis*: analyse, compare, evaluate, visualise, adapt, research, investigate • *Materials*: wood (and potentially the name of the specific wood used), plastic, card • *Joining techniques*: screw, nail, glue, dovetail, moulded nail, screw, joint, joint, corner, bracket, cross member	• Children's engineering worksheet

Living things and habitats 101

Activities

Designing
- Identify and design three main ideas for products to be made.
- Draw up plans for three potential products.
- Evaluate and assess which of these ideas best meets the requirements of the selected organism and which idea is best suited to the habitat that it would be used in.
- Explain product choice to others in the class and share reasoning about why this product has been chosen.
- Identify how the separate parts of the product will be joined together.
- Identify how the product will be made strong and stable.
- Outline the process and order that the components and overall product will be constructed in.
- Ask the children to identify additional materials and resources required.
- Complete the 'designing ideas' section on the children's engineering worksheet.

Tinkering
Tinkering allows children to play with an idea, skill, or tool. Tinkering with tools and materials at this design stage will enable children to try out skills and techniques and evaluate which they will be able to use in their products.
- Ask children to join two pieces of wood together using screws/nails/glue or a combination of these. Test which of these methods of joining produces the most stable join.
- Explore various mechanisms for making their joins stronger (see 'design and technology content' section above in this chapter.

Assessment
Children can select a design from a range and articulate why this is the most suitable choice.
  Children can explain how they will join the separate components together and make their product strong and stable.

 ## EDP stage: Making, testing, and improving ideas

Science Content Learning Objectives:
• To apply scientific understanding within a 'real-world' context.
Design and Technology Learning Objectives:
• To develop explicit skills (e.g., sawing, joining, etc.).
• To be aware of a variety of health and safety considerations.
• To turn a design into a final product.
• To test a product against a set of pre-determined criteria.
• To share ideas and use and adapt the ideas of others.
Thought Processes/Engineering Habits of Mind (EHOM)
Analyse, compare, evaluate, improve

Key Questions	Vocabulary	Resources
• Does your product meet the identified needs of your	• Test, improve, evaluate, improve, appraise	• Children's engineer worksheet

organism or help to solve its problem? • Did you encounter any problems when making? • What solutions to these problems did you find? • Did other groups encounter similar problems? What solutions did they produce? • Did you choose the most appropriate material to make your product out of? Why/why not?	• *Materials:* wood (and potentially the name of the specific wood used), plastic, card • *Joining techniques:* screw, nail, glue, dovetail, moulded nail, screw, joint, join, corner, bracket, cross member	• Children's engineer worksheet • Safety glasses • Wood • Pencils • Rulers/tape measures • Table clamps • Brackets • Pull saws • Hammers, screwdrivers (Phillips head) • Nails and screws (Phillips head) • Wood glue • Bench hooks • Other materials that may be required such as wire/fabric mesh, plastic, etc.

Activities

Explicit Skills Teaching
- Skills teaching for measuring, cutting, and joining (see 'design and technology content' above in this chapter for tips and techniques).

Health and Safety
- Demonstrations/watch videos of how to use various tools safely.
- Make safety posters or warning signs for the various tools to be used.
- Teachers will need to decide which pieces of equipment are suitable for the children in their classes based on the age and skills level of the children, and how the room and equipment is organised.
- Close adult supervision will be required for sawing and hammering.

Making Activities
- Time for children to make their designed product.

Testing and Appraising Ideas
- Testing of the products durability in the environmental conditions of the habitat. Place the product under a light source or out in the heat (NB not under a direct heat source), in water or in wind etc for a designated period.
- Use a toy of comparable size and shape to the chosen organism and evaluate ease of access and use.
- Real-life testing. Place or use the product in the habitat for which it was designed. Monitor use through in-person observation or through camera equipment. What went well, which parts of the design did not work so well, what needs to be improved?

Improving Ideas
- Following initial testing, children may need to revisit some aspects of their product. Here, research on waterproofing or selection of a more appropriate material might be needed.

Share ideas, using and adapting the ideas of others
- Create flat-pack furniture style instructions for how to make your product.
- Children write a blog, keep a diary, or write a report on how the product is being used/how effective it is in the habitat.

Living things and habitats 103

- Use the Children's engineering worksheet to evaluate.
- Children then return to their own designs and products and adapt considering this new information.

Assessment

Children can describe what they like and do not like about their product.
They can describe why their product is suitable for the habitat that it will be used in.
Children can describe how their product has been designed and made to support their selected organism.
They can evaluate if they have met the design brief and if they have solved the original challenge set.
They can offer solutions to various problems encountered.
Their product shows the application of the relevant scientific principles.

| *Linked Scientific Investigations* | **Investigating through observation:** behaviours and preferences
It would be unethical to alter the conditions within a habitat to investigate the impact. However, comparisons of organisms found in different naturally occurring conditions would make an excellent investigation.
    Making observations is a useful way to gather scientific data. Here, this could be a number of factors, such as:

- The numbers of bees visiting different types of plants and flowers
- Plant populations in different locations
- Minibeasts numbers (or specific animals such as woodlice) found in dry/damp/sunny/dark conditions
- The quantity of different types of food eaten by birds
- Times of day certain species are seen

Investigating through modelling; changes to populations and interdependence
We must be cautious with the use of models as they can never truly represent real life; however, they are useful for simulating and demonstrating phenomenon where it is impossible to examine the real thing.
    For this activity, you will need a selection of coloured counters. Each counter represents a plant or animal found in one of the local school habitats. See the example given below:

- Green = dandelion plant
- Yellow/orange = slug
- Blue = starling (bird)

Remind the children about food chains and pyramids. Can they identify the producer, the consumer, and the tertiary consumer? If these three organisms were in a food chain, what numbers of each would you expect to see (i.e., many for the dandelion, fewer for the slug, and very few for the starling). Give out the counters to the children in these proportions (one counter per child) to play the population game:

- Ask the children holding the green cubes (dandelions) to run around.
- After a minute, ask the children holding the yellow/orange cubes (slugs) to chase them. When a slug catches a dandelion, the dandelion must sit out of the game.
- Pause the game and ask the children what they expect to happen (eventually there will be too many slugs competing for small numbers of dandelions and the dandelion population will die out). |

- Repeat the game with the starlings and the slugs, pausing to examine what is happening to the populations.
- Now ask all three groups to join in. Again, pause the game to examine what is happening to the populations of each of the three species.

In a large space, line up the children in their different species. Tell them that you are going to have a look at how the populations of these three species might be affected by changes to the habitat and what this might do to the other animals in the food pyramid. Read the following scenarios out to the children:

Scenario 1 - The school places a large shed next to the habitat. This stops the light getting to the plants and reduces their growth. Ask the children holding some of the green cubes to sit down to represent this. Ask the children what will happen to the population of slugs and ask some children holding the yellow/orange cubes to sit down to represent this. Ask what will happen to the population of starlings and again represent this by asking some children to sit down.

Scenario 2 - The slug population have been exposed to high levels of pest killer left out by a gardener (some children holding yellow cubes sit down to represent the reduced numbers). Ask the children what they think will happen to the population of the dandelions (increase) and the population of starlings (decrease) and show this with the cubes.

Scenario 3 - The starling population has been hit by a disease that is reducing their numbers. Ask the children what they think will happen to the population of the slugs (increase as the starlings are eating less) and the population of dandelions (decrease as there will be more slugs) and show this with the cubes.

Investigating data - populations and population change
In this activity, we will use data that has already been gathered.

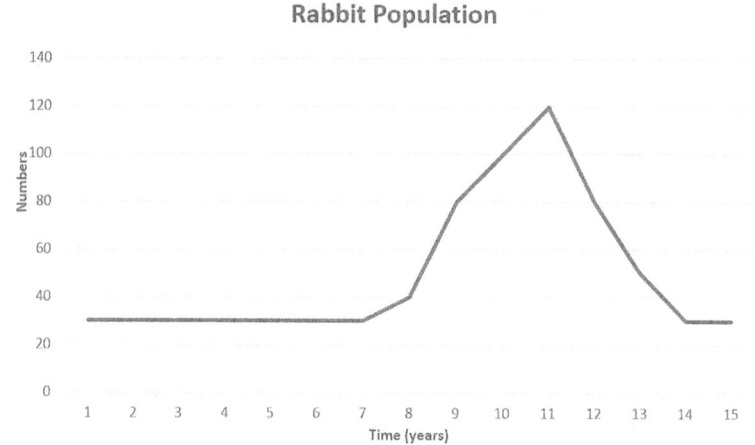

Figure 6.3 Rabbit population

Show the children the graph in Figure 6.3 and ask:

- How many rabbits were there to start with?
- What is the highest number of rabbits?

- How long was it before the rabbit population stated to grow?
- When was the highest population of rabbits?
- What is the difference between the highest and lowest population numbers?
- Can you describe what happens in years 7 and 8?
- Why might this have happened (e.g., better growth of grass so more food available, disease eradicated, fewer predators)?
- Can you describe what happens in years 11 to 14? Why might this have happened (disease, increase in predators, reduction in food)?

Show the population graph in Figure 6.4. Repeat the above questions, this time looking at the population of foxes. Ask the children what happens to the rabbit population when the population of foxes alters. Ask why this might be.

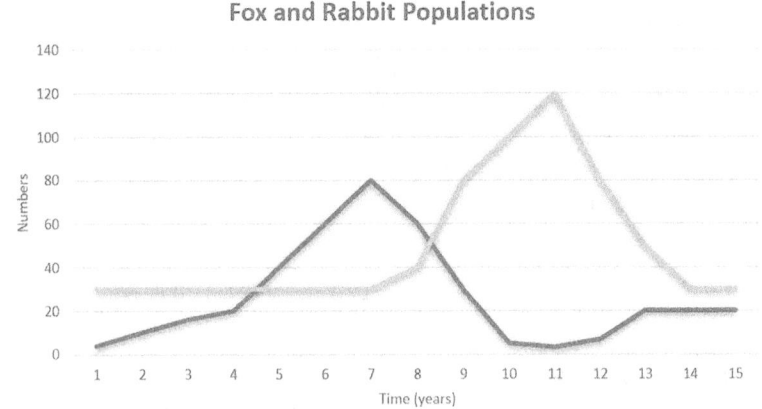

Figure 6.4 Fox and rabbit population

Show the children the graph in Figure 6.5. This represents the population of frogs in a school pond. Ask the children to discuss what is happening and what may have caused the changes in populations.

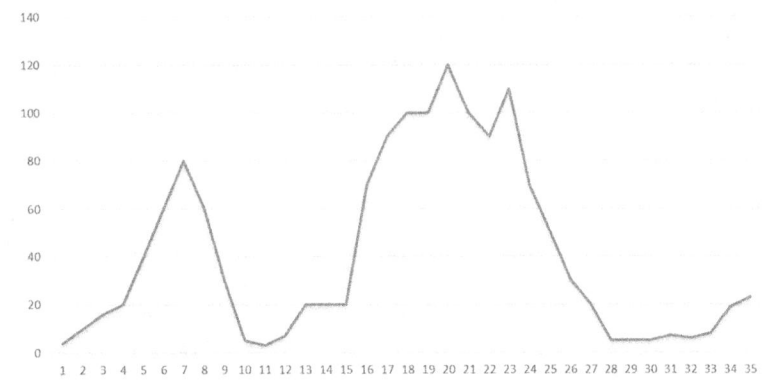

Figure 6.5 Frog population

Resources

- Children's engineering worksheet
- Safety glasses
- Wood (different types if possible)
- Pencils
- Rulers/tape measures
- Table clamps
- Brackets
- Pull saws
- Hammers, screwdrivers (Phillips head)
- Nails and screws (Phillips head)
- Wood glue
- Bench hooks
- Other materials which may be required such as wire/fabric mesh, plastic, etc.
- Magnifying glasses
- Pond dipping equipment
- Equipment for working with mini beasts (trays, pooters, tweezers, etc.)
- Measuring equipment
- Counting equipment
- Drawing equipment
- Identification keys (age and location appropriate)
- Identification pictures or cards for younger children
- Access to books/internet
- Access to real-life products such as bird feeders, seed sprinklers, bug hotels, etc.

Health and safety

General safe classroom practices and behaviours should be at the heart of any woodwork activity. Children should have longer hair tied back, jewellery removed, and they should not run. Eye protection should be worn and loose ties (e.g., on aprons) should be secured. The tools used and adult/child ratios should be selected at the teacher's discretion, depending on the age, skill, and experience of the children. First aid equipment should be maintained and readily available.

All trip hazards should be removed with bags and coats should be stored away from the working area and chairs pushed under tables. Tables should be at an appropriate height for the children to work at safely (i.e., they are not having to stretch up to see adequately or bend over their work to reach it).

Some woods and techniques may produce a lot of dust and so masks could be provided for children who have respiratory problems, and gloves for those who have skin conditions. Avoid using rough, splintery wood and sand down any particularly rough edges before use. All floors and tables should be thoroughly cleaned afterwards to ensure that no sharp objects are left out.

Full instructions and demonstrations on how to use each tool should be given and children should be free to ask questions about this to check their understanding. Videos and safety/instruction posters can also supplement this. Children should not be allowed to use a tool unless they have engaged with this first. Equipment should be well maintained and in full working order and counted out and in again after use so that the teacher is sure that all equipment has been returned. After use, equipment should be stored safely and away from access by the children. Children should be taught that they should not move around the classroom with tools and sharp objects in their hands and should instead place them into the centre of the table when not in use.

When cutting, both hands should be kept behind the cutting edge and when using saws, hammers, or screwdrivers all wood being worked on should be securely clamped to a bench. Finally, make sure that risk assessments are in place and that all staff and adults are aware of the hazards and procedures laid out in this assessment.

Wider resources related to living things and habitats

- Building a bug hotel: https://www.rspb.org.uk/get-involved/activities/nature-on-your-doorstep/garden-activities/build-a-bug-hotel/ or https://www.wildlifetrusts.org/actions/how-build-bug-mansion
- BBC bitesize: https://www.bbc.co.uk/bitesize/topics/z6wwxnb
- National Geographic Kids: https://kids.nationalgeographic.com/nature/habitats

Common misconceptions

Many children think that adaptation is a conscious decision made by organisms that happens within a short timeframe. In fact, this process can take many thousands of years, arising through spontaneous mutations (see 'Science explained' section above).

Other example activities for living things and habitats

- The school gardening club is concerned about the lack of flying insects to pollinate their crops. The school playground has very few places for insects to overwinter as it is mostly tarmac and buildings. Design a bug hotel area for a range of insects to overwinter and have shelter during the winter and be able to access water in the summer.
- The school pond is overgrown, and the plants and animals are dying off. What can we do to clean it up?

Bibliography

BBC. https://www.bbc.co.uk/news/explainers-60823267
ICUN Red List of Endangered Species. https://www.iucnredlist.org/en
Natural History Museum. What is mass extinction and are we facing a sixth one? | Natural History Museum (nhm.ac.uk).
UN Biodiversity Goals. https://www.un.org/sustainabledevelopment/blog/2022/12/press-release-nations-adopt-four-goals-23-targets-for-2030-in-landmark-un-biodiversity-agreement/
UN SDGs. https://sdgs.un.org/goals/goal12
Unicef. https://www.unicef.org/globalinsight/stories/why-biodiversity-important-children

7 Forces

DT focus: Levers

> **The Engineering Challenge**
>
> *Letter from the school council*
>
> Dear Owl Class,
> The Badger class (ages 4-5) teacher has come to us with a problem. The class would like a car track. However, when the teacher went to look in the shops, the car tracks were all made of plastic. You will know that the school is trying to reduce the use of plastic. Can you help by designing and making a car track from recycled materials? The Badger class wants the cars to be able to travel fast and they also want a mechanism to start the cars at the same time from a starting point for races. Will you take on the challenge?
>
> Best wishes
> The School Council.

Aim of this challenge

The aim of this engineering challenge is to help children understand the ways in which forces act on an object and influence the speed and distance that it is able to move. This will encompass gravity, friction and air resistance. There are multiple opportunities for linked scientific investigations throughout this challenge, enhancing the scientific understanding to be applied.

The design and technology focus is on levers, how these work, and the forces applied and used. This challenge could therefore be used as an introductory challenge to the one presented in Chapter 8, which examines a wider range of mechanisms.

A photocopiable Childrens' Engineering Challenge Sheet can be found in the Appendix.

Sustainable development goals

This challenge sits within the UN's sustainable development goals:

Goal 12: Ensure sustainable consumption and production patterns.

As described in the beginning of Chapter 5, the United Nations' Sustainability Goals (https://sdgs.un.org/goals/goal12) encourage the world to reduce its consumption of resources. Toys can form an aspect of this waste.

Toys and waste

In the United Kingdom, parents spend £370 M on toys every year; 80% of those toys will be made of plastics. However, children often lose interest in a toy after a month, which may mean that a working toy quickly ends up in landfill. Toy manufacturers say that plastic toys last between 10-15 years, so one of the best solutions if the children lose interest is to pass the toy on to other children (https://www.greenmatters.com/p/environmental-impact-plastic-toys).

However, second-hand plastic toys have their pitfalls. For a start, the manufacturer of the toy uses fossil fuels, a diminishing resource, and the process often releases polluting chemicals into the environment. It is often impossible to know where the toy comes from, making issues such as fake safety stickers and toys now considered hazardous a problem.

Toys are also difficult to recycle. They are often made from a mixture of varied materials and plastics, each of which may have a different method of recycling. Even if the plastics are recycled, this may result in a higher concentration of toxins in the next product (https://www.theguardian.com/environment/2023/may/24/recycled-plastic-more-toxic-no-fix-pollution-greenpeace-warns).

One alternative is to reduce the purchase of buying new toys, by joining a toy library or by buying toys made of materials such as wood, cork, or natural fabrics. One construction toy manufacturer has been trialling pieces made of a flexible plastic from sugar cane. Another alternate action is to reduce the number of toys, trying to purchase those that will last for many years.

See:
https://www.zerowastescotland.org.uk/resources/what-do-toys-and-games
and
https://www.toys4life.co.uk/about/

For further information on the problems of landfill, see Chapter 5.

Potential solutions

The challenge involves exploring materials, mechanisms, friction, gravity, and levers.

Having surveyed Badger Class for their views on the kind of track the young children want, the solutions could be a track with a slope made from cardboard or wood. The children could experiment with the steepness of the slope.

Adaptations could be to include lanes on the track to keep the cars from moving across one another or from falling off the track, with cardboard rails or dowelling.

Other adaptations could be the surface of the track; some surfaces allow the cars to travel quicker than others.

The children may want to include something that will stop the cars at the end of the track, such as a sponge to reduce impact.

Other designs could include devices to make sure all the cars start at the same time. These could include a lever to release the cars down the slope or a lifting barrier or revolving barriers on a straw to release the cars.

Some of the reception children may want parts of the track with potential for imaginary play, for example some shops for the cars to visit or a car park. These could be made with individual cereal packets or small boxes covered in paper with details drawn on the fronts.

The children may want to incorporate bridges or bends into the track.

Science content

The scientific content for this challenge sits within the fields of forces and materials and their properties. This firstly involves being able to describe the properties of the materials.

Materials

Children aged 5-7 years

Younger children could use everyday terms such as:

- Rough/smooth
- Stretchy/stiff
- Bendy/not bendy
- Shiny/matt or dull

Children should be encouraged not only to describe these properties but also to group materials according to these properties. For this challenge, this could involve sorting the materials into two piles (e.g., those with rough surfaces that may slow down toy cars and those with smooth surfaces that might speed up the passage of toy cars). Children will also need to be able to explain why they have chosen a particular material for a purpose (or why they have rejected another one). In this challenge, this may involve identifying material that reduces or increases the friction of the wheels on the car with the surface.

Children aged 7-11 years

Older children will need to be able to use and apply a range of more technical terms such as flexible, malleable, or rigid (see list below).

Again, they will need to be able to describe and classify materials according to their properties and discuss potential uses for materials based on these properties, but they may also be expected to test these materials. For example, which tracks allow the cars to move fastest over the same distance?

Vocabulary

- Flexible
- Rigid
- Strength
- Malleable
- Ductile
- Floppy
- Elastic
- Stretchy
- Supple
- Bendy
- Pliable
- Firm
- Dense
- Bendable
- Soft
- Spongy

Forces

Children aged 5-7 years

Many curricula do not identify forces as a topic of study for younger children. However, the children could gain a range of experiences that would be helpful to their growing understanding such as looking at pushes and pulls of toy cars or in playgrounds. Noticing speeding up or slowing down, throwing balls, and watching them fall, running cars down slopes, and exploring rough and smooth surfaces as stated above.

Vocabulary

- Push
- Pull
- Speed up
- Slow down
- Rough
- Smooth
- Steep surfaces
- Flat surfaces

- Heavy
- Light

Children aged 7-11 years

Children could explore falling objects of varied sizes and masses. They should be starting to experience how gravitational forces act on all objects. They could look at how objects can speed up and slow down and the role of friction and air resistance in altering the speed of objects across surfaces. They could experience how friction is used to stop the movement of objects, for example, in car and bicycle tyres and on the bottom of training shoes.

The science explained

Gravity

Gravity is often thought of when considering planets or large objects, like rockets. But every single particle in the universe has its own gravitational pull, attracting other particles in the universe. The extent of this gravitational pull is increased by the mass, the amount of stuff, in the particle. We do not really notice the tiny forces between small particles, but we do notice the impact of a huge mass like the Earth on objects or people on Earth. The moon is a smaller body than the Earth but still exerts a gravitational force on objects but at a lesser extent, therefore astronauts need to increase their mass using heavy boots to stay on the moon's surface.

Mass and weight

One of the issues in understanding gravity is the distinction between mass and weight. Mass is the amount of stuff in an object. If an object is very dense there will be more stuff in it than if the object was like a sponge with air holes in it. Weight is the force that acts on mass due to gravity.

Cars travelling down slopes

When a toy car travels down a car track or slope there are several forces always acting on it. One force is gravity which is trying to pull the toy car through the slope towards the Earth. However, the surface is resisting with an equal force in the opposite direction, preventing the car from falling through. If the car is moving it has a momentum in the direction of the slope. The car will have more energy the higher the starting point on the track and the angle of the slope. This means it will travel faster and further.

Friction

The interaction between the surface of the slope and the car's wheels also acts as another force called friction, slowing the car down. This can be explained with the analogy of trying to pull two hairbrushes apart. Air resistance acts as another friction force as the particles in the air rub against the surface of the car as it travels. There will also be a small amount of air resistance as a force acting on the toy car, slowing it fractionally.

Design and technology content

One of the first design and technology skills that can be developed through this challenge is giving children the opportunity to examine a range of materials so that they can make informed choices about what is most suitable for the product. Other skills and knowledge from setting up a simple mechanism for releasing the cars at the same time.

Levers

A lever is a simple machine that helps us to lift objects with less effort. When you push on one end of the level, it lifts the other end. This could either be resting on a pivot point (Figure 7.1) or attached within a pivot point (Figure 7.2).

The pivot point of the lever is called the fulcrum. By changing the position of the fulcrum, you can make it easier or harder to lift the object on the end of the lever. Examples of levers in everyday life are scissors, tweezers, and seesaws.

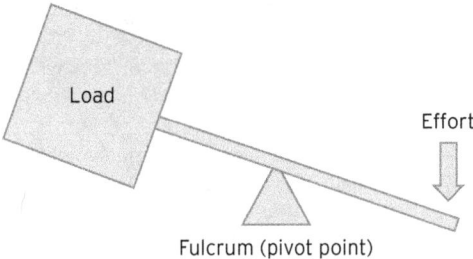

Figure 7.1 A simple lever

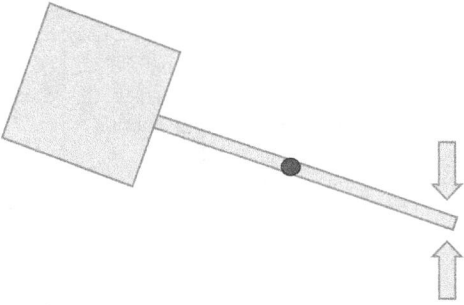

Figure 7.2 A lever with an attached pivot point

114 Forces

Below we have provided some examples of how levers could be explored and understood for all children. These activities will help the children understand how the mechanisms work before they can then be used as part of their designs and products.

Age	Levers
	Levers allow us to use a smaller force to have a greater effect and change motion. The object you are lifting (here, the barrier) is the load, and the force used to make the object move is called effort. Think about using a stick or screwdriver to lever open a tin of paint. The load is the lid, the effort is you pushing down on the end of the stick/screwdriver and the fulcrum is the edge of the tin.
Younger children (ages 4-7)	Start by exploring everyday levels such as a seesaw, balance weighing scales or even a home made lever using a ruler balanced over a large pen or tube of glue. The children can explore what happens when they push and pull either side of the lever up and down, how much force they need to move different loads etc.
Older children (ages 6-11)	As above and also: Try identifying levers in everyday life (stapler, pegs, scissors, etc). Where is the load, effort, and fulcrum? Why and how is the lever used? Explore moving the load or the effort point closer to or farther away from the fulcrum. What happens to the effort needed to lift the load? (see suggested scientific investigation below) Investigate how far you can fire a pompom (or cotton wool ball) by changing the effort applied to the level and the position of the load (the pompom) or the fulcrum.

For more general design and technology guidance for the challenge, see below:

Age	Skills	Example Product for this Challenge
Ages 3-6	For very young children, the skills required should be kept as simple as possible. This could involve making a track from carboard boxes and painting lanes or road features. Glue can also be used to attach additional add-ons and decorative motifs.	Adapt a cardboard box into a racetrack
Ages 6-8	Older children can be taught cutting cardboard in straight lines and gluing barriers between lanes.	Adding lane and edge barriers for cars.
Ages 8-11	At these ages, children can be taught to make several types of levers. A simple lever on a pivot or a rotating lever on a straw that raise individual car	Design and make racetrack with starting barriers and lanes.

Forces 115

	barriers. Children should have the experience of connecting dissimilar materials together with a glue gun or glue. Children can design and make decorations for the track including finish lines for a racetrack or sponsorship decals.	

Teacher guidance (lesson and activity plans)

The tables below set out how the science and design and technology content could fit within the EDP. This is not an exhaustive list, and you may well be able to think of alternatives or different ways of organising the content for your own class.

These tables also give example activities to do at each stage of the EDP and key questions to ask. Again, these are ideas for you to use, adapt, and add to for your own classes.

EDP stage: Igniting ideas

Learning Objectives To be able to identify a presented need or requirement. To be able to articulate what is needed as an outcome of the challenge set.		
Key Questions	*Vocabulary*	*Resources*
• What have the reception class asked the children to do? • What does reception class want us to design and make? • What features do the reception class want on their racetrack? • Why do they want the children to make something rather than to buy a racetrack?	• Recycle/reuse/ repurpose • Product/solution • Racetrack • Barriers • Start line • Finish line • Fixings	• Copies of the children's engineering challenge page
Activities • Share the challenge with the children. • Discussions to clarify the need presented in the challenge. • What kind of features do the children think are important to have on a racetrack? • Discuss how the class can find out about the features Badger class want on their racetrack.		
Assessment Children can define the challenge that has been set for them, showing that they understand the need presented and how they can find out more about the wishes of the children in Badger class.		

 **EDP stage: Exploring ideas**

Science Content Learning Objectives
- To be able to identify the effects of friction that act between moving surfaces.
- To be able to explain how all objects are subject to the pull of the Earth's gravitational field. As the object cannot fall through the racetrack, it acts on accelerating the cars down the slopes.

Design and Technology Learning Objectives
- Understand and use mechanical systems in their products (for example, gears, pulleys, cams, levers, and linkages).
- Explore and use mechanisms (for example, levers, sliders, wheels, and axles), in their products.
- To be able to recognise that some mechanisms, including levers, allow a smaller force to have a greater effect.

Key Questions	Vocabulary	Resources
• What might you need to know about friction to help design a racetrack? • What do we need to know about the angle of the slope? • Can you describe what this material is like? What are its properties? How might this affect what we use it for?	• Friction • Slopes • Gravity • Cardboard • Track • Lane • Levers • Survey • Data • Products • Fixings • Angle of slope • Surface • Fulcrum • Pivot • Mechanism	PE bench Books for raising the slope Toy cars Silver foil Kitchen roll Fabric length to cover bench Timers or tape measure Selection of objects with levers: scissors, stapler, tweezers, picture of wheelbarrow, nut crackers Class ruler, erasers for pivot, weight, or coins Paper fasteners and card

Activities
Identifying the requirements and constraints of the set challenge
- Discuss what the children need to know to provide a solution to the challenge set.
- In groups, each group composes three questions to ask about the parameters of the challenge set.
- Children write lists of challenge constraints and requirements.
- Children complete the 'exploring ideas' section on their EDP worksheet.
- Examine the range of materials and tools available to use.
- Teachers may need to prompt and guide children on any missed information (e.g., time allowance, conditions that the product will be used in, materials available etc.).

Exploring Friction
- Ask the children what they think friction is.
- Ask children to run hands together and notice the heat that comes from the action.

- Pour a teaspoon of oil on hands and try rubbing together again. What happens now? Why do they think it has changed?
- Show an analogy of two hairbrushes fixed together by processing together the two sides containing bristles. Try to pull the hairbrushes apart. What do the children think is happening? Interleave two books together by their pages and ask the children to explain what is happening. How does this relate to cars going down slopes? What is happening between the tyres and the road?
- Show the BBC Bitesize video https://www.youtube.com/watch?v=P6_VUfHzaaM
- Investigate: Take the same toy car and time it travels down three different slopes of the same angle of steepness. Use a timer at start and end.
  - On slope 1 use silver foil on the surface
  - One slope 2 use kitchen roll
  - One slope 3 use fabric
  - Repeat the test
  - Record results in a table

Surface	Time test 1	Time test 2

- What do the results suggest about racetrack surfaces?
- How will this affect your design?

Exploring Gravity Down Slopes
- How will the height of the slope affect the speed of the car? What is making the car travel fast down the slope?
- Ask the children to predict what will happen to the toy car if the slope gets steeper.
- Set up an investigation where the children raise the slope by either intervals of 10 cm or two paperback books of the same thickness.
- Using a table for results below, record the time it takes to travel down the slope. Repeat readings.

Height of slope	Time test 1	Time test 2

- Ask the children what they noticed.
- Was there a height where the car spun off as it was travelling too fast? Which is the best height of slope for the toy car?

Exploring Levers
- Examine a range of objects that use levers (e.g., door handle, scissors, tweezers, nut crackers, tennis racket with arm, wheelbarrow). How do the children think they work? Where is the force applied and where does the force end up? Where is the pivot for the lever? Are they all the same?
- Using a class ruler, eraser, and some weights, make a simple lever like a seesaw. Change the position of the weights. What do the children notice?
- How can we use our knowledge of levers to make a barrier that lifts at the start line?
- Use paper fasteners and card to make simple models of the human arm demonstrating how it is a lever with an elbow pivot!

Assessment
Can children apply the science knowledge on slopes, friction, and levers to their design?
   Children understand and can appropriately use a range of vocabulary associated with forces, slopes, friction, and levers.
   Children are able to describe why a racetrack surface is a suitable choice drawing on their tests.

EDP stage: Developing ideas

Science Content Learning Objectives:
- Investigate the type of surfaces for the racetrack and relate these to forces, friction and gravity.
- Investigate the relationship between height of the slope and the speed of the car.

Design and Technology Learning Objectives:
- To investigate how comparable products have been made. (How have the materials been joined together? How have attachments been added on?)
- To use information from a variety of sources to generate ideas for potential solutions (e.g., looking at home-made racetracks on the internet).
- To investigate the use of levers to act as a start line.

Key Questions	Vocabulary	Resources
<ul><li>What is the racetrack made from? Why do you think that this material was chosen?</li><li>How have the parts been joined together?</li><li>What may help you to develop ideas?</li><li>What do the reception class say about features they want on the racetrack?</li></ul>	<ul><li>Friction</li><li>Slopes</li><li>Gravity</li><li>Cardboard</li><li>Track</li><li>Lane</li><li>Levers</li><li>Survey</li><li>Data</li><li>Products</li><li>Fixings</li><li>Angle of slope</li><li>Surface</li><li>Fulcrum/ pivot</li><li>Mechanism</li></ul>	<ul><li>Children's engineer worksheet</li><li>Access to laptops or tablets, etc. for research</li><li>Paper copies of survey to collect data from the reception class</li><li>Cardboard boxes, toy cars, books as supports, shiny paper, newspaper, corrugated cardboard</li></ul>

Activities
- Survey the class to find out what features they would like on their racetrack. Make a tally to report results (if this is not possible, provide the children with this information).
- Brainstorm imagination activities in small groups to produce wild and whacky solutions.
- Sharing of ideas discovered or imagined.
- Complete the 'developing ideas' section of the photocopiable children's engineering page.

Examine the properties of materials used in comparable products/discuss why these materials have been chosen
- Ask the children to examine what they have found from images of racetracks (toy and real) found on the internet. What are these items made from?
- Conduct internet or literature-based research about designs or products that could provide ideas for the children's designs.
- Using cardboard and cars, try out different heights for the slopes. Which angle slope is best for running toys cars down without them flipping or getting stuck? Discuss and explain why.

Forces 119

Investigate how comparable products have been made
- Looking at homemade toy racetracks on the internet – how have the parts been joined? How do they make a barrier for the start line? What materials do they use?

To use information from a variety of sources to generate ideas for potential solutions
- Drawing on the children's knowledge from internet research and running the cars down the cardboard, how could the product be improved?
- Which ideas could you take to use in your own product?

Assessment Indicators
Can the children use the data from their survey of the Badger class and identify patterns in the data to inform their product design?

Can they make a reasonable and relevant choice of design of racetrack relating to the materials available to them and can justify this choice based on the properties of the material(s) and their own initial tests?

Are they able to research comparable products and identify features that they could incorporate into their own designs and products?

Are they able to articulate a range of ideas about potential products and solutions?

EDP stage: Designing ideas

Science Content Learning Objectives:
- To investigate the properties of materials (could also be covered during the 'developing ideas' stage or the 'making, testing, and improving ideas' stage).

Design and Technology Learning Objectives:
- To be able to draw and design a set of plans relating to an intended product.
- To be able to analyse and evaluate plans and potential products for their suitability in meeting the requirements of the challenge set.
- To be able to evaluate methods of joining.
- To be able to apply understanding of levers as a mechanism.

Thought Processes/Engineering Habits of Mind (EHoM)
Analyse, compare, evaluate, visualise, adapt

Key Questions	Vocabulary	Resources
- Why have you decided on your final product design? - What makes this one better than your other options? - How does your design meet the challenge and the constraints/requirements set out in the 'explore' stage? - Do you anticipate any problems or issues when making your product?	- Analyse, compare, evaluate, visualise, adapt - Research, investigate	- Children's engineer worksheet - A range of fabrics and materials - A range of materials for track: cardboard/plastic/paper/kitchen roll - Scissors/craft knives and cutting mat

120 Forces

		• Fabric glue/glue guns • Adhesive tape • Paper fasteners • Staples and stapler • Tape measures, rulers • Materials and objects for decoration • Toy cars • Timers • Tape measures

Activities
- Identify and design three main ideas for products to be made.
- Draw up plans for three potential products.
- Evaluate and assess which of these ideas best meets the requirements set out in the 'ignite' and 'explore' stages of the EDP.
- Explain product choice to others in the class and share reasoning about why this product has been chosen.
- Identify how the separate parts of the product will be joined together or how any attachments will be added on.
- Explain how a lever mechanism will be used within the design.
- Complete the 'designing ideas' section on the children's engineer worksheet.

Assessment
Children are able to select one design from a range and articulate why this is the most suitable choice.
　Children can explain how they will join the separate components of their product together and explain why they have chosen this method.

 ## EDP stage: Making, testing, and improving ideas

Science Content Learning Objectives: • To investigate the properties of the racetrack. • To be able to apply scientific understanding within a 'real-world' context.		
Design and Technology Learning Objectives: • To be aware of a variety of health and safety considerations. • To be able to turn a design for a solution to a set problem into a racetrack. • To be able to test a product against a set of pre-determined criteria (from the 'exploring ideas' stage). • To be able to share ideas and use and adapt the ideas of others.		
Thought Processes/Engineering Habits of Mind (EHoM) Analyse, compare, evaluate, improve		
Key Questions	*Vocabulary*	*Resources*
• Does your racetrack have all the features requested by Badger class?	• Test, improve, evaluate, improve, appraise • Product • Research, investigate	• Children's engineer worksheet • Scissors

• Does your product meet all the specifications set out in the 'exploring ideas' stage? • Did you encounter any problems when making your product? • What solutions to these problems did you find? • Did other groups encounter similar problems? What solutions did they produce? • Did you choose the most appropriate material to make your race track out of? Why/why not?	• Requirements/parameters/constraints • Gravity and friction • Strength, malleable floppy, elastic, stretchy, supple, bendy, pliable, firm, dense, bendable, soft, spongy • Speed, acceleration, slowing down. • Lanes • Barriers • Starting line • Finishing line	• A range of materials for track: cardboard/plastic/paper/ kitchen roll • Scissors/craft knives and cutting mat • Fabric glue/glue guns • Adhesive tape • Paper fasteners • Staples and stapler • Tape measures, rulers • Materials and objects for decoration • Toy cars • Timers • Tape measures

Activities

Explicit Skills Teaching
- Using the glue gun to fix parts together.

Health and Safety
- Demonstrations of how to use glue guns or craft knives safely.
- Teachers will need to decide which pieces of equipment are suitable for the children in their classes based on the age and skill level of the children.

Making Activities
- Time for children to make their designed product.

Testing and Appraising Ideas
- Testing of tracks to judge the start line barrier's effectiveness. Observe whether all cars leave at same time.
- Timing of toy cars running down different slopes to find out which track has the best surface for travel (less friction). If no timers are available, the children could measure how far the toy cars travel when leaving the slope.
- Older children could calculate the speed that the cars travel at using different slopes and materials. Time how long it takes each car to travel a set distance. The speed can be calculated by dividing the distance travelled (e.g., 150 cm) by the time taken to travel (e.g., 25 seconds). This would give a speed of 6 cm/second (0.06 m/second).
- The class could take their tracks to the younger children and watch the them playing with track. Asking children about the track. What do they like about it? What would they want that is different?
- Use the Children's engineering worksheet to evaluate.
- What went well, which parts of the design did not work so well, and what needs to be improved? What features do the children like and what do they want changed?
- See also the linked scientific investigations below.

Improving Ideas
- Often, during this stage, the children encounter problems with their product. This provides an opportunity to revisit the science involved to help them to solve these issues. For example, if slope is too steep the cars may skid and fall off track. In which case the slope could be reduced or the surface if the track could have better grip.

122 Forces

- The starting line barrier may advantage some toy cars over others so the design may need to be altered.
- Again, when encountering issues this would be a good opportunity for children to go back to do some further research (e.g., What other kinds of starting barriers could they use? Why could these be more effective?).

Sharing ideas, using and adapting the ideas of others
- Children display their part or fully completed racetrack alongside their designs. All children move around the classroom to examine the work of others. Encourage the children to note down innovative ideas that they could use in their own designs and racetracks.
- Ask each child/group of children to share an issue or triumph that they have had with their design and racetrack. The rest of the class can either use the idea that worked or offer a solution to the issue experienced.
- Children then return to their own designs and products and adapt considering this new information.

Assessment
Children should be able to make some evaluation of their design relating to the design criteria.

Linked Science investigations	**Friction in Surfaces (Shoes)** Collect some shoes of the same shoe size, wellington boot, training shoes, slippers, or school shoes. Look at the tread on the shoes. Ask the children to predict which shoe will grip best on the test surface. Place a 500 g weight in the shoe and attach a Newton meter to the laces. Pull the shoes along the same surface the same distance. Repeat the test two to three times. Record the force needed to pull the different shoes along. Change the surface and repeat. The surface could be wet or dry. Relate the roughness of the surface to the force required and apply this understanding to the surfaces used in the car tracks. *Gravity* Many children (and adults) believe objects fall faster if they are heavier. Using two small tubs (of the same size and shape), one full of plasticine to increase the mass, drop the tubs at the same time from a desk or table. Film the drop with a phone camera. Slow the video down to show how both tubs hit the ground at the same time, even though one has more mass. Get the children to repeat the test exploring their own ideas. *Air resistance* Make cones out of paper the same diameter and launch them from an empty plastic lemonade bottle that is quickly compressed. Ask the children to make different nose cones including those with decoration on the surface to explore air resistance. They could use different materials on the cone (e.g., silver foil or fabric) and observe which flies highest. The children may need to get the same child to launch each cone to make the test fair. Repeat the test for more consistent results. What do the children notice about air resistance?

Health and safety

If cutting card or paper with a craft knife, children should be shown how to hold the paper away from the knife and how to use a cutting mat.

Glue guns may be used by children depending on their age, but try to use the cold glue gun versions and only have these available under close adult supervision. Make sure the cable is not in a position where it can catch on children or objects.

Make sure toy cars are not left on the floor for children to slip on.

Common misconceptions

Gravity

By the age of 11 years, many children have a little understanding of gravity; it is just the way things are. If they do have some awareness of gravity, it tends to be applied in limited situations; if something is falling. Children are often not aware that gravity is acting on an object even if it is not moving, or that all objects (regardless of how small they are) exert a gravitational force. They often believe that heavy items drop faster than lighter objects. They will sometimes state that there is no gravity on the moon.

Friction

Children are starting to have some ideas about the effects of friction through their own experiences of riding bikes or playing ball games. They are often aware that applying something that rubs two surfaces together can slow movement, like brakes. They are not aware that friction also has an impact on objects that are not moving.

Other related challenges

- Mrs. Clark, a new member of the staff with a mobility disability, joins the school and often needs to use the lift. Could you design a system to take small items like the register from the ground floor to the second floor to reduce the number of stairs she has to climb (e.g., a pulley system)?
- The school wishes to encourage children to use bicycles and scooters to ride to school. Can you design a bicycle stand to hold the bikes/scooters?
- Levi's mum is always complaining that he wears through his school trousers too quickly on the knees. Can the class investigate which materials are the most hard wearing? Using a sanding block and sandpaper, test different materials and record how many rubs with the sandpaper block the fabric takes before getting holes. Record the results in a table and write to Levi's mum with your results. Tell her about what kind of fabrics are the most hard wearing. See Chapter 5 for linked ideas.

Wider resources related to forces, gravity, and levers

One of our favourite resources for teaching children about gravity is the sequence of Brian Cox dropping feather and a weight in an air vacuum.
https://www.youtube.com/watch?v=E43-CfukEgs

Physicists in primary schools (PIPS) have some good activities that teach about forces acting on objects that are not moving with ping pong balls and straws!
https://www.stem.org.uk/resources/elibrary/resource/33017/forces-and-gravity#&gid=1&pid=1

The Engineer Project has a different engineering challenge that involves designing and making a mobile. This involves children in a lot of work on levers and balance.
https://www.stem.org.uk/resources/elibrary/resource/35620/fine-balance-building-hanging-sculpture

Experiment with Rocket balloons with the Institute of Physics 'Do try this at Home':
https://www.iop.org/explore-physics/at-home/episode-7-rocket-balloon

Science at Home has a firing rocket that is powered by baking soda and vinegar. This would be a great scenario for exploring the forces acting on the rocket:
https://pstt.org.uk/resources/science-fun-at-home/?_sft_science_topics=forces

For those children who always want a bit more, Grace has created an animation of the world showing variation in the strength of gravity!
https://grace.jpl.nasa.gov/resources/6/grace-global-gravity-animation/

8 Light and sound

Design and technology focus: Mechanisms

The Engineering Challenge

The children in Mohammed's gardening club love to grow vegetables and fruits that they can cook with. This year, they are trying to grow tomatoes, which need to be grown in a greenhouse as they need just the right amount of warm sunlight. Unfortunately, they are having some difficulties and their tomato plants have shrivelled leaves, are wilting, and are turning brown. Mohammed has done some research about what might be happening and thinks that the tomato plants may be getting too hot, and the leaves are becoming scorched as it has been very sunny and hot recently.

Mohammed would like to know if you can create anything to shade the plants when it is too hot but will allow plenty of sunlight to reach the plants when it is a little cooler.

Aim of the challenge

This challenge asks children to create a product which will shade tomato plants grown in a greenhouse from intense sunlight. The product will need to incorporate a mechanism so that it can be moved to allow sunlight through during cooler times and provide shade during periods of more intense heat. The children can explore different mechanisms (levers, sliders, wheels, axles, pulleys, or even cams) and incorporate this into their design and product.

The scientific focus of this challenge is to explore the relationship between light and shadows (how light travels, how shadows are formed, how the distance between the light source and an object will affect the size of a shadow), and how different materials (opaque, translucent, and transparent) will allow different amounts of light through to cast different shadows.

This challenge also encourages children to consider how plants grow and the requirements that they have. It also promotes locally and seasonally grown foods.

A photocopiable Childrens' Engineering Challenge Sheet can be found in the Appendix.

DOI: 10.4324/9781003325826-8

Sustainable development goals

This challenge sits within two of the UN's sustainable development goals:

>Goal 3: Good health and wellbeing.
>Goal 12: Ensure sustainable consumption and production patterns.

The journey which our food goes through from farm to plate is a long and complex one involving harvesting, transport, storage, and processing. Each of these stages consumes energy and adds to the carbon footprint of the product that we eventually use. To add to this, food is also lost or wasted at each of these stages meaning that much of the food that we grow is never consumed. More information can be found on the environmental costs of food production in the Sustainable Development Goals section in Chapter 9. Unsustainable patterns of production and consumption need to be addressed and one way that we can address this at an individual or community level is to grow more of our own food.

Calculating the environmental cost of our food is a complex business. Whilst it seems logical to select foods which are lower in food miles these may not always be the options with the lowest energy footprint. For example, it may often take less energy to import tomatoes to a cooler country from a warm climate than it does to grow them in heated greenhouses. The mode of transport used will also impact the energy footprint. Foods with a shorter shelf life (such as tomatoes) are more likely to be transported by air. This is confusing for the customer and makes trying to eat with a lower carbon footprint complicated. What is clear is that home grown will always have a lower environmental impact.

Sourcing and growing local and seasonal foods can also make good economic sense. The United Nations (sustainable goals https://sdgs.un.org/goals/goal2) estimates that soaring food prices have affected 47% of countries in 2020. Careful thought and planning could save money on food costs with home grown alternatives. For example, *Which* magazine (https://www.which.co.uk/reviews/grow-your-own/article/growing-vegetables/save-money-by-growing-your-own-veg-a8zgZ4G3O3AC) estimates that the cost of a kilogram of home-grown tomatoes would be roughly 0.5 p, whereas the cost of a supermarket bought kilogram would be £3.19.

The following points could help you or your school save money when growing your own produce:

- Which are the more expensive foods that you buy? Crops like potatoes or carrots may be easy to grow, but the space could be used to grow higher value crops. For instance, a packet of lettuce or kale seeds is cheap and will yield the equivalent of may bags of more expensive salad leaves. This also has the advantage that you will only pick what you need at the time and will have a continual, fresh supply.
- Invest in small fruit bushes, such as blackberries, raspberries, blackcurrants, gooseberries, and redcurrants. Each year, these will provide a crop of fruits that are quite expensive at the supermarket. Surplus crops can also be frozen and used throughout the year.
- Herbs can be expensive to buy; even with little outdoor space, herbs can be grown easily for a quick and inexpensive supply.

- Try to grow your crops from seed rather than buying more expensive seedlings. One packet of seeds will grow many plants.
- Try to source free seeds or seedlings. Many gardeners plant more seeds than they need and are happy to give away any surplus that they do not need, especially to schools. Put the word out that you are looking for crops to parents, local neighbours, and even on social media.
- The equipment needed to grow your own food can be costly, but free or cheap alternatives can be found. When growing seedlings, use paper pots, clean old pots, yoghurt pots, margarine tubs, or takeaway containers rather than buying new plant pots. Also keep an eye out for second-hand tools; ask for donations to a school gardening club within your local community.

When growing fruit and vegetables in school, there are additional considerations to bear in mind:

- Try to consider what the children would like to eat. Berries and fruits work well here, but vegetables such as tomatoes are also popular.
- Think about foods that are easy to prepare and cook for eating. Lettuce is great as it can easily be picked, washed, and used in a salad. Tomatoes can be sliced and used to top a pizza or in a sandwich. Peas are delicious eaten straight from the pod.
- Remember to consider when your fruit and vegetables will be ready to harvest. Try to plant crops that will ripen and be ready to eat during the term time rather than during longer holidays.
- Use your produce for cookery activities within class.

Potential solutions

The variety of solutions for this challenge lie in the type of mechanism used in the product. The selected mechanism will contain movable parts which will then allow the shade to be put in place or removed to let in sunlight. Simple mechanisms that could be used are suggested in the table below. Further information about how these could be used or built in the classroom is given in the design and technology content section below.

Children can also vary their product by varying the type of material that they choose to create the shadow which will block the light and shade the plants. They may choose an opaque material (to offer complete shade), a translucent material (to offer partial shade) or a transparent material (to offer no shade at all).

Science content

The scientific content for this challenge primarily sits under the topic of light, although some understanding of the requirements that plants have for life will also be required and can be covered through this challenge.

128 Light and sound

Mechanism	Example	Description
Levers	*Figure 8.1* A simple lever (showing Load, Fulcrum (pivot point), Effort) *Figure 8.2* A lever with a fixed pivot point	This is a simple mechanism where a shade can be attached to one end of a lever and the other end pushed up or down to move the shade to the appropriate position. This could either be resting on a pivot point (a fulcrum) (Figure 8.1) or attached within a pivot point (e.g., with a split pin) (Figure 8.2).
Sliders	*Figure 8.3* A simple sliding mechanism	Simple sliding mechanisms (Figure 8.3) can be made by younger children where it is attached to a surface by a strap which holds it in place.

Light and sound 129

Pulley	A pulley (Figure 8.4) could be attached to a ceiling or the roof of a greenhouse.	*Figure 8.4 A simple pulley mechanism*
Cam	The misshaped wheel in a cam (Figures 8.5 and 8.6) will push up or cause the main stem in the mechanism to move up or down. This vertical movement will then cause the shade to move up or down into position.	*Figure 8.5 A cut-out cam mechanism* *Figure 8.6 A bevelled cam mechanism*

Mechanism	Example	Description
Axle/ wheel	*Figure 8.7* An axle and wheel mechanism	This mechanism involves an axle with an attached wheel (Figure 8.7). When the wheel is turned, the axle also turns. Any object attached to the axle via a string or a rope, etc. can then be wound up or down into position.

Within the topic of light, children will need to understand how light travels, how shadows are formed (and what factors affect the type of shadow cast), as well as the differences between opaque, translucent, and transparent materials.

Children aged 5-7 years

Plants
Younger children will need to understand that plants need water, light, and a suitable temperature to grow and stay healthy. They may also make some simple observations of how plant growth and health is affected by a lack of or too much sunlight.

Light
Children will need to understand that light travels from a source to the eye, or to an object and then to the eye. This challenge will also help younger children to understand how shadows are formed when the passage of light is blocked.

Children aged 7-11 years

Plants
Older children can explore the requirements of life for plant growth (air, light, water, nutrients from soil, and room to grow) and how these requirements can vary from plant to plant (for example, those plants that survive well in a warm greenhouse compared to those with thrive outdoors). They could also investigate the effects of differing amounts of light on plant growth and health.

Light
Like the younger children, older children will need to recognise that light travels in straight lines and that shadows are formed when the light from a light source is blocked by an opaque object. This knowledge will help them to explain why shadows have the same shape as the objects that cast them. They can explore and find patterns in the way that the size of shadows change (e.g, angle of opaque object, distance between a light source and an opaque object, angle of the light source, distance between the opaque object and the place where the shadow is cast). Ideas for investigating these factors are provided later in this chapter.

Some understanding of how we see objects will also be of use in this challenge (e.g., using the idea that light travels in straight lines to explain that we see things because light travels from light sources to our eyes or from light sources to objects which is then reflected off these objects into our eyes).

Vocabulary

- *Light*: day (daytime), night (night-time), light, dark, source, sun, opaque, translucent, transparent, block, beam, reflect, shadow, shine, straight line, eye, absorb, material, bright, bright (brightness, brightest), direction, reflection, travel

- *Plants*: leaves, flowers, petals, fruit, roots, bulb plant, plants, branch, stem, flower, leaf, leaves, seeds, weeds, grow, growing, living, alive, not-living, not alive, dead, healthy, light, warmth, water, height, germinate, fertiliser, nutrients, stamen, stigma, sepal, petal, ovary, pollen, style, germinate, germination, fertilise, fertilisation, pollinate, pollination, disperse, dispersal

The science explained

Opaque/translucent/transparent

When light travelling from a source hits an object, three things can happen. The light can either pass through the object, be absorbed, or can be reflected off it. The amount of light that passes through and the amount that is absorbed or reflected determines whether an object is opaque, translucent, or transparent.

Opaque materials do not let any light through at all. They block light any light travelling from a light source that hits them by absorbing and reflecting it and therefore cast complete, dark shadows.

Translucent materials (such a thin fabrics, tracing paper, or coloured glass, etc.) both reflect and absorb some light and let some light through and therefore cast partial shadows. The more light a translucent material lets through, the fainter the shadow it casts will be. Transparent materials (such as transparent glass or plastic) let almost all light through; almost no light is reflected or absorbed and therefore almost no shadow is cast.

It is easy to identify opaque, translucent, and transparent materials, but what is that makes some materials opaque and some transparent? Light is a form of energy which, when it hits an opaque material, is absorbed whereas in transparent materials this energy can pass through without any dispersion making the material see through. Whether or not the light energy gets absorbed depends on the energy levels of the atoms, or more specifically the electrons, inside the material. The greater the difference in energy between the incoming light and the electrons in the material, the more transparent the material will be.

Shadows

A shadow is simply an absence of light. If the light travelling towards a surface (such as the ground or a wall) is blocked, then that portion of the surface will be darker than the rest of the surface that the light has been able to reach. Light can only travel in straight lines and can therefore not bend around an object.

Shadows are the same shape as the object that has blocked the light; however, the size of shadows can be changed. This is affected by the position of the light source, the object blocking the light, and the surface that the shadow is cast onto.

An object blocks more light when the light is at a lower angle (side on), making longer shadows; when the light source is at a higher angle (overhead), the shadows are shorter. Think about the shadow that would be cast if you held a torch directly above your head and then moved it round to your side. More light is blocked when the light source is side on and therefore the shadow cast is longer. You can see this outside on a sunny day as the sun's position in the sky affects the length of the shadow. When the sun is low, the shadows are long, whereas when it is high in the sky, the shadows are much shorter.

The size of a shadow can also be altered by changing the distance between the light source and the object casting the shadow. When the object is closer to the light source, more light is blocked and so the shadow is larger. When there is a larger gap between the light source and the object, less light is blocked and so the shadow is smaller. The size of the shadow is also determined by the distance between the object and the surface that the shadow is cast on. Again, when the distance between the object and the surface is small, the shadow is small as less light is blocked. When the object is further away from the surface, the shadow is larger as more light is blocked.

Design and technology content

This challenge focusses on understanding and using mechanical systems such as levers, sliders, pulleys, cams, and axles/wheels. This technical knowledge can seem like a challenging aspect of the curriculum to take on, but the concepts are simple, and the mechanisms involved can be made easily with everyday classroom materials. Most mechanisms are simply systems designed to change smaller input forces and motion into greater output force and motion (i.e., a movement or force at one end creates a movement or force at the other).

Below we have provided some examples of how each of these mechanisms could be explored and understood for all children. These activities will help the children understand how the mechanisms work before they can then be used as part of their designs and products.

Age	
	Levers (Figures 8.1 and 8.2)
	Levers allow us to use a smaller force to have a greater effect and change motion. The object you are lifting (here, a shade) is the load, and the force used to make the object move is called effort. Think about using a stick or screwdriver to lever open a tin of paint. The load is the lid, the effort is you pushing down on the end of the stick/screwdriver and the fulcrum is the edge of the tin.
	For this challenge, we suggest that you use a simple (Figures 8.1 and 8.2) type of lever where the load (in this case the shade to be moved) and the effort (the point which will be used to move the mechanism) are at either side of the fulcrum (the pivot point).
Younger children (ages 4-7)	Start by exploring everyday levels such as a seesaw, balance weighing scales, or even a home-made lever using a ruler balanced over a large pen or tube of glue.
	The children can explore what happens when they push and pull either side of the lever up and down, how much force they need to move different loads, etc.

Older children (ages 7-11)	As above and also:
	Try identifying levers in everyday life (stapler, pegs, scissors, etc). Where is the load, effort, and fulcrum? Why and how is the lever used?
	   Explore moving the load or the effort point closer to or further away from the fulcrum. What happens to the effort needed to lift the load? (See suggested scientific investigation below.)
	   Investigate how far you can fire a pompom by changing the effort applied to the level and the position of the load (the pompom) or the fulcrum.

Age	*Sliders* (Figure 8.3) Sliders are simple mechanisms that can move objects horizontally or vertically. An object is attached at one end. The diagrams in the 'Potential Solutions' section of this chapter show two simple mechanisms that could be used.
All children	Investigate pop-up and interactive books. Which have sliders that have been used? How have these been constructed? Why have they been made in this way?

Age	*Pulleys* (Figure 8.4) A pulley is a wheel with a groove in it. A string or cable is attached to the object you want to lift and looped over the pulley (into the groove) and the other end pulled. The pulley changes the amount of force that is needed to lift an object.
Younger children (ages 4-7)	You can see an excellent example of a pulley system at work in *The Lighthouse Keeper's Lunch* by Ronda and David Armitage. Discuss how the pulley is used and why it is needed.
Older children (ages 6-11)	Try identifying pulleys in everyday life (cranes, curtain/blind mechanisms, flag hoists, gym equipment). Why and how are they used? You can investigate the role of a pulley in changing the amount of force required by making a simple pulley system. Take an empty container (e.g., a yogurt pot) and attach it to a long piece of string at three points to form a basket in which a load can be carried. Loop the string around a cotton thread wheel (or similar) and add weights to the pot. The amount of force needed to lift different loads can then be measured.

Age	*Cams* (Figures 8.5 and 8.6) A cam is an odd- or even-shaped wheel that pushes a rod in contact with its edge to move up vertically at different rates, distances, or intervals.

Light and sound

Younger children (ages 4-7)	Ask younger children to simply play with toys or pop-up mechanisms involving cams so that they become familiar with how they work.
Older children (ages 6-11)	Examine a range of mechanical toys. Can the children identify a cam mechanism, how it works, what movement this results in, and why it has been used? Children can make prototype cam mechanisms out of thin card or paper to become further familiar with how they work.

Age	Axles and wheels (Figure 8.7) This mechanism is similar to the pulley mechanism described above. An axle is simply a bar onto which wheels are attached to allow them to rotate freely. Here, the string is attached to the axle and is wound round rather than pulled.
All	Examine a range of toy vehicles. Can the children identify the axle and the wheel? Can they use construction toys to build a vehicle with wheels and axles? Can they build a wheel and axle system to move a load?

Teacher's guidance (lesson and activity plans)

The tables below set out how the science and design and technology content could fit within the EDP. This is not an exhaustive list, and you may well be able to think of alternatives or different ways of organising the content for your own class.

These tables also give example activities to do at each stage of the EDP and key questions to ask. Again, these are ideas for you to use, adapt, and add to for your own classes.

EDP stage: Igniting Ideas

Learning Objectives:
To be able to identify a presented need or requirement.
To be able to articulate what is needed as an outcome of the challenge set.

Key Questions	Vocabulary	Resources
• What problem does Mohammed have? • What does Mohammed need us to do to help him? • Have you seen any fruit or vegetables being grown? Where they in a greenhouse or just outside? Why do you think some plants are grown in a greenhouse?	• Product/solution • Light, heat, growth	• Copies of the children's engineering challenge page

136 *Light and sound*

Activities
- Share the challenge with the children.
- Discussions to clarify the need presented in the challenge.
- Discuss fruit and vegetable growing. Where/what/how/when, etc.

Assessment
Children can define the challenge that has been set for them, showing that they understand the need presented and what they are required to do to provide a solution.

 **EDP stage: Exploring ideas**

Science Content Learning Objectives:
- To understand that different materials allow different amounts of light through to cast different shadows.

Design and Technology Learning Objectives:
- To be able to ask questions about the conditions, needs, and purpose of the challenge set.
- To be able to identify requirements and constraints of the set challenge.
- To understand how mechanism work (lever, slider, pulley, cam, and wheel/axle).
- To understand where mechanisms are used in everyday life and why they are used.

Key Questions	Vocabulary	Resources
- Can you describe Mohammed's problem in your own words? - What might you need to be able to provide a solution to Mohammed's problem? - Why do we need to use a mechanism in our product? - How do the different mechanisms work? - Why and when are the different mechanisms used in everyday life? - Which mechanism might be best to use to solve Mohammed's problem and why? - Which materials block the most light? - Which materials would be best to shade plants?	- Requirements/parameters/constraints - Lever, slider, pully, cam, axle, wheel, load, force, effort, fulcrum, pivot, movement - Opaque, transparent, translucent, shade, shadow, block, light source	Everyday classroom materials Scissors Sticky tape Paper Card Rulers A range of opaque, translucent, and transparent materials (card, tracing paper, glass (safety), tin foil, fabric, clear and coloured plastic, wood, etc.

Activities
Identifying the requirements and constraints of the set challenge
- Discussions about what the children need to know to provide a solution to the challenge set.
- In groups, each group composes three questions to ask about the parameters of the challenge set.
- Children writing lists of challenge constraints and requirements.
- Children complete 'exploring ideas' section on their EDP worksheet.
- Examine the range of materials and tools available to use.
- Teachers may need to prompt and guide children on any missed information (e.g., time allowance, conditions that the product will be used in, materials available, etc.).

Exploring mechanisms
- Introduce the children to the range of possible mechanisms.
- Use the diagrams in the 'Potential Solutions' section of this chapter as models and with the children make simple versions of these (levers: a ruler balanced over a tube of glue/pen etc.; slider: simple card and paper mechanism; pulley: a small pot attached to some string which is looped over a cotton reel or other cylindrical object; cam: simple card and paper mechanism; axle/wheel: a small pot attached to some string which is looped over and attached to a cotton reel or other cylindrical object). Each group of children could make a different mechanism and present how it could be used to move a load to the rest of the class.
- For each mechanism, ask the children to research everyday objects which use the mechanism. How does the mechanism help to lift or move a load? Again, this can be done with different groups focussing on different mechanisms and the findings presented to the class.
- Investigate systems which use multiple mechanisms such as pop-up books or Rube Goldberg (USA)/Heath (UK) machines. Can the children identify the different mechanisms being used? Can they explain how and why they are being used?

Exploring materials
This challenge requires a shade for the plants. Children may decide that fully opaque materials are the most suitable for this or may choose to use a translucent material so that some light can still reach the leaves.
- Show a range of opaque, translucent, and transparent materials (card, tracing paper, glass [safety], tin foil, fabric, clear and coloured plastic, wood, etc.). Hold them up to the light (not the direct sun) and rank them in order of which are easier to see through. Categorise the materials into three groups as follows: those that block the light completely (i.e., cannot be seen through at all); those that block some light; and those which do not appear to block any light and label as opaque, translucent, and transparent.
- Look around the classroom/school and find other materials that would fit into these categories.
- Discuss which materials would be best to make a shade from the plants from. Do they want a shade that completely blocks out the light (and what impact might this have on plant health and growth) or one that partially blocks the light?

Assessment
Children can identify the needs set by Class 5 in their challenge and can describe a set of quantifiable requirements.
  Children can name the different mechanisms and briefly describe how they work.
  Children can identify opaque, translucent, and transparent materials.
  Children understand and can appropriately use a range of vocabulary.

138 *Light and sound*

 EDP stage: Developing ideas

Science Content Learning Objectives:
• To understand how the size of a shadow can be altered.

Design and Technology Learning Objectives:
• To investigate how comparable products have been designed and made.
• To use information from a variety of sources to generate ideas for potential solutions.

Key Questions	Vocabulary	Resources
• Does the size of a shadow always stay the same? • How could we change the size of a shadow whilst still using the same object and light source? • What have you seen or used before that may help you to develop ideas? • What can we find out about what other, similar products are made of? • What have you found out from your research/looking at other products which could help you with your own designs?	• Research, investigate, analyse, compare, evaluate • Vocabulary to describe shadows e.g., light source, surface, object, block, distance, travels, shadow, opaque, translucent, transparent • Lever, slider, pully, cam, axle, wheel, load, force, effort, fulcrum, pivot, movement	• Children's EDP worksheet • Access to laptops or tablets, books, etc. for research • Light sources such as lamps or torches

Activities
- Brainstorm imagination activities in small groups to produce wild and whacky solutions.
- Share ideas discovered or imagined.
- Complete the 'developing ideas' section of the photocopiable children's engineering page.

Investigate how comparable products have been designed and made.
- Ask the children to examine what they have at home or what they have seen before or use internet- or literature-based research about designs or products.
- What are these products made from and why have these materials been chosen?
- Which mechanisms have been used? Examine and discuss how these products work.
- What is the same about all these products? What is different?
- How could these products be improved?
- Which ideas could you take to use in your own product to.

Explore the size of shadows
The position of the shade in relation to the plants (and the sun!) will affect the size of the shadow (shade) that is cast. Children will need to consider this when designing their product and deciding where to place it in the greenhouse. In this challenge, the position of the light source (the sun) and the plants is fixed and so the only variable is the position of the shade.
- See linked scientific investigations below for ideas about how to investigate the relationship between the position of the shade and the size of the shadow.

Light and sound 139

Assessment
Children can make a reasonable and relevant choice of product relating to the materials and mechanisms available to them and can justify these choices.
  Children can investigate comparable products and identify features that they could incorporate into their own designs and products.
  Children can articulate a range of ideas about potential products and solutions.
  Children can explain how the position of their product will affect the size of the shadow cast.

 EDP stage: Designing ideas

Science Content Learning Objectives:
- To be able to apply understanding of light and shadows to a product design and selection of materials.

Design and Technology Learning Objectives:
- To be able to draw and design a set of plans relating to an intended product.
- To be able to use scientific ideas and understanding within a design.
- To be able to incorporate plans for an appropriate mechanism into a design.
- To be able to analyse and evaluate plans and potential products for their suitability in meeting the requirements of the challenge set.

Thought Processes/Engineering Habits of Mind (EHoM)
Analyse, compare, evaluate, visualise, adapt

Key Questions	Vocabulary	Resources
• Why have you decided on your final product design? • What makes this one better than your other options? • How does your design meet the challenge and the constraints/requirements set out in the 'explore' stage? • Do you anticipate any problems or issues when making your product?	• Analyse, compare, evaluate, visualise, adapt • Research, investigate • Vocabulary to describe shadows (e.g., light source, surface, object, block, distance, travels, shadow, opaque, translucent, transparent) • Requirements/parameters/constraints • Lever, slider, pully, cam, axle, wheel, load, force, effort, fulcrum, pivot, movement	• Children's EDP worksheet

Activities
- Identify and design three main ideas for your product to be made.
- Draw up plans for three potential products.
- Evaluate and assess which of these ideas best meets the requirements set out in the Ignite and explore stages of the EDP.

140 *Light and sound*

- Explain product choice to others in the class and share reasoning about why this product has been chosen.
- Identify the mechanism being used, explain how this works in this product, and justify choice of mechanism.
- Complete the 'designing ideas' section on the children's engineer worksheet.

Assessment
Children can select on design from a range and articulate why this is the most suitable choice.
  Children can explain how they will join the separate components of their product together and explain why they have chosen this method.

 EDP stage: Making, testing, and improving ideas

Science Content Learning Objectives:
- To be able to apply scientific understanding of light and shadows within a 'real-world' context.

Design and Technology Learning Objectives:
- To use understanding of how mechanisms work to produce a functioning lever/slider/pulley/cam or axle/wheel.
- To turn a design for a solution to a set problem into a product.
- To test a product against a set of pre-determined criteria.
- To share ideas and use and adapt the ideas of others.

Thought Processes/Engineering Habits of Mind (EHoM)
Analyse, compare, evaluate, improve

Key Questions	Vocabulary	Resources
• Does your mechanism work as you intended it to? • Does your product answer Mohammed's problem? • Does your product meet all the specifications set out in the 'exploring ideas' stage? • Did you encounter any problems when making your product? • What solutions to these problems did you find? • Did other groups encounter similar problems? What solutions did they come up with? • Did you choose the most appropriate mechanism to incorporate into your product? Why/why not?	• Test, improve, evaluate, improve, appraise • Vocabulary to describe shadows e.g., light source, surface, object, block, distance, travels, shadow, opaque, translucent, transparent • Requirements/parameters/constraints • Lever, slider, pully, cam, axle, wheel, load, force, effort, fulcrum, pivot, movement	• Children's engineer worksheet • Tin foil (aluminium) • Paper • Glue • Split pins • Scissors • Thin plastic • Card and cardboard • String/cord/wool • Cylindrical objects for wheels or pulley such as cotton reels, snack tubes • Lamps • Torches • Ice cubes/chocolate • Everyday classroom objects

Activities

Making Activities
- Time for children to make their designed product.
- Children could prototype and test their chosen mechanism before making their final product so that any issues can be addressed.
- The strength and stability of the mechanism can also be tested. Can it be moved 10, 20, 30, 40 times without breaking or malfunctioning? How long does the shade hold in place once the mechanism has been moved?

Testing and Appraising Ideas
- Use light metres to measure the amount of light before and after use of the product.
- Place a piece of chocolate/ice cube on a plate underneath a light source. Time how long it takes to melt with and without use of the shade.

General
- Use the Children's engineering worksheet to evaluate.
- What went well, which parts of the design did not work so well, and what needs to be improved?

Improving Ideas
- Often, during this stage, the children encounter problems with their product. This provides an opportunity to revisit the science involved to help them to solve these issues. For example, if the shade does not hold in place once the mechanism has been used, what could be added to the product to stabilise this?
- Again, when encountering issues this would be a good opportunity for children to go back to do some further research (e.g., When using a pulley mechanism for curtains how is the cord held in place?).
- Children display their part or fully completed products alongside their designs. All children move around the classroom to examine the work of others. Encourage the children to note down innovative ideas that they could use in their own designs and products.
- Ask each child/group of children to share an issue or triumph that they have had with their design and product. The rest of the class can either use the idea that worked or offer a solution to the issue experienced.
- Children then return to their own designs and products and adapt considering this new information.

Assessment

Children can describe what they like and do not like about their product.
    They can describe what worked well and what did not work so well.
    They can evaluate if they have met the design brief and if they have solved the original challenge set.
    They can offer solutions to various problems encountered by themselves and others.
    Their product incorporates a working mechanism suitable for the task.
    Their product shows the application of the relevant scientific principles.

Linked Scientific Investigations	*Light measurements:* Shine a light on a range of opaque, translucent, and transparent materials and use a digital light sensor measure the amount of light shining on the materials and the amount passing through. Rank the materials in order of how much/little light they let through. (NB the light measurement taken underneath the material will also measure ambient light as well as the light passing through the material)

	Shadow size:
	Investigate the relationship between the position of the shade and the size of the shadow cast either by going outside or by using lamps and torches (in a fixed position).
	    Hold the object being used to cast the shade close to the surface where the shadow will be cast and measure the size of the shadow cast (the children can discuss if this should be the length, perimeter, or area). Move the object farther away, measure this distance and again, and measure the size of the shadow cast. Repeat this until enough data has been gathered. Older children can represent their findings in a line graph.
	    This investigation can be adapted to investigate the relationship between the size of the shadow and the distance between the light source and the object blocking the light.

Resources

- Children's engineer worksheet
- Tin foil (aluminium)
- Paper
- Glue
- Split pins
- Scissors
- Thin plastic
- Card and cardboard
- String/cord/wool
- Cylindrical objects for wheels or pulley such as cotton reels, snack tubes
- Lamps
- Torches
- Ice cubes/chocolate
- Laptops/books
- Staples/stapler
- Ruler and tape measures

Health and safety

Light sources

Take care when using lamps as they have trailing cables and so should be placed carefully in the classroom. They also often have exposed bulbs that can become hot. When using the sun as a light source, remind children not to look at the sun directly.

Allergies, intolerances, and poisonous plants

Regularly update lists of any food allergies and intolerances and send out a letter to parents and guardians outlining any foods to be used in school.

Only harvest from identified and cultivated plants rather than wild plants.

Common misconceptions

Light

A common misconception amongst children is that we see things through light being emitted through our eyes (in pictures they may draw an arrow leaving the eye and moving towards the object being seen). Children should be encouraged to see that light travels from a light source to our eyes. This can be shown in diagrams or demonstrated practically. Try shining a torch in a darkened room. Sprinkle a fine powder over the beam of the torch so that it can be seen.

Shadows

Children may also hold several misconceptions about shadows. They may firstly think that thicker objects will cast darker shadows. This idea can be challenged by demonstrating the shadow cast by a thin piece of opaque card or a sheet of aluminium foil and a thick piece of transparent glass and discussions can be held about the blocking of the light.

Some children may also think that a shadow is a form of reflection as it has the same shape as the object. Show the children a reflection of, and the shadow of, an opaque, colourful object and discuss the differences. In the reflection, the colour and detail can be seen as the light is bounced off the object. In the shadow, only the shape can be seen as the light is blocked. You could use the torch and powder, as described above, to show the light being blocked.

It is easy to understand why some children may think that there are no shadows when the light intensity is low (e.g., on an overcast day). This is simply because they are less obvious as there is less contrast between the shadow where the light has been blocked and the rest of the surface.

Wider resources related to materials, their properties and uses

There are many excellent sources of support and resources for the topic of light and sound. For further support with mechanisms, see the resources below:

- BBC Teach (Science KS2 Mechanisms) provides an interesting video that outlines how various mechanisms work for children and also notes for teachers https://www.bbc.co.uk/teach/class-clips-video/science-ks2-mechanisms/zfhr96f
- For further activities involving simple mechanisms, see STEM learning https://www.stem.org.uk/resources/community/collection/466474/ks1-mechanical-systems
- Northumbria University also provide some useful overviews of how mechanisms work and a range of engaging activities: https://nustem.uk/activity/ase-2015-simple-mechanisms-primary/

Other Example Activities for Light and Sound

- At playtime, the school can be very noisy. Some of the children want a quiet space/want something to block out the noise. What could you design and make that would help them?
- The class has bought a solar-powered battery charger for their class laptops. How can the children maximise the amount of sunlight reaching the charging pads? (reflection)

9 States of matter

Design and technology focus: Food technology

The engineering challenge

> **An email from Class 5:**
>
> Hi,
> Our class would really like to cut down on the amount of waste we produce. So far, we have reduced our paper use and we bring our lunches in reusable wrappers rather than disposable ones. However, we have noticed that our bins contain a lot of tea bags!
>
> Our teacher, Mr. Nowak, loves to drink tea. We have asked him if he can cut down on the number of tea bags that he uses and throws away, but he says that he cannot do without his favourite drink! Is there something that we could do to help to reduce the amount of waste his tea habit produces?
>
> We hope that you can help,
> Class 5

Aim of the challenge

Children can work with two possible themes as a solution.

1. **Theme 1** - Produce an alternative to tea bags so that loose leaf tea can be used.
   This challenge draws on concepts around dissolving, sieving, and filtering and applies understanding of these to find possible solutions. This will initially focus on how a tea bag works in filtering out the flavour but retaining the tea leaves, and how this can be replicated for loose leaf tea. Much of the design and technology focus for this challenge will be on the examination of existing products and solutions, which can then be used to inform designs and products.
2. **Theme 2** - Making fruit and herb teas as alternatives to traditional teas
   This second theme encourages children to consider more local and seasonal alternatives to traditional tea, and therefore focusses on food technology, with children

146 *States of matter*

designing their own tea recipes. These could be made using the products designed in the first theme.

A photocopiable Childrens' Engineering Challenge Sheet can be found in the Appendix.

Sustainable development goals

This challenge sits within two of the UN's sustainable development goals:

Goal 3: Good health and wellbeing.
Goal 12: Ensure sustainable consumption and production patterns.

The United Nations states that (https://sdgs.un.org/goals/goal12) around 13.3% of food is lost after harvesting, before reaching retail markets, with a further 17% wasted at consumer level. These patterns of production and consumption are unsustainable and so an alternative may be to look at more local sources of food, even considering home-grown possibilities. The Natural Resources Defence Council (2010) (https://www.nrdc.org/sites/default/files/eatgreenfs_feb2010.pdf) recommends that we buy seasonal, fresh, and locally grown goods to eliminate food miles and processing steps, which have a large carbon footprint.

According to the *Guardian* newspaper (2010), the carbon footprint of a cup of white tea is around 13 g CO_2. Much of this comes from the milk and boiling of the water, but some also comes from the distance that the tea has travelled, the packaging, and transportation (https://www.theguardian.com/environment/green-living-blog/2010/jun/17/carbon-footprint-of-tea-coffee).
Much of the tea consumed in Europe and northern America is transported from sub-Saharan Africa and India by air. This typically creates around 10 times more carbon emissions than road transport and around 50 times more than shipping (BBC, https://www.bbcgoodfood.com/howto/guide/facts-about-food-miles). Once goods have reached their destination, they are distributed within the country, again, increasing carbon emissions. Even then there are still further carbon costs through the way in which we transport ourselves to purchase our food.

The environmental cost of food packaging should also be considered. For most brands of tea, up to 25% of each tea bag is made from plastic. This plastic content helps the tea bag to retain its shape and to seal shut effectively but this has an implication for the disposal and breakdown of used and discarded tea bags; 11.6 billion minuscule particles known as "microplastics" and 3.1 billion "nano plastics" are released into each cup of tea through the plastic content of the tea bag (https://pubs.acs.org/doi/abs/10.1021/acs.est.9b02540#).

Whilst the solution to many of these issues appears to be a simple 'cut down on tea consumption,' the answer may not be so straightforward. Many tea-producing countries rely on this as a major source of income. In India, this is estimated to bring in US$670 million in foreign exchange earnings whilst also providing large-scale employment for many workers (Fairtrade, 2015. Fairtrade_Tea_Report2.pdf). A reduction in this trade would have serious economic impacts. More locally grown alternatives should also be carefully considered as crops grown in heated greenhouses in more temperate climates may also have a significant environmental cost. The following suggestions may provide some answers.

- Try to purchase teas that have been sea freighted rather than air freighted (e.g., Darjeeling tea is often transported by air as it needs to be fresher for consumption).

- Compost food waste (including used tea) at home. The BBC good food website has some excellent suggestions and guidance: https://www.bbcgoodfood.com/howto/guide/how-compost-food-home
- Choose plastic-free tea bags
- Choose brands with reduced packaging
- Try tea crystals. These are made from a process that transforms tea leaves into crystals that instantly dissolve in water, creating a quicker and more potent drink.
- Reduce the use of milk in your tea.
- Use loose leaf tea (see activity below).
- Use alternatives to tea (see activity below).

Potential solutions

Theme 1 - Produce an alternative to tea bags so that loose leaf tea can be used to cut down on waste.

Children will need to consider how the loose tea leaves can be contained to prevent them from being drunk whilst still providing enough space for the tea leaves to move around in the water to let the flavour infuse. Possible solutions could consider ideas where the tea sits within a compartment within a tea pot or are held within a container (i.e., an infuser). Such infusers are usually made of metal, but classroom alternatives could be made from aluminium, plastic, or certain fabrics such as silk. Other solutions could encompass systems where the tea leaves are filtered out when the tea is poured, or a container holding the tea leaves through which the water is poured being used, or even a product containing the tea being used as a stirrer.

Some children may want to incorporate additional features into their product, such as a squeezing device to extract maximum flavour, a timer to ensure that the tea does not become overly brewed, or a measurer so that the correct amount of tea is used.

Theme 2 - Alternatives to traditional teas

There are many plants, herbs, and fruits that can be used an alternative to tea. These can be dried or even used fresh. Depending on what grows locally, try experimenting with some of the following:

- *Leaves:* goldenrod, bergamot, mint, lemon verbena, feverfew, lemon basil, rosemary, sage, raspberry or blackcurrant leaves, thyme, spearmint.
- *Fruits*: berries, lemon, cucumber, apples, oranges, strawberries.
- *Spices:* cloves, cinnamon, nutmeg, allspice, ginger, vanilla.
- *Roots*: chicory, ginger, liquorice.

Science content

The scientific content for this challenge sits within the field of states of matter. This focusses on the concepts of dissolving and separation (filtering, sieving, filtration), but also encompasses elements of human life and plants.

148 States of matter

Ages 5-7

Theme 1 - Produce an alternative to tea bags
The challenge could be used to introduce solids and liquids, asking children to describe the different properties of these states of matter. They will also need to be able to identify and name everyday materials and describe simple properties of these materials (see Chapter 5 for further ideas).

Theme 2 - Alternatives to traditional teas
Children can be taught the basic requirements for keeping healthy, how we obtain food from plants, and naming various sources of food. They will also need to identify the basic structure of a plant and the different constituent parts.

Ages 7-11

Theme 1 - Produce an alternative to tea bags
Again, children will need to describe the different properties of the states of matter, but will need to also include ideas about dissolvable and non-dissolvable substances. They will also need to be able to identify and describe how mixtures can be separated through sieving or filtering using their knowledge about solids and liquids and understand the differences between reversible and non-reversible changes.

Theme 2 - Alternatives to traditional teas
As above, children should describe the basic requirements for keeping healthy and also how we obtain food from plants and naming various sources of food. They will need to recognise the impact of diet on the way their body functions and how our bodies may become damaged through unhealthy choices.

Vocabulary

- States of matter: solids, liquids, gasses
- Changes in materials: dissolvable, non-dissolvable, solution, soluble, non-soluble
- Mixtures and separation: filter, filtration, separate, sieve, strain
- Plants: leaves, roots, stalk, stem, flower, tuber
- Health: diet, food chain, food source, nutrition, nourishment, carbohydrates, vitamins, minerals, fibre, dairy, fruits, vegetables

The science explained

Dissolvable (soluble)/non-dissolvable (non-soluble). Can tea dissolve in water?

All tea has soluble and insoluble elements. The insoluble elements such as fibre, cellulose, fats, and starches are the bits that are left behind when you make a cup of tea. However, unless some compounds from the tea leaves dissolved our tea would be flavourless. These soluble compounds (such as polyphenols, amino acids, theine, and caffeine) are what gives the tea its flavour. Almost all chemicals are more soluble at higher temperatures than they are at lower temperatures, meaning that the flavour of the tea infuses more quickly when we use hot water.

Whether a substance will dissolve in water or not depends on the charges between its molecules. Water molecules are polar, meaning that one end carries a positive charge and the other a negative charge. When a substance such as salt is added to water, these charges interact with the polar molecular bonds within the salt. This reduces the charges within the salt molecules so that they no longer attract each other as strongly and so the salt is dissolved.

In non-dissolvable materials such as metal or plastic, the molecules are attracted to each other much more strongly than they attract the water molecules and so they stick together and do not dissolve.

Filtration, sieving

Filtration involves the use of filter paper but filtration and sieving work on the same principle i.e., that the barrier (the filter paper or the sieve) contains holes which are big enough to let the water through but small enough to prevent the undissolved material (the tea leaves) through. Any material which has been dissolved (the flavour) is also small enough to pass through the holes. These processes therefore help us to make the perfect cup of tea where the flavour is retained but there are no bits left floating around!

Identification of plant parts (leaves, flowers, stalks, roots, tubers, etc.)

Leaves, stalks, and flowers are easy to identify, but there may be some confusion when it comes to roots and tubers as both are found under the ground. Both draw moisture and nutrients from the soil and anchor the plant in place in the soil. However, tubers are also used as storage vessels and to grow new plants (e.g., potatoes, sweet potatoes, and yams).

Other vegetables such as carrots, beetroots, and turnips are true root crops and not tubers. These vegetables are modified roots that store energy, but they do not propagate new plants. If you cut up a tuber into sections, you would be able to grow new plants that you would not be able to do with a root crop.

Design and technology content

Theme 1 - Produce an alternative to tea bags
Here, much of the focus will be on the exploration of existing products. They will need to evaluate these products against the design criteria for this challenge and apply their new learning to their designs.

Theme 2 - Alternatives to traditional teas
Food, nutrition, and cookery in school can seem like a daunting task to take on, but a cookery activity does not have to be an entire class cooking a hot dish from scratch. Instead, cookery activities can be broken down into smaller steps of learning and shorter, more simple activities. These could include:

150   States of matter

- Conducting taste tests of existing products
- Researching products and potential ingredients online
- Chopping up cutting up ingredients
- Picking or shopping for ingredients

Age	Skills	Example Product for This Challenge
Ages 3-7	Develop simple skills such as chopping soft fruits using a butter, dinner, or adapted knife. Picking fruits, flowers, stalks, etc to use in teas. Adults can then use these products to brew the teas. Children should also be taught basic hygiene activities such as hand washing and preparation of surfaces.	Chopping fruits to make a fruit tea

Ages 7-11	Older children can build on these early skills and be taught to use equipment, including knives, more safely. This includes the bridge and the claw hold (https://www.youtube.com/watch?v=rHacroXxNPk).
	   Older children can also start to brew their own teas using hot water after being taught how to handle this safely.
	   At this age, we would encourage children to start to prepare food to their own preferences. Encourage children to try out a recipe and adjust this according to taste. Tea flavours can be enhanced or adapted by adding or removing ingredients or through the addition of extra ingredients such as honey.
		Optimising a fruit or herbal tea recipe

Teacher's guidance (lesson and activity plans)

The tables below set out how the science and design and technology content could fit within the EDP. This is not an exhaustive list, and you may well be able to think of alternatives or different ways of organising the content for your own class.

These tables also give example activities to do at each stage of the EDP and key questions to ask. Again, these are ideas for you to use, adapt, and add to for your own classes.

 EDP stage: Igniting ideas

Learning Objectives
- To be able to identify a presented need or requirement.
- To be able to articulate what is needed as an outcome of the challenge set.

Thought Processes/Engineering Habits of Mind (EHOM)
Understand, empathise, connect. Problem Finding

Key Questions	Vocabulary	Resources
• What problem does Class 5 have? • What does Class 5 need us to do to help them?	• Diet, nutrition • Product/solution	• Copies of the children's engineering challenge page

States of matter 151

| • What hot drinks do you or the people in your home drink? How do they make these drinks? | | |

Activities
- Share the challenge with the children
- Discussions to clarify the need presented in the challenge
- Discussions about which theme of solutions you will be following

Assessment
Children can define the challenge that has been set for them, showing that they understand the need presented and what they are required to do to provide a solution.

 **EDP stage: Exploring ideas**

Science Content Learning Objectives:
Theme 1
- To begin to explore the principles of sieving and filtration.
- To begin to explore the principles of dissolving.

Theme 2
- To be able to name and identify simple plant parts.

Design and Technology Learning Objectives:
- To be able to ask questions about the conditions, needs and purpose of the challenge set.
- To be able to identify requirements and constraints of the set challenge.
- To be able to identify appropriate ingredients.

Thought Processes/Engineering Habits of Mind (EHoM)
Question, refine, focus, apply logic and Systems thinking. Creative problem solving

Key Questions	Vocabulary	Resources
• Can you describe Class 5's problem in your own words? • What might you need to know to be able to provide a solution the problem? • Why do people use tea bags? What purpose do they serve? • How do tea bags work? • Does the tea dissolve? • What materials and tools do we have to use? How might we use them?	• Requirements/parameters/ constraints • *States of matter*: solids, liquids, gasses • *Changes in materials*: dissolvable, non-dissolvable, solution, soluble, non-soluble • Filter, filtration, separate, sieve, strain • *Plants*: leaves, roots, stalk, stem, flower, tuber	• Children's EDP worksheet • The range of materials and tools on use for each theme of the challenge. Theme 1 Mesh food bags Plastic Aluminium foil Paper Cotton String Glue Loose leaf tea

152   States of matter

		Cotton thread Cardboard Staples/stapler Wire *Theme 2* Sieves Strainers Range of fresh or dried berries, leaves, herbs, spices (see section above for ideas)

Activities

Identifying the requirements and constraints of the set challenge
- Discussions about what the children need to know to provide a solution to the challenge set
- Compose three questions about the parameters of the challenge
- Write lists of challenge constraints and requirements
- Complete the 'exploring ideas' section on their EDP worksheet
- Examine the materials and tools available to use
- Teachers may need to prompt and guide children on any missed information (e.g., time allowance, conditions that the product will be used in, materials available, etc.)

Theme 1

Filtering/Sieving: How do tea bags work? Exploring filtration/sieving and dissolving
- Demonstrate or get groups of children to make a cup of tea (without milk). Ask them to watch what happens to the tea bag, tea leaves, and water.
- Ask if the tea dissolved. (They are likely to say no here as the tea leaves remain. Prompt them to think about what has happened to the water, i.e., some material from the tea leaves has dissolved).
- Ask how the flavour has got out of the tea bag.
- Give the children a range of tea bags to explore; use magnifying glasses so that the pores can be seen more clearly.
- Ask the children if they can think of 3 things that they would need to think about when designing and making a tea bag? See the 'Thinking Like An Engineer' activity in Chapter 1 for ideas.

Theme 2:
- Name and identify simple plant parts.
- Ask the children which parts of plants we eat.
- Give the children a range of fruits, leaves, roots, seeds, etc., which could be used to make a fruit or herbal tea. Ask them to match each item to a diagram of a plant to show which part of a plant they came from.
- Group all the ingredients that are leaves together, repeat for fruits, flowers, roots, stalks, etc.
- If possible, go to a local garden or allotment to pick ingredients, or to a shop to buy ingredients. Discuss which parts of the plants are being used.

Scientific Investigation- make the best cup of tea (see section below)

Assessment

Children can identify the needs set by this challenge and can describe a set of quantifiable requirements.

Children understand and can appropriately use a range of vocabulary associated with either separation of materials or plant parts.

States of matter 153

 EDP stage: Developing ideas

Science Content Learning Objectives:
Theme 1
• To explore the principles of sieving/filtration/dissolving by investigating solutions and discuss why and how these work.
Theme 2
• To understand seasonal availability of plants.
• To know the flavours of each of the potential ingredients to use.
Design and Technology Learning Objectives:
• To investigate how comparable products have been designed and made.
• To use information from a variety of sources to generate ideas for potential solutions.

Key Questions	Vocabulary	Resources
Theme 1: • What is the item made from? Why do you think that this material was chosen? • How have the parts of the item been joined together? • What have you seen or used before that may help you? • What can we find out about what other, comparable products are made of? • What have you found out from your research/other products which could help you?	• Research, investigate, analyse, compare, evaluate • States of matter: solids, liquids, gasses • Changes in materials: dissolvable, non-dissolvable, solution, soluble, non-soluble • Mixtures and separation: filter, filtration, separate, sieve, strain • Plants: leaves, roots, stalk, stem, flower, tuber • Vocabulary to describe flavours (e.g., sweet, bitter, spice, aromatic, savoury, etc.)	• Children's EDP worksheet • A range of products (or pictures of products) related to the challenge (e.g., tea strainers, infuser teapots, etc.) • A range of herbal and fruit teas (either commercial or home-made) to taste • Access to laptops or tablets, books, etc. for research • Range of fresh or dried berries, leaves, herbs, spices (see section above for ideas)
Theme 2: • What teas have you tasted before? • What flavours do you like? • What might we be able to find in the garden or shops that we can use?		

Activities
- Brainstorm imagination activities in small groups to produce wild and whacky solutions.
- Share ideas discovered or imagined.
- Complete the 'Developing Ideas' section of the photocopiable children's engineering page.

Theme 1
- Examine or research other products/solutions to this challenge.
- What are these made from? Why have these materials been chosen?
- Discuss how these products work.
- What is the same/different about all these products?
- How have the materials been joined together? How have attachments been added on?
- How could the product be improved?
- Which ideas could you take to use in your own product?

Exploring the principles of sieving/filtration/dissolving
- Take a range of insoluble materials in a range of sizes (e.g., sand grains, seeds, tea leaves, small stones, marbles, etc.) and a range of filter paper (coffee filters work well here if you do not have filter paper), sieves, strainers, and colanders. Ask the children to predict which materials will be retained by each sieve/filter and which will be able to pass through. Ask the children to explain and justify their thoughts in terms of comparing the size of the holes to the size of the material.
- Ask the children to predict which filter/strainer the tea leaves will be able to pass through.

During this stage, the children may need to test out some of the materials/ingredients to be used. See also the linked scientific investigations below.

Theme 2
Seasonal availability of plants
- Ask the children to conduct literature of internet-based research about what grows in your area at different times of the year.
- Visit a local garden to see what is available at the time of year.

To investigate how comparable products have been designed and made.
- Visit a shop or conduct internet research about different fruit or herbal teas. Which ingredients are used and which flavours are combined?
- Select teas and combine fruit and herbal teas to investigate preferences.
- Pick or buy a range of local produce, make teas, and conduct taste tests.

To know the flavours of each of the potential ingredients to use:
- Describe the smell of different ingredients.
- Make a tea infusion with individual ingredients, taste, and describe the flavour. Categorise each of the ingredients as to whether they provide a sweet, bitter, spice, aromatic, savoury flavour.

Assessment
Children can make a reasonable and relevant choice of product and can justify this choice based on the properties of the material used, the functionality and purpose of the product.

Children can investigate comparable products and identify features that they could incorporate into their own designs and products.

Children can articulate a range of ideas about potential products and solutions.

EDP stage: Designing ideas

Science Content Learning Objectives:
- To be able to apply understanding of the principles of separation techniques.

Design and Technology Learning Objectives:
Themes 1 and 2
- To be able to draw and design a set of plans relating to an intended product.

- To be able to analyse and evaluate plans and potential products for their suitability in meeting the requirements of the challenge set.

Theme 2
- To be able to design a recipe based on understanding flavour combinations and personal preferences.

Thought Processes/Engineering Habits of Mind (EHoM)
Analyse, compare, evaluate, visualise, adapt

Key Questions	Vocabulary	Resources
<ul><li>Why have you decided on your final design?</li><li>What is this the best choice?</li><li>How does your design meet the challenge and the constraints/requirements?</li><li>Do you anticipate any problems or issues when making your product?</li></ul>	<ul><li>Analyse, compare, evaluate, visualise, adapt</li><li>Research, investigate</li><li>States of matter: solids, liquids, gasses</li><li>Changes in materials: dissolvable, non-dissolvable, solution, soluble, non-soluble</li><li>Mixtures and separation: filter, filtration, separate, sieve, strain</li><li>Plants: leaves, roots, stalk, stem, flower, tuber</li></ul>	<ul><li>Children's EDP worksheet</li></ul>

Activities
For **Theme 2**, children will be required to write recipes rather than draw plans
- Identify and design three main ideas for products/recipes to be made.
- Draw up plans for three potential products (for recipes, include quantities).
- Evaluate and assess which of these ideas best meets the requirements of the challenge.
- Explain product choice to others in the class and share reasoning about why this product has been chosen.
- Identify how the separate parts of the product will be joined together or how any attachments will be added on.
- Complete the 'designing ideas' section on the children's engineer worksheet.

During this stage, the children may need to test out some of the materials/ingredients to be used. See also the linked scientific investigations below.

Assessment
Children can select one design from a range and articulate why this is the most suitable choice.

EDP stage: Making, testing, and improving ideas

Science Content Learning Objectives:
- To be able to apply scientific understanding of separation and dissolving within a 'real-world' context.

Design and Technology Learning Objectives:
- To develop explicit skills (e.g., chopping, mixing, etc.).
- To be aware of a variety of health and safety considerations.

States of matter

- To turn a design for a solution to a set problem into a product.
- To test a product against a set of pre-determined criteria (from the 'exploring ideas' stage).
- To share ideas and use and adapt the ideas of others.

Theme 2
To be able adjust a recipe according to own tastes and preferences.

Thought Processes/Engineering Habits of Mind (EHoM)
Analyse, compare, evaluate, improve

Key Questions	Vocabulary	Resources
• Does your product answer Class 5's problem? • Does your product meet all the specifications? • Did you encounter any problems when making your product? • What solutions to these problems did you find? • Did other groups encounter similar problems? What solutions did they produce? • Did you choose the most appropriate material to make your product out of? Why/why not?	• Test, improve, evaluate, improve, appraise • Fabric, material • Seam, hem, join • Stitch, sew/sewn • Running/cross/blanket stitch • Product • Research, investigate • Requirements/parameters/constraints • Absorbent, waterproof, permeable, porous, impervious • Flexible, rigid, strength, malleable, ductile, floppy, elastic, stretchy, supple, bendy, pliable, firm, dense, bendable, soft, spongy • Opaque, translucent, transparent, clear, see-through, dense • Fabric, material	• Children's engineer worksheet **Theme 1** • Mesh food bags • Plastic • Aluminium foil • Paper • Cotton • String • Glue • Loose-leaf tea • Cotton thread • Cardboard • Staples/stapler • Wire • Kettle/ hot water source • Cups, spoons • Scissors • Elastic bands • Sewing tools **Theme 2** • Sieves • Strainers • Range of fresh or dried berries, leaves, herbs, spices (see section above for ideas) • Chopping boards • Knives (varied type, depending on age of children) • Kettle/hot water source • Cups • Spoons

Activities
Teachers will need to decide which pieces of equipment are suitable for the children in their classes based on the age and skill level of the children.

Theme 1

Explicit Skills Teaching and Health and Safety

- If children wish to punch a hole in a material, this must be done at a table with a protective covering and with a soft material such as play dough placed under the material for the sharp object to be punched through. Children should be taught how to use a suitable, sharp objects safely.
- Some children may wish to produce a mesh-like material and may need to be shown how to weave this.
- If using wire, the children will need to be shown how to use wire snippers safely (or have an adult do this for them). They should understand that wire ends are sharp and so should not be carried around the room.

Theme 2

Explicit Skills Teaching and Health and Safety

- Skills teaching for safe and effective use of knives. This includes the bridge and the claw hold (https://www.youtube.com/watch?v=rHacroXxNPk).
- Teaching how to use loose ingredients to make a cup of tea (i.e., using s strainer or infuser) and taking care when using hot water.

Making Activities

Themes 1 and 2

- Time for children to make their designed product.
- During this stage, the children may need to test out some of the materials/ingredients to be used. See also the linked scientific investigations below.

Testing and Appraising Ideas

Theme 1

- Use your product to make a cup of tea. Count how many parts of tea leaves (if any) have gotten through your product into the tea.
- Keep your tea in the product to infuse (or brew) for longer periods of time. Time how long your product holds together.
- Place your product into water at different temperatures. Can your product withstand a full range of temperatures?
- How many cups of tea can you make with your product? Remember, the purpose of the activity was to cut down on the number of tea bags wasted. Products which can make the most cups of tea are the most successful.
- Do a taste test survey. Which products make the best tasting tea? Consider why.

Theme 2

- Do a taste test survey. Which is the most popular tea with children or adults?
- Taste your own tea. Do you like it? What could be added to enhance the flavour or make it taste better? What would you leave out? Go back to the categories of flavours produced earlier to adapt recipes.
- Which tea recipe looks or smells the most appealing?

General

- Use the Children's engineering worksheet to evaluate.
- What went well, which parts of the design did not work so well, and what needs to be improved?
- Often, during this stage, the children encounter problems with their product. This provides an opportunity to revisit the science involved to help them to solve these issues. For example, if making a tea which is too bitter, they may need to go back and investigate which of the ingredients would give a sweeter taste.

158   States of matter

- Again, when encountering issues, this would be a good opportunity for children to go back to do some further research (e.g., What materials are used to make tea bags? Why are these chosen?).

Sharing ideas, using and adapting the ideas of others
- Children display their part or fully completed products alongside their designs. All children move around the classroom to examine the work of others. Encourage the children to note down innovative ideas that they could use in their own designs and products.
- Ask each child/group of children to share an issue or triumph that they have had with their design and product. The rest of the class can either use the idea that worked or offer a solution to the issue experienced.
- Children then return to their own designs and products and adapt in light of this new information.

Assessment
Children can describe what they like and do not like about their product.
    They can describe what worked well and not so well.
    They can evaluate if they have met the design brief.
    They can offer solutions to various problems encountered by themselves and others.
    Their product shows the application of the relevant scientific principles.

Linked Scientific Investigations	**Developing scientific investigation skills: Making the 'best' cup of tea**
	1 *Posing a scientific question to be answered.*
	   What we mean by the 'best' is ambiguous and therefore cannot be measured, so the children will need to set their own question to be answered and decide how this can be measured (e.g., the strongest cup of tea, the best tea to milk ratio, optimum temperature, etc.).
	2 *Controlling variables*
	   Making the 'best' cup of tea could also involve considering which variables need to remain the same and which can be changed (e.g., the type of tea used, the tea/water/milk ratio, infusion time, temperature, etc.). Children will need to decide which of these factors that they would like to test and keep all the other factors as the non-changing variables.
	3 *Taking measurements, recording, and displaying results.*
	   Children will also need to decide what to measure and how to record this. If they are investigating people's opinions on the taste of their tea, they may need to do a survey, temperatures may require a series of readings over time, or strength of tea could be recordings of colour and changes in colour, etc.
	4 *Drawing and recording conclusions.*
	   Children will need to describe what they have learnt as an outcome of their investigation. Comparative statements can work well here. For example, the hotter the temperature of the water, the stronger the tea.
	
	Dissolving:
	Rate of dissolving
	Factors that affect the rate and extent of dissolving sugar in tea could include water temperature, the sugar to water ratio, amount of stirring, and surface area of the solid to be dissolved (e.g., caster sugar, granulated sugar, sugar cubes). Children could set up a series of cups where all variables other than the one to be tested were kept the same. They could measure the time taken for the sugar to dissolve.

States of matter 159

	Soluble/non-soluble Keeping all other variables the same, children could add a range of materials to water to test if they will dissolve (i.e., are soluble or non-soluble). The extent or solubility of the materials could be tested in a number of ways including; taste tests (if safe), observations of the colour of the water or observations of the amount of solid left over. Add some water into a glass of water and stir until the sugar dissolves, pour this through a filter paper, and ask the children to predict what will be left behind. Can they explain why there is no residue? *Separation (filtering and sieving)* Use a mixture of insoluble solids (of various sizes) in water (e.g., mud, sand, stones, plastic bricks, paper clips, etc.) and present them also with a variety of filtration, sieving and separation devices. Ask children to produce the clearest water possible.

Resources

Theme 1

- Mesh food bags
- Plastic
- Aluminium foil
- Paper
- Cotton
- String
- Glue
- Loose leaf tea
- Cotton thread
- Cardboard
- Staples/stapler
- Wire
- Kettle/hot water source
- Cups spoons
- Scissors
- Elastic bands
- Sewing tools
- Kettle/hot water source
- Cups
- Spoons

Theme 2

- Sieves
- Strainers

160 *States of matter*

- Range of fresh or dried berries, leaves, herbs, spices (see section above for ideas)
- Chopping boards
- Knives (varied type, depending on age of children)
- Kettle/hot water source
- Cups
- Spoons

Health and safety

Knives

The use of kitchen items should always be done at the discretion of the class teacher and under the general health and safety policies of any school. These decisions can be made based on the age of the children, the level of adult supervision, and any special of behavioural needs.

Children need to be taught how to use the correct equipment in the correct way. Sometimes, using incorrect equipment which would appear to be safe can, in fact, be more dangerous (imagine trying to cut a raw carrot using a butter knife). Children should be taught how to hold a knife correctly and how to hold the item to be chopped correctly. This includes the bridge and the claw hold, as seen in the following video and pictures below (https://www.youtube.com/watch?v=rHacroXxNPk) (Figures 9.1 and 9.2).

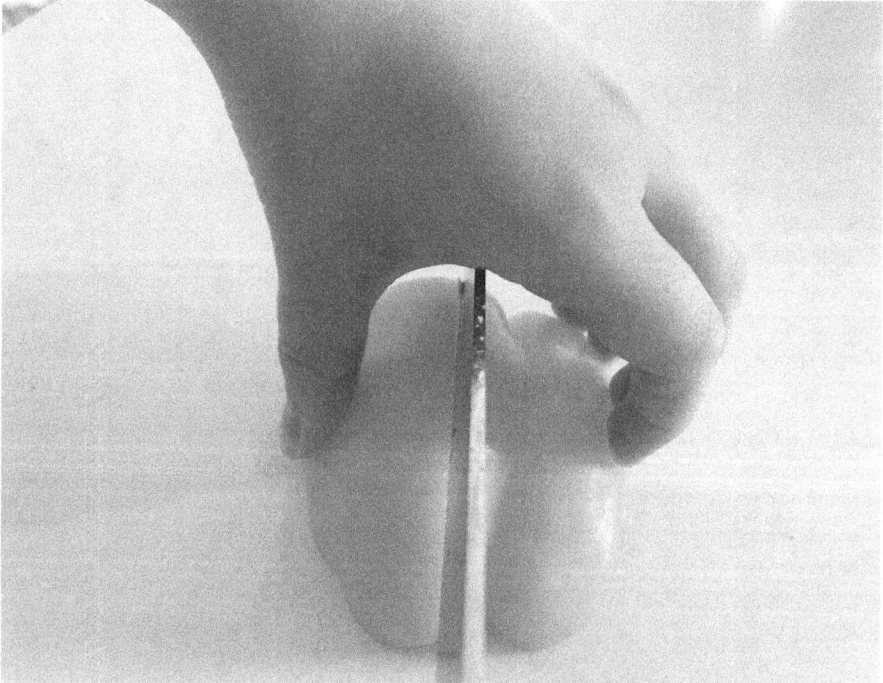

Figure 9.1 Bridge hand position

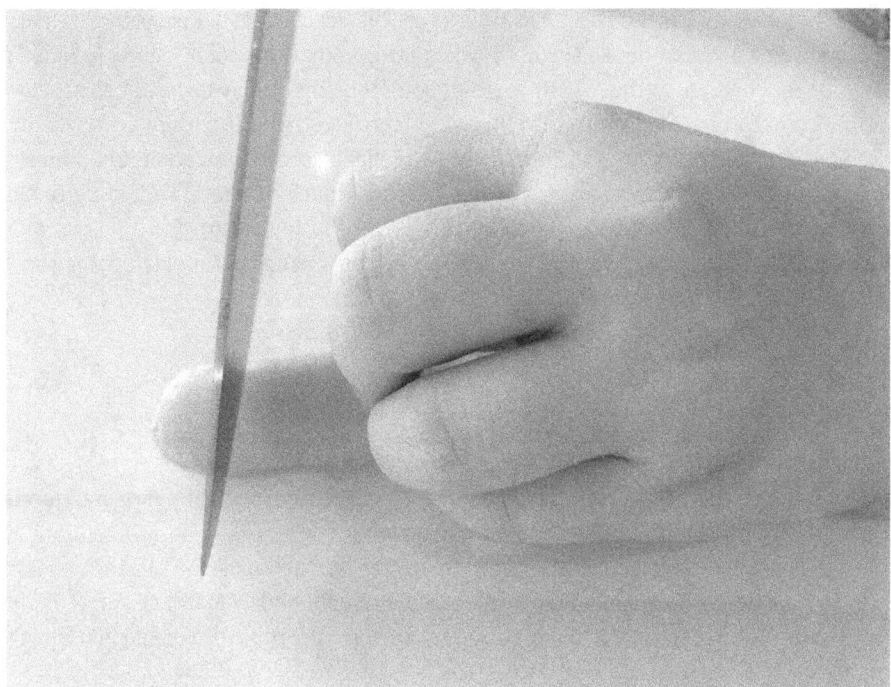

Figure 9.2 Claw hand position

Knives should be used with an appropriate chopping board and never carried around the classroom. Teach children to place knives onto the table and then move themselves around the table before they pick the knife up again. This is also a safe method for passing knives between children.

Knives that have been adapted for use by children are available. These have rounded rather than pointed ends, or serrated edges rather than sharpened edges. Others have chunkier handles that are easier to grip for smaller hands. A variety of safety devices are also available to make cutting and chopping activities safer for younger children or those with coordination difficulties.

Teachers will need to keep track of how many knives (or other potentially dangerous pieces of equipment) that they have put out for use. Teachers should count out knives at the start of an activity and then count them back in again at the end of an activity.

Hot water kettles and pans

Again, these resources should be used at the discretion of the teacher, depending on the age, skills, and behaviour of the children and the level of adult supervision.

You may decide to let older children heat their own water. If this is the case, teach children how to use kitchen appliances safely. Use kettles with a short cord and keep them well back from the edges of tables. If using a saucepan to heat water turn the saucepan handles towards the back of the cooker and use the back rings where possible. As children get older, they can also be taught to pour safely from the kettle (not holding the cup that the water is to be poured into).

For younger children, or those with coordination problems, it may be better to provide the children with hot water. Make sure that this is not carried around the room or moved by the children but is instead brought to a safe place near the children by an adult. Children should be taught not to test the temperature of the water by touching it and should be reminded that steam can also burn and so to avoid looking over the hot water.

If a microwave is used to heat the water, it should be stirred thoroughly as this can heat water unevenly, leaving areas of scalding water.

If a child gets burnt or scalded, medical advice should be sought.

Hygiene

Children must be taught good hygiene habits. Encourage them to wear aprons, as these provide a barrier to keep their clothes clean and a barrier between the dirt and germs on their clothes and the food. Aprons should be removed for visits to the bathroom. Good hand washing is necessary and gloves (possibly latex free for allergies) or plasters should be provided for children who have broken skin or cuts on their hands. Finally, all surfaces should be wiped down with soap and water, followed by an anti-bacterial spray and children should be encouraged to wash all produce before use.

Allergies and Intolerances

Schools should keep an up-to-date list of any food allergies and intolerances that children have. It is good practice to instead send out a letter to parents and guardians with a list of potential ingredients to be used so that they can inform you of anything that should be avoided.

Dangers of picking wild plants

If picking produce to use in your tea recipes, avoid picking wild plants. It cannot be fully guaranteed that you have the correct edible plant, and you may inadvertently expose the children to certain toxins. Always use plants grown in gardens where you can be sure of their identity.

Common misconceptions

Diet and nutrition

There are a great many misconceptions around food, nutrition and diet held by children. In fact, the term 'diet' itself is often only understood to be related to the foods eaten when trying to lose weight, whereas the *Cambridge English Dictionary* defines it as 'the food and drink usually eaten or drunk by a person or group'.

We should be wary of labelling certain foods as healthy or unhealthy. An apple, for example, would be seen as a healthy food, but if a person only ever ate apples, this would be an unhealthy, unbalanced diet (it would not contain enough protein, fats, or calcium, etc.). Likewise, chocolate would be seen as unhealthy, but it is perfectly acceptable in the correct portions as part of a balanced diet. Children therefore need to learn the types of foods that they should be eating and in what proportions. This will help them to navigate the myriad of (sometimes misleading) food and nutrition messages they receive from a wide range of sources.

Fruits/vegetables

The scientific definition of a fruit is the part of a plant that has developed from the ovary of a flowering plant. The fruit therefore contains or encloses the seed(s). This means that foods commonly viewed as vegetables, such as tomatoes, beans, sweetcorn, or cucumbers, are actually fruits.

Dissolving

Many children think that when a substance is dissolved in water it disappears or has melted. Tasting salt or sugar dissolved in water disproves this misconception. The soluble substance has just been broken down into such small parts that they are no longer visible. Try dissolving a colourful sweet so that the colour can still been seen in the liquid. If large enough quantities are used or sensitive cooking scales are used, you should also be able to detect a change in the mass of the solution after the material has been added and dissolved.

Wider resources related to materials, their properties and uses

There are many excellent sources of support and resources for the topic of materials, their properties and uses.

- The Institute of Engineering technology has a range of educational resources. The resource called 'Materials and their Properties' encourages children to consider the suitability of materials for various products: https://education.theiet.org/primary/teaching-resources/materials-and-their-properties/
- STEM (Science, Technology, Engineering, and Mathematics) learning also has a range of resources and links for this topic. For children aged 5-6, try exploring: https://www.stem.org.uk/resources/community/collection/12725/year-1-everyday-materials
- For those aged 6, 7, or 8, try: https://www.stem.org.uk/resources/community/collection/12724/year-2-uses-everyday-materials
- The Hamilton trust has a range of interesting investigations related to materials and their properties for your children to try out: https://www.hamilton-trust.org.uk/science/year-5-science/properties-materials-music-festival-materials/

Other example activities for everyday materials, their uses and properties

- On hot days Mr Nowak likes to drink iced tea. Can you design a reuseable cup which will keep the ice cubes in his drink from melting for as long as possible?

10 Science focus
Electricity

Design and technology focus: Understanding and using electrical systems in products

> ### The Engineering Challenge
>
> Kasper has noticed that people in his school sometimes forget to turn the lights off when they leave a room. He is worried that his school is wasting electricity. Can you design an alarm that buzzes when the door closes to remind people to switch off the light?

Aim of the challenge

The aim of this challenge is an electrical engineering task to design and test an alarm system for a door. The activities will look at circuits and different switches and encourage thinking about breaking and connecting circuits as well as conductors and insulators.

A photocopiable Childrens' Engineering Challenge Sheet can be found in the Appendix.

Potential solutions

There are many potential solutions to this challenge, which focus on different ways of making and connecting switches in a circuit.

Children could produce a simple pressure switch under the carpet. This is a folded piece of card with two sides covered in foil, attached to the wires in a circuit, including a buzzer. When a person walks on the carpet or mat, the two sides of the card touch together, completing the circuit and setting off the buzzer. This alerts them to check if the lights have been switched off (e.g. Figure 10.1).

An alternate pressure switch can be made by covering two CDs covered in foil in a circuit with a buzzer and putting a bit of foam between the surfaces. When someone walks on the CDs, they flex, causing the surfaces to touch and the buzzer to sound (Figure 10.2).

DOI: 10.4324/9781003325826-10

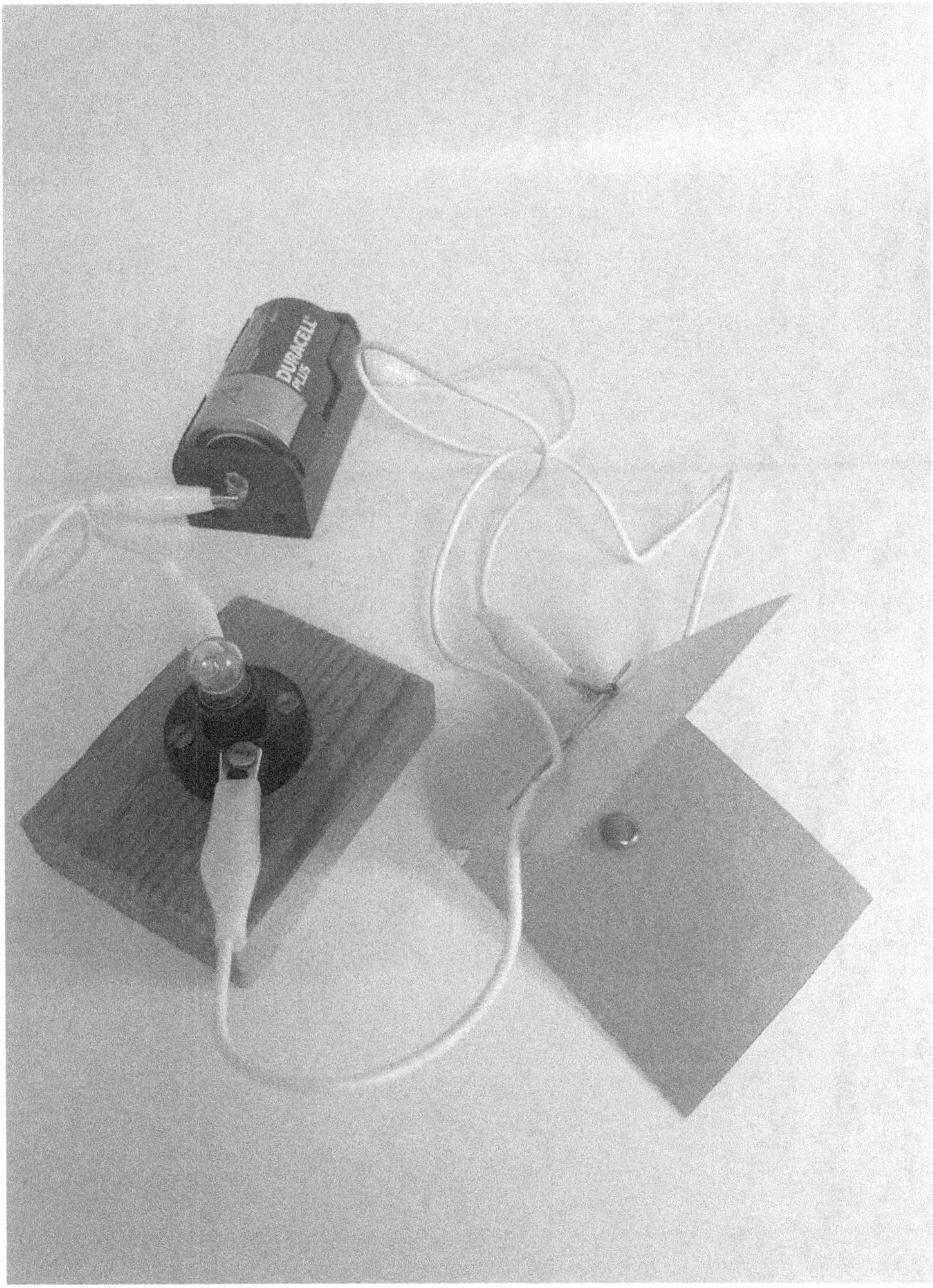

Figure 10.1 Cardboard pressure switch

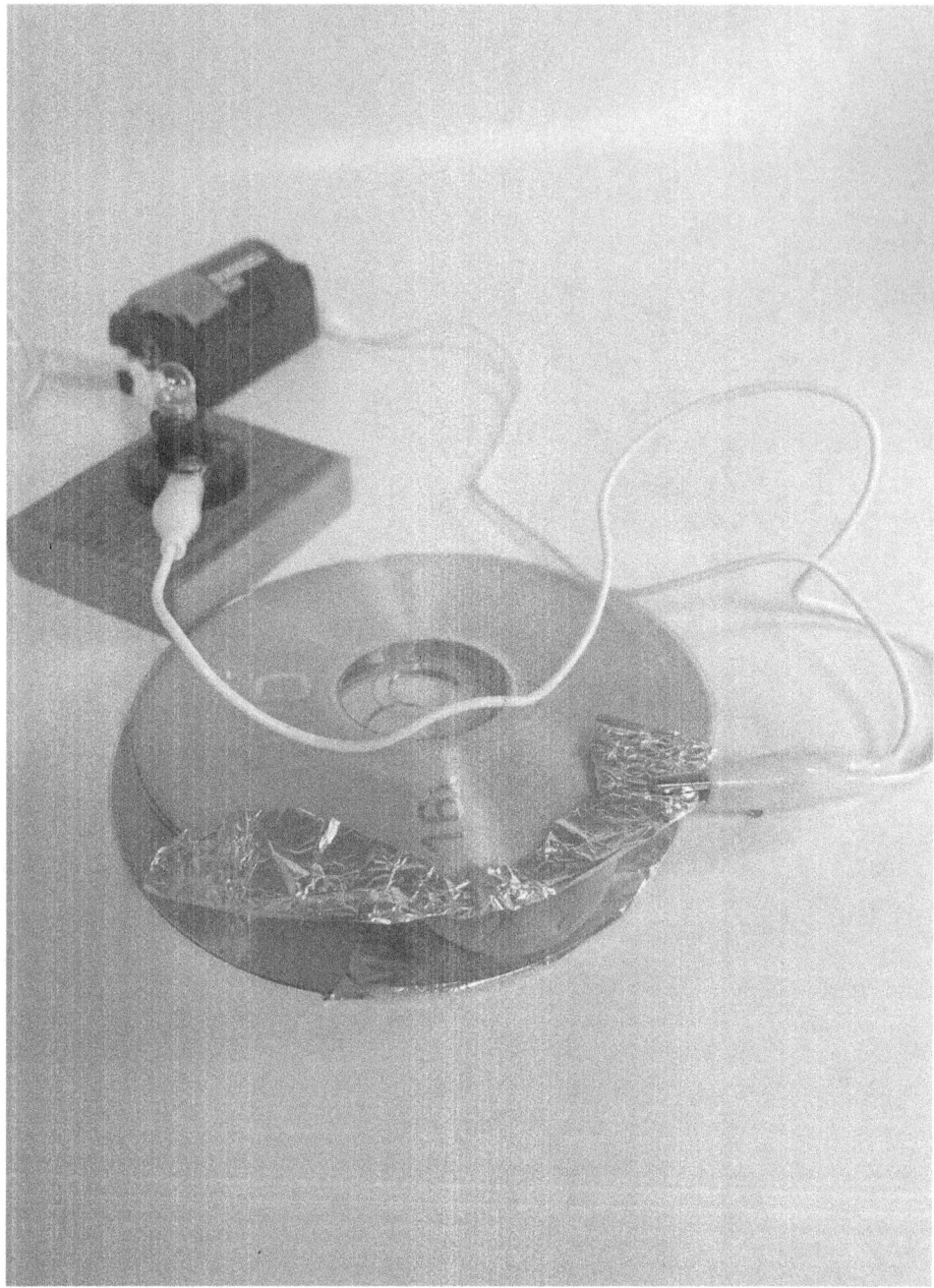

Figure 10.2 CD pressure switch

Another solution could be a circuit with clothes pegs and the ends covered in foil. When the clothes peg is closed, the circuit is complete and the buzzer will sound. However, the circuit can be broken by having a small piece of card on a string attached to the door, placed in between the ends of the clothes peg. When the door closes the card will be pulled from the clothes peg and the circuit will be complete, sounding the buzzer.

A further solution is to place some silver foil on the door frame and on the door. When the door closes, these two pieces of silver foil touch, connecting a circuit to sound an alarm.

A tilt switch could be attached to a door handle consisting of a film canister with two paper fasters attached at one end and a ball of silver foil in a circuit with a buzzer attached to the door handle. When the handle is turned, the ball of foil falls to the end of the canister connecting the two terminals and completing the circuit (Figure 10.3).

Sustainable development goals

This challenge connects to the UN sustainable development goals (2013) of:

   Goal 7: Energy. Affordable and clean energy
   Goal 12: Ensure sustainable consumption and production patterns.

There is a large disparity in the amounts of energy used per head around the world. In 2021, the USA used 76,634 kWH compared to 889 kWh in Uganda. Many of the wealthiest countries in the world used 100 times the amount of energy as some of the poorest countries (Our World in Data, 2021).

Although 91% of the world's population has access to electricity, that still leaves 733 million people, mostly in sub-Saharan Africa, with no access (UN, 2023).

As countries become wealthier, there is a bigger demand on energy and around the world. Much of this increasing demand is still met by fossil fuels, resulting in disastrous effects on the environment.

To reduce the impact of fossil fuels on climate change, many countries are looking to renewable sources to produce the energy they need. Wind, solar, nuclear, tidal, and hydro-electric power can all be used to replace fossil fuels, although each has limitations (e.g., solar power on a cloudy day).

This video explains different energy sources and identifies the issue for the future but with hopeful suggestions of ways forward for the future.

https://www.youtube.com/watch?v=tjwrG4Debc4

Energy efficiency is also a key aspect to reducing our fossil fuel emissions and an effective way to cut down our household costs. Energy efficiency can be a significant factor in bringing our emissions down to net zero. One way to do that is to ensure you are using LED lightbulbs and replacing halogen, incandescent, and old strip lighting. A short Newsround video of the history of the invention of the lightbulb can be found here:

https://www.bbc.co.uk/newsround/21995663

However, even better would be to reduce usage as much as possible. This includes turning off electrical appliances and systems when not in use. A typical household can save UK £20 a year by turning off the lights when not in use in a year; obviously, the gains are greater in a

168 *Science focus*

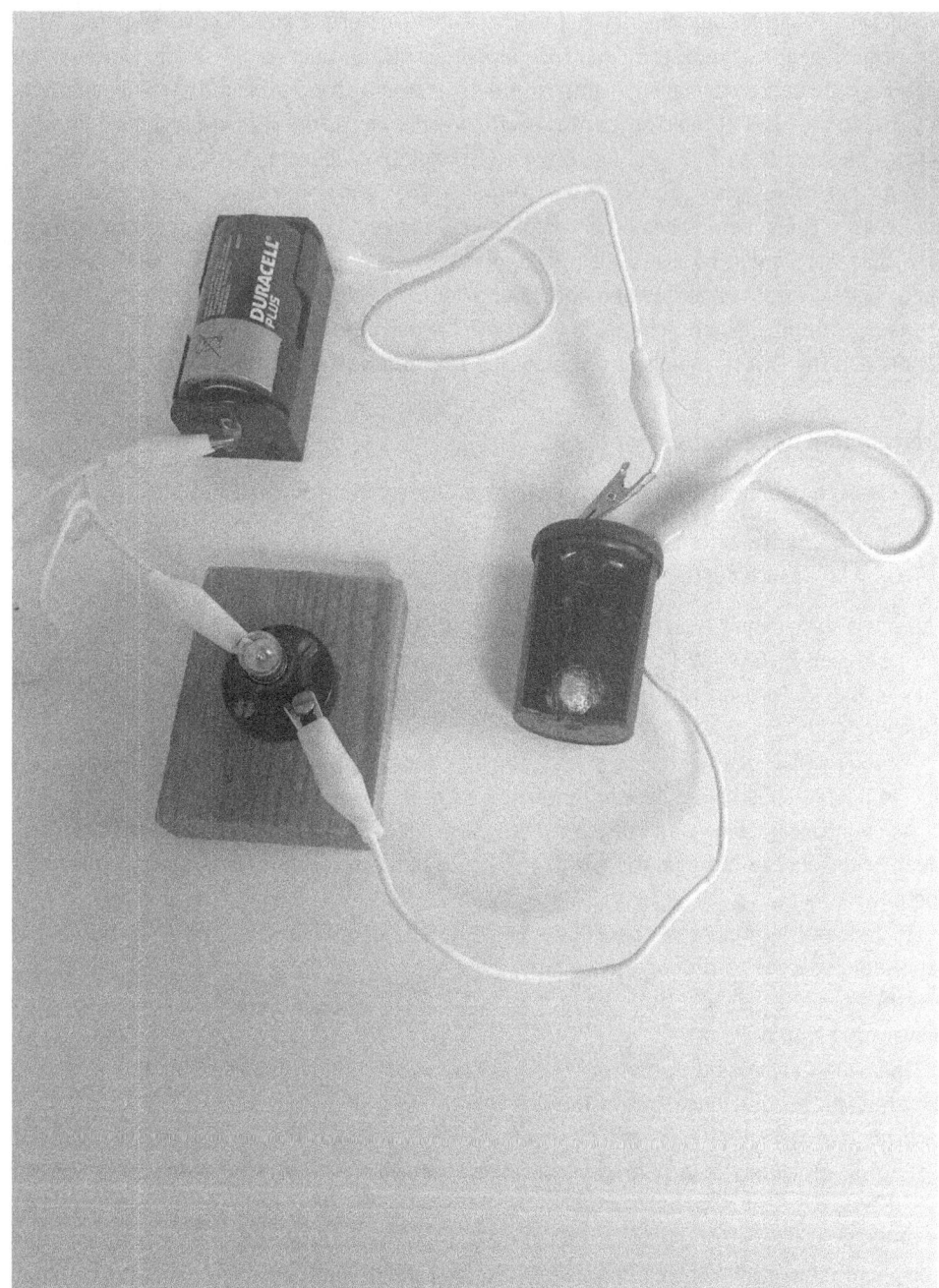

Figure 10.3 Tilt switch

Science focus 169

school building. For further information, go to the energy saving trust at https://energysavingtrust.org.uk/advice/lighting/.

Science content

The science content for this challenge lies in subject knowledge on electrical circuits and switches.

Children aged 5-7 years

Identify appliances that use electricity.
Understand health and safety issues around electricity usage at home or in school.
Understand the role and use of switches.

Children aged 7-11 years

a Identify common appliances that run on electricity.
b Construct a simple series electrical circuit, identifying and naming its basic parts, including cells, wires, bulbs, switches, and buzzers.
c Identify whether a lamp will light in a simple series circuit, based on whether the lamp is part of a complete loop with a battery.
d Recognise that a switch opens and closes a circuit and associate this with whether a lamp in a simple series circuit will light up or not.
e Recognise some common conductors and insulators, and associate metals with being good conductors.
f Associate the brightness of a lamp or the volume of a buzzer with the number and voltage of cells used in the circuit.
g Compare and give reasons for variations in how components function, including the brightness of bulbs, the loudness of buzzers, and the on/off position of switches.
h Use recognised symbols when representing a simple circuit in a diagram.

Vocabulary

Circuit
Current
Voltage
Switch
Battery/cell
Bulb/lamp
Conductor
Insulator
Wires
Buzzes

Series circuit
Power
Repel
Attract
Magnetic forces

The science explained

Batteries and circuits

Atoms are made up of a central nucleus containing protons and neutrons with tiny particles known as electrons orbiting. The electrons are negatively charged and are attracted by the positive electrical charge of the atom's centre or the nucleus. Atoms make up every material on Earth.

Atoms and their electrons are therefore always present in batteries and in the wires and components of a circuit even if the circuit is not complete or in use. When a circuit is complete the battery exerts a push on the electrons in a circuit. The electrons begin to move towards the positive battery terminal along the wires by bumping into each other a bit like a row of dominoes. This is known as current. The more able a component of a circuit is at conducting electricity, the more loose electrons it will move and bump into other electrons. Copper is a good example of a very conductive material as it has 2% of electrons that are free to move and therefore conduct electricity.

A battery is another name for two or more cells. Cells are units that produce electrical power. To produce the push in the battery to move the electrons around there are chemicals or electrolytes inside (sealed in the battery cover) and two battery terminals that you connect the wires to. When the battery is connected in a circuit a chemical reaction between the electrolytes and the terminals pushes electrons towards the negative terminal pushing them out into the wires. The higher the voltage of a battery, e.g., 4.5 V rather than 1.5 V, the greater the push of the electrons around the circuit. The greater the push, the more energy the electrons have, so the bulbs will be brighter and the buzzer louder with a higher volt battery.

When the chemicals in a battery have been used up in the chemical reactions or the circuit disconnected, the push stops and the battery is dead.

When the electrons move through the components in a circuit, they bump into particles that are not free to move. The movement from these tiny forces is what we call heat. In a filament in a bulb or lamp, the heat becomes so great it glows giving off light. If the wires in the lamp get too hot, they melt, and the lamp is blown. The bumping into other particles causes the electrons to lose some of their energy.

Switches

A switch is a physical break in a circuit stopping the electrons moving. A switch can be just the removal of a wire from a terminal or a mechanical device that joins and detaches two wires. An easy switch can be made with a paper clip and two paper fasteners pushed into cardboard as part of your circuit. Attach the wires to the paper fasteners and then use the paper lip looped around one paper fastener to connect and disconnect the circuit.

When all the components in a circuit are in a line coming from the battery and back to the battery, this is called a series circuit. The current passes through all the components in the circuit. The electrons in a series circuit will lose energy from bumping into non-moving particles, as discussed above, and then have less energy. In a parallel circuit, components often have their own route to and from the battery, making the loss of energy less. Bulbs in a series circuit may be dimmer than those in a parallel circuit.

Design and technology content

Age	Skills	Example Product for This Challenge
Ages 3–6	For young children, the skills required should be kept as simple as possible. This could be identifying appliances that use electricity around the classroom or school. Sort those that use main electricity and batteries. Make a simple circuit using batteries and lamp.	Make a light for a dolls' house using battery, wires, bulb, and bulb holder. Make a shade.
Ages 6–8	Older children start to design simple switches with paper fasteners and explore ways of breaking circuits.	Make a switch for your lamp.
Ages 8–11	At this stage, the children could explore different types of switches, tilt switch, and pressure switch. They could explore materials that conduct electricity and those that insulate electricity to support making different switches.	Design and make a switch that lights up a bulb when someone stands on a mat.

Teacher's guidance (lesson and activity plans)

The tables below set out how the science and design and technology content could fit within the EDP. This is not an exhaustive list, and you may well be able to think of alternatives or different ways of organising the content for your own class.

These tables also give example activities to do at each stage of the EDP and key questions to ask. Again, these are ideas for you to use, adapt, and add to for your own classes.

Science focus

EDP stage: Ignite

Learning Objectives:
To be able to identify a presented need or requirement.
To be able to articulate what is needed as an outcome of the challenge set.

Thought Processes/Engineering Habits of Mind (EHOM)
Understand, empathise, connect, problem finding

Key Questions	Vocabulary	Resources
• Why do we want to warn a person that they have left the light on? • What is the problem set out in the challenge? Why is this a problem? • Are there other ways that we waste electricity in school or at home? • What will happen if the light is left on overnight? • How do we warn the person they have left the light on, through a buzzer or warning light? • What actions happen when someone leaves a room? What forces are exerted on the door frame, carpet, etc.? • Where is the person looking when they leave the room? • How can we alert their attention?	• Requirements/ parameters/ constraints • Wires, batteries/cells, bulb/ lamp/lamp holder, crocodile clips, wires, battery holder, switch, cardboard, buzzers, silver foil. Paper fasteners, string. • Circuit, conductors, insulators, voltage • Connection, power, flow	• Batteries • Bulbs • Bulb holder • Crocodile clips • Battery holder • Masking tape • Buzzers • Cardboard • Scissors • Aluminium foil • Paper fasteners. • Small screwdrivers • Wire • Strippers/cutters • Foam • Cardboard • Clothes pegs • Button magnets • Magnetic coins or washers

Activities

Identifying the requirements and constraints of the set challenge
- Discussions about what the children need to know to provide a solution to the challenge set
- In groups, each group composes three questions to ask about the parameters of the challenge set
- Children writing lists of challenge constraints and requirements
- Children complete 'exploring ideas' section on their EDP worksheet
- Examine the range of materials and tools available to use
- Teachers may need to prompt and guide children on any missed information (e.g., time allowance, conditions that the product will be used in, materials available, etc.)

Assessment

Children can define the challenge that has been set for them, showing that they understand the need presented and what they are required to do to provide a solution.

 **EDP stage: Exploring ideas**

In this stage, we help the children understand about switches, conductors, and insulators.

Exploring Switches in Circuits
Science Content Learning Objectives:
- To construct a simple series electrical circuit, identifying and naming its basic parts, including cells, wires, bulbs, switches, and buzzers.
- To recognise that a switch opens and closes a circuit and associate this with whether a buzzer buzzes in a simple series circuit.

Design and Technology Learning Objectives:
- To be able to discuss the potential solutions to the idea of breaking circuits.
- To be able to ask questions about the conditions, needs and purpose of the challenge set.
- To be able to identify requirements and constraints of the set challenge.

Thought Processes/Engineering Habits of Mind (EHOM)
Communication, systems thinking

Key Questions	Vocabulary	Resources
• What actions happen when someone leaves a room? What forces are exerted on the door frame, carpet, etc.? • How can we secure our alarm, so it does not get knocked off? • What materials do we have to carry out the problem? • How far will the alarm be from the switch? • How can we make the alarm loud enough? • How can we make the warning light bright enough?	• Circuit • Switches • Bulb • Battery • Conductor • Insulator • Current • Attract • Repel • Magnet	• Batteries • Bulbs • Bulb holder • Crocodile clips • Battery holder • Masking tape • Buzzers • Cardboard • Scissors • Aluminium foil • Paper fasteners. • Small screwdrivers • Wires • Wire strippers/cutters • Foam • Cardboard • Clothes pegs • Button magnets • Magnetic coins or washers

Identifying the requirements and constraints of the set challenge
- Discussions about what the children need to know to provide a solution to the challenge set
- In groups, each group composes three questions to ask about the parameters of the challenge set
- Children writing lists of challenge constraints and requirements
- Children complete 'exploring ideas' section on their EDP worksheet
- Examine the range of materials and tools available to use
- Teachers may need to prompt and guide children on any missed information (e.g., time allowance, conditions that the product will be used in, materials available, etc.)

Thinking about circuits and switches
- Children are asked to draw how they would make a lightbulb light up if they had a battery, bulb, and wires in a circuit. Teacher to check levels of understanding.
- Give children wires, batteries, bulb holder, and bulbs and see if they can light up the bulb.
- For a further challenge, see if they can light a bulb with one wire and a battery.
- Ask the children what they think is happening in the wires.

Investigating Conduction
In a small group of about 3, each with a simple circuit with a bulb and battery and two crocodile clips. Use the simple circuit to explore objects around the classroom and whether they conduct electricity.

Activity 1
Go around classroom with exploring items which conduct electricity and those that do not and what they are made of. Items could be radiators, desks, taps, metal spoons, wooden paintbrush, scissors, paper, cardboard, pencil case, etc.

Activity 2
Present the children with a selection of materials and ask them to predict which would conduct electricity and which would not. Test which actually do conduct electricity with a simple circuit. These materials could include: the inside of a graphite pencil, an aluminium foil take-away dish, aluminium foil backed take away pot lid with foil on one side, a button magnet, coins, washers, cotton wool, plastic bottle lids, drinks can, cardboard, Sellotape, paper fastener, twig, foam, etc.

What do the children notice? Is it only metals that conduct electricity?

Activity 3
Ask 4 groups to make a different switch to put into their simple circuit.

Group 1 - Make a switch with cardboard and paper fasteners.

Group 2 - Make a pressure switch with cardboard and foil on either side connected to the circuit. When the card is folded, it completes the circuit.

Group 3 - Make a magnetic switch. Fasten two button magnets to a washer and wires in a circuit. When the magnets are attracted to each other, the switch closes.

Group 4 - Make tilt switches with a film cannister, paper fasteners, and a piece of aluminium foil.

Bring the children together and ask the groups to explain how their switches work to the rest of the class. Emphasise that they are breaking and completing the circuit allowing the flow of current. Which materials in the switches are conductors and which are insulators?

Assessment
Children can draw a complete circuit with power source.
  Children understand that a switch is a break in the circuit.
  Children can identify conductors and insulators and recognise some features of conductors.

Science focus

 EDP stage: Developing ideas

Science Content Learning Objectives:
To gain some ideas of the possible solutions that exist.

Design and Technology Learning Objectives:
- To investigate how comparable products have been made (how the alarms work, how they complete a circuit and break the circuit).

- What materials/processes are used to connect the door or person to the alarm.
- To use information from a variety of sources to generate ideas for potential solutions.

Key Questions	Vocabulary	Resources
• What is the alarm made from? Why do you think that this material was chosen? • How does the circuit get broken or joined? • What have you seen or used before that may help you to develop ideas? • What can we find out about what other, comparable products are made of? • What have you found out from your research/looking at other products that could help you with your own designs?	• Circuit • Switches • Bulb • Battery • Conductor • Insulator • Current • Attract • Repel • Magnet	• Children's engineer worksheet • Access to internet • List of search terms that could be used • School project alarm • Simple alarm

Activities
- Brainstorm imagination activities in small groups to produce wild and whacky solutions.
- Share ideas discovered or imagined.
- Complete the 'developing ideas' section of the photocopiable children's engineering page.

Examine the properties of materials used in comparable products and discuss why these materials have been chosen.

- Ask the children to examine what they have at home or what they have seen before and what they have researched online. What are these items made from?
- Have a selection of switches available for children to examine. What are they made from and why? How do they break the circuit?
- Internet or literature-based research about designs or products that could provide ideas.
- Using real items or internet searches, investigate the range of materials used to made comparable items. Which material would be best for the product and why?
- Look at the clothes peg alarm or pressure switch (Figure 10.1). Ask the children:
  - How could these switches be used when someone opens a door?
  - How could the product be improved?
  - Which ideas could you take to use in your own product?

Assessment
Children can make a reasonable and relevant choice of product relating to the materials available to them and can justify this choice.
   Children can investigate related products and identify features that they could incorporate into their own designs and products.
   Children can articulate a range of ideas about potential products and solutions.

176 Science focus

EDP stage: Designing ideas

Science Content Learning Objectives:
To be able to apply understanding of the principles conducting and insulating electricity in their designs.

Design and Technology Learning Objectives:
- To be able to draw and design a set of plans relating to an intended product.
- To be able to analyse and evaluate plans and potential products for their suitability in meeting the requirements of the challenge set.

Thought Processes/Engineering Habits of Mind (EHOM)
Analyse, compare, evaluate, visualise, adapt

Key Questions	Vocabulary	Resources
• Why have you decided on your final product design? • What makes this one better than your other options? • How does your design meet the challenge and the constraints/requirements set out in the 'explore' stage? • Do you anticipate any problems or issues when making your product?	• Analyse, compare, evaluate, visualise, adapt • Research, investigate • Conduct • Insulate • Attract • Repel • Wires • Battery or cell • Bulb • Current • Voltage • Buzzer • Motor	• Children's EDP worksheet

Activities
- Identify and design three ideas for products to be made.
- Draw up three different plans for a potential product.
- Evaluate and assess which of these ideas best meets the requirements set out in the 'ignite' and 'explore' stages of the EDP.
- Explain product choice to others in the class and share reasoning about why this product has been chosen.
- Identify how the separate parts of the product will be joined together or how any attachments will be added on.
- Complete the 'designing ideas' section on the children's engineer worksheet.

During this stage, the children may need to test out some of the materials/ingredients to be used. See also the linked scientific investigations below.

Assessment
Children can select on design from a range and articulate why this is the most suitable choice.
   Children can explain how they will join the separate components of their product together and explain why they have chosen this method.

Science focus

 EDP stage: Making, testing, and improving ideas

Science Content Learning Objectives:		
To be able to apply scientific understanding of conductors, insulators, and switches within a 'real-world' context.		
Design and Technology Learning Objectives:		
• To develop explicit skills connecting a circuit using wire strippers, cutter, screwdrivers. • To be able to turn a design for a solution to a set problem into a product. • To be able to test a product against a set of pre-determined criteria (from the 'exploring ideas' stage). • To be able to share ideas and use and adapt the ideas of others.		
Thought Processes/Engineering Habits of Mind (EHOM) Analyse, compare, evaluate, improve		
Key Questions	Vocabulary	Resources
• Does your product answer Kasper's problem? • Does your product meet all the specifications set out in the 'exploring ideas' stage? • Did you encounter any problems when making your product? • What solutions to these problems did you find? • Did other groups encounter similar problems? What solutions did they produce? • Did you choose the most appropriate material to make your product out of? Why/why not?	• Test, improve, evaluate, improve, appraise • Evaluate • Criteria • Conduct • Insulate • Break circuit • Switch	• Children's engineer worksheet • Batteries/cell • Wires • Wire cutters/strippers • Screwdrivers • Battery holders • Buzzers • Bulbs • Clothes pegs • Silver foil • Card • Sponge • Cd's • String • Crocodile clips • Bulb holders • Motors • Film cannisters or small pots • Ball bearing or marble covered in silver foil • Paper fasteners • Balsa wood • Compass or bradawl • Blue tack • Tape, Elastic bands • Craft knife • Cutting board • Magnets

Activities

Explicit Skills Teaching and Health and Safety
- Teach children to use wire strippers and cutters. Explain how to attach wires to crocodile clips and/or bulb holders.
- Explain to children why you are using low-voltage batteries and not to try this with the mains electricity at home. Children could make safety posters or warning signs.
- Teachers will need to decide which pieces of equipment are suitable for the children in their classes based on the age and skills level of the children.
- Demonstrations of how to use various tools such as scissors, glue guns, or craft knives safely.

Making Activities
- Time for children to make their designed product.
- During this stage, the children may need to test out some of the materials/ingredients to be used.
- Children will need to think about how they intend to fix the alarm to the door.

Testing and Appraising Ideas
- Set up design on desk or table at first; use cupboard door as well a classroom door if there are many children wanting to test their designs at the same time.
- Set up the alarm system and ask a group of children to sit away from view. Can they tell when someone has stepped on the doormat or closed the door stc by hearing the alarm sound?
- Use the Children's engineering worksheet to evaluate.

What went well, which parts of the design did not work so well, what needs to be improved?
- During this stage, the children may need to test out some of the materials/ingredients to be used.

Improving Ideas
- Often, during this stage the children encounter problems with their product. This provides an opportunity to revisit the science involved to help them to solve these issues. For example, if their switch is on all the time under a carpet, they need to use an insulator to keep the contacts apart unless pressure is applied.
- Again, when encountering issues this would be a good opportunity for children to go back to do some further research (e.g., How are homemade alarms fitted to doors and what with)?
- During this stage, the children may need to test out some of the components to be used.

Share ideas, using and adapting the ideas of others
- Children display their part or fully completed products alongside their designs. All children move around the classroom to examine the work of others. Encourage the children to note down good ideas that they could use in their own designs and products.
- Ask each child/group of children to share an issue or triumph that they have had with their design and product. The rest of the class can either use the idea that worked or offer a solution to the issue experienced.
- Children then return to their own designs and products and adapt considering this new information.

Assessment

Children can describe what worked well and what did not work so well.

They can evaluate if they have met the design brief and if they have solved the original challenge set.

They can offer solutions to various problems encountered by themselves and others.

Their product shows the application of the relevant scientific principles.

Linked Science Investigations	**Investigating Electricity** There are three different activities the class could do here. The children could do each activity, or groups could each do one activity and report back to the class on their findings: • Explore the effect of greater voltage batteries on buzzers and bulbs. • Explore the impact of more buzzers/bulbs in a circuit with the same battery source. • Explore series and parallel circuits. *Activity 1* Make a circuit with a bulb, a battery, and two wires. Connect the circuit and see how many layers of tracing paper you can see the light through or use a light meter to measure the brightness. Put another battery into the circuit in the same circuit. What happens to the bulb brightness? Measure through the tracing paper or with the light metre. Try the same activity with one buzzer in your circuit. What happens to the buzzer sound? *Activity 2* Make a simple circuit with a bulb, bulb holder, battery, battery holder, wires, and crocodile clips. See how many layers of tracing paper the children can see the bulb shining through. Put two bulbs in the circuit. Test with tracing paper or light metre. What happens to the brightness of the bulbs? Why do you think this happens? *Activity 3* Build a circuit with two bulbs, a battery, and wires all in one circle. Now try to build a circuit where each bulb has its own route to the battery with separate wires. Measure the brightness of the bulbs with the tracing paper of light meter. What do you notice? Why do you think this happens?

Health and safety

Children are often concerned about electrical shocks when studying electricity. Primary/elementary classrooms should not use above a 9 V battery. There is little likelihood of getting a shock that will burn with this voltage.

Children should be taught the difference between using a 3 V battery and main electricity. There are some good electrical safety materials: https://www.switchedonkids.org.uk/electrical-safety-in-your-homePrimary classrooms or https://www.bbc.co.uk/bitesize/topics/zj44jxs

However, there is a small risk of fire if a 9 V battery is used as an electromagnet. Just make sure the wires are disconnected when the magnet is not in use or if the battery is getting very warm.

Reusable batteries should not be used in primary/elementary classrooms.

Children should be careful with stripped electrical wire as this can be a bit sharp. It will not harm children much, but they should be careful when handling and avoid holding it near their faces and eyes.

When punching holes in materials it is good practice to have something behind to push against that will not harm children or surfaces. Cork, class erasers, and plasticine can all be useful materials.

Common misconceptions

One key misconception that children hold is that current gets used up, that electricity goes into a bulb, the bulb shines, and the electricity has been depleted. This is not helped by the fact that batteries or cells only have a limited amount of chemicals to make an electrical push; when this is used up, they stop producing the power.

The energy may have transferred into another sort of energy, such as light energy or heat, but the current (the movement of the electrons) still exists.

Children also may not understand the importance of an electrical circuit. They often draw pictures of one wire running from a battery to a bulb or motor. This is not surprising when you look around your home and see one wire running to an appliance. The wires also contain another wire to return the current. Children would benefit from activities where they construct different circuits.

Other children may hold an idea about clashing currents. They see the two wires travelling to a bulb and believe that the electricity coming down each wire will clash and make energy! The use of analogies can help understanding as could add some drama with children in a circle with a rope acting as the current.

Good resources for teaching electricity

The STEM learning website has some useful links to materials for teaching aspects of electricity. Electrical systems such as designing doorbells and an electric billboard.
https://www.stem.org.uk/system/files/elibrary-resources/legacy_files_migrated/19315-billboard-8345.pdf

The Engineer project has another engineering challenge where the children design a small vacuum cleaner for a desk.
https://www.stem.org.uk/system/files/elibrary-resources/legacy_files_migrated/37574-36530-Sweden%20-%20Super%20Sucker.pdf

The Institute of Engineering and Technology has a fun activity where you can make a battery from fruit.
https://www.stem.org.uk/resources/elibrary/resource/446795/fruit-lights

Festive light challenge:
https://www.hamilton-trust.org.uk/science/unit/558-electrical-festive-challenge/

Ideas about energy conservation, especially lightbulbs:
https://energysavingtrust.org.uk/advice/lighting/

Other engineering challenges related to electricity

- The school has planned a summer fair. You have been asked to run a stall. Design and make a game using batteries.
- You class has been studying the sea as a class topic. Can you design and make a lighthouse model that shines?
- You live with an older relative who is not too steady on their feet. Use a tilt switch design and an alarm that sounds a buzzer if they fall.

Bibliography

Our World in Data (2021) at https://ourworldindata.org/
The Energy Savings Trust (2023) at https://energysavingtrust.org.uk/advice/lighting/
United Nations (2013) Sustainable Development Goals at https://sdgs.un.org/goals/goal7
United Nations (2023) United Nations Development Programme Sustainable Development Goals accessed at https://www.undp.org/sustainable-development-goals/affordable-and-clean-energy

11 Summary and key thoughts

The challenges and activities set out in this book strive to present a true picture of how the STEM subjects (science, technology, engineering, and maths) are experienced in the real world. It is impossible to engineer a solution to a problem without drawing on the all aspects of STEM. Likewise, in this book, we have presented challenges that require children to draw on and and apply their scientific, design and technology skills, and knowledge to solve the engineering challenges set. This differs greatly from other approaches to engineering or design and technology where children are required to make a set product and are often given a set of instructions about how to do this.

In order for this approach to be successful, there are a few key points to remember:

1 **Explore the solutions to a similar problem and similar products.**
   Imagine being asked to design a balloon-powered car. Off the top of your head you may be able to come up with a few ideas and a reasonable solution, but spending some time researching designs and models made by others would result in a much more detailed and plausible solution. Often when we undertake design and technology work with children, we tell them what product they are going to make and ask them to draw up a plan. This leaves out the opportunity to research and therefore diminishes powerful learning opportunities.

   Researching similar solutions and products can offer children rich opportunities to extend their understanding of suitable materials, mechanisms, and construction skills as well as how scientific principles can be applied. Research activities should therefore be at the forefront of any design and technology activity.

2 **Do not tell the children what product to make.**
   By prescribing the product to be made, we not only restrict the creative responses that children may come up with but we also deny them the opportunity to experience how scientists and engineers work in the real world. By allowing the children freedom of choice about the product that they will make to address the engineering challenges, they will come up with a range of potential solutions, some of which you will not think of yourself.

   For example, when given a challenge of producing a cup holder for a day at the beach from newspaper, a group of students came up with the following solutions (Figure 11.1):

DOI: 10.4324/9781003325826-11

Summary and key thoughts 183

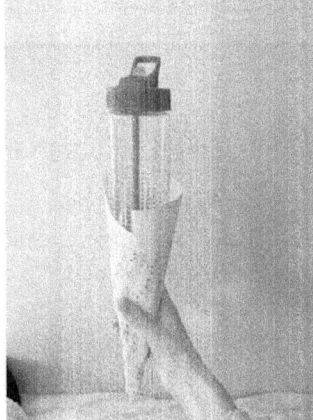

Figure 11.1 A range of cup holder solutions

- A traditional table with rolls of newspaper serving as the four table legs.
- Newspaper rolled into a cone shape. One end of which holds the cup and the other is set into the sand.
- A holder that hooks onto the side of a sun lounger.
- A holder with a handle which could either be carried or worn around the neck.
- A tripod holder.
- A woven basket which hooks onto a chair.
- A paper hat incorporating a cup holder and long straws!

Each of these potential solutions tackles the original engineering challenge in a unique way and applies scientific principles in a slightly different manner. The potential advantages and disadvantages of each potential solution can be discussed, emulating how engineers in the real world work more realistically.

3 **Before you start, consider the scientific understanding that the children will need to know and apply.**

The scientific principles underpinning the engineering challenges presented in this book need to be considered carefully before you introduce the children to the activities. Teachers will need to consider what prior knowledge the children have and where there may be gaps. This does not mean that all of the science has to be taught before starting the challenge, but instead that the teacher will need to plan which aspect of the scientific understanding will need to be understood and applied at different points. Teaching the skills and understanding as they are needed can help to show their relevance and importance to children.

4 **Share ideas.**

In the real world, engineers do not work in isolation. They take inspiration from the work of others and draw on the expertise of others when they face challenges. Emulating this way of working may be difficult for some children who view this as copying. However, sharing ideas and solutions to problems faced can be a powerful learning tool. Ideas of how children can be encouraged to share their ideas and incorporate the ideas of others into their own work are given in Chapter 2.

Using the engineering and science model for other challenges

In this book, we have suggested many design challenges that cover many areas of the science curriculum across physical, biological, and chemical sciences. However, it is always possible to use the engineering design process model to create your own challenges for your class. Some of the key issues to consider are what the science is, how to cover some significant science content in the challenge, and to keep the challenge open-ended in its remit. As stated previously, if you give children a very closed challenge, an engineering task can easily become a making task which will not engage the children in the range of thinking skills and engineering habits of mind.

In designing an engineering task, it is desirable to have a context that is familiar to the children. Contexts can come from everyday occurrences or fictional starting points. Everyday occurrences could be the teacher's coffee going cold on playground duty, the kindergarten toys getting wet in the rain, or a large energy bill for the school. If the school is investing in a new outbuilding or shelter or place to park a bicycle, the children can be involved in researching the problem and perhaps given a role in informing or briefing the architect. The occurrences may be spotted by the children or the teacher. In either case, it provides a real-life challenge to investigate.

In some cases, the real-life challenge may prove difficult as there may be a danger to children. For example, making large waterproof signs to slow traffic near the school may involve children being out on the road to research the issue. It may also contravene local traffic rules as the signs can prove to be a distraction to driver and may need to be approved by the local council. The activities may need a risk assessment.

Other inspiration can come from children's fiction. The books can be read, and then the challenger proposed to the class. Here are some current children's fiction and some ideas of areas for challenges:

Using Fiction as Inspiration

Aardema, V (2019) *Bringing the rain to Kapiti Plain*. Macmillan. Could we devise a watering device?

Armitage, R and D (2022) The lighthouse keeper's lunch. Scholastic. How can we help the lighthouse keeper? Design a pulley to transport the Lighthouse keeper's lunch. Design a cover for a basket that is seagull-proof.

Burroway, J (2010) *The giant jam sandwich*. Red Fox. How can we keep the wasps away from jam sandwiches?

Davies, B (2022) *The storm whale*. Simon and Schuster. Can we design and make something to transport a small whale?

Donaldson, J (2017) *Room on a broom*. Macmillan. Can we come up with a solution for the witch to carry her wand and hat when in the air?

Jeffers, O (2027) *The way back home*. Harper Collins. Can we design something will allow the boy to land safely on Earth?

Murphy, J (2018) *Peace at last*. Macmillan. How can we design something to block out sounds for the bear so he can sleep?

Sustainability Inspiration

The sustainability focus used in this book can raise many challenges for the classroom as it does for humankind. It can be an effective approach in learning about environmental issues without the emphasis on the lack of power that the children have in addressing some huge global issues. Ecoanxiety can negatively affect children (Baker et al., 2021). A sustainable engineering approach can model the global community in taking on the challenges of climate change and its impact. Technology could be one way of addressing global problems, but personal responsibility and actions can also be another way of addressing environmental issues. The knowledge and understanding accompanying the challenges in this book may help to inform and help children make decisions about their future actions and behaviours.

Some significant areas of school life can be considered for study within the classroom or from the child's home. The Eco-schools project identifies areas for study, some of which are:

Biodiversity and nature – within the school environment and school grounds.

Climate change – how the school community's actions affect the production of carbon dioxide.

Energy – within the classroom and around the school.

Water – consumption in schools.

Litter – in and around school.

Transport – to and from school.

Waste – from the school community (https://www.eco-schools.org.uk/).

Within these themes, there is a range of challenges and possible solutions that the children could develop.

If you feel that this focus is too local, and you want the children to have a wider perspective, Practical Action has excellent challenges from developing countries, e.g., finding hand-washing solutions (https://practicalaction.org/schools), which provide an understanding of some of the challenges of living in certain areas of the world and offers low-tech solutions to the issues.

Cross-curricular learning

Teaching science and engineering together is a form of cross-curricular learning. Knowledge, skills, and understanding do not fit neatly into the subject boxes ascribed by curricula. We also know there is overlap in science and other subjects such as maths, geography, and even music; for example, data handling and sounds. This book uses a cross-curricular approach, combining design technology or engineering with science. It can be tempting to think what other subjects you can squeeze into the topic; this should, however, come with a word of caution as there are pros and cons of a cross-curricular approach.

The advantage of this approach is that, as stated before, it presents knowledge in a more natural form; it can be highly motivating for children if it draws on their interests or if it gives them an amount of autonomy (Barnes, 2015). It can foster transferable skills in a range of contexts that may better prepare children for adulthood than atomised teaching (Laurie, 2015). It can also be a convenient way to deliver an overcrowded curriculum.

However, it requires sound teacher subject knowledge across the disciplines and careful planning to make sure one subject is not diluted to such an extent that there is little meaningful learning happening (Barnes, 2018; Rowley and Cooper, 2009). In this book, we have tried to present models of dual-focus cross-curricular teaching (Barnes, 2015); the design technology skills and processes are complemented by the science. In many countries, science and technology are taught together. When the teacher tries to incorporate several subjects together, it can be harder to keep the integrity of each subject intact and the learning meaningful. Colouring in a design is different from being taught art skills.

Extending engineering and science learning

Through this work, you and your children may want to explore the world of engineering or the scientific principles covered in more depth. There are many ways of doing this, but taking learning outside of the classroom through making external links is a great way of entrenching learning in a real-world context. Try exploring the following:

- Draw on the expertise of parent and carers
  If the parents or carers of the children in your school work within STEM-based industries, invite them into school to talk to the children. This can be about their work and how they use STEM within their work, but it can also be a wider look at their career (what they had to study and when, what they enjoy doing in their free time, TV programmes that they watch, etc.). This can help the children to see STEM specialists as real people whom they can connect to and have things in common with.
- Local businesses and industry
  Many STEM-based industries will have STEM outreach workers who can come into schools to run activities based on their work. They may also offer trips and visits to their sites. Not only does this show children how the subjects that they learn about at school are used in real jobs, it also gives them an opportunity to meet and get to know scientists and engineers. For children who do not have the opportunity to talk to scientists and engineers within their own families or communities, this can be a valuable experience.
- Look out for local STEM or engineering events locally.
  Local museums often run speciality days, where additional events are laid on for the general public. There may also be local festivals with a STEM theme that run annual basis such as a festival of nature that are worth looking out for. Even just informing parents and carers about these is a good step to take.
- Investigate institutions such as the IOP or IMechE.

Institutions such as the Institute of Physics (IOP) or mechanical Engineers (IMechE) (UK) produce a range of resources and ideas for use in the classroom. These are usually available for free and have been designed by a range of experts.
- Museums, etc.
  Don't forget your local museums and galleries. They have their regular exhibitions to visit but also often offer additional workshops on specific themes for classes of children.
- Community resources.
  Some farms offer visits and activities that explore forces (e.g., tractor pulling) or old mills offer opportunities to see mechanisms such as levers or pulleys in action.

Bibliography

Baker, C. *et al*. (2021) Educating for resilience: Parent and teacher perceptions of children's emotional needs in response to climate change. *Environmental Education Research [Online]*, 27(5), 687–705.

Barnes, J. (2018) *Applying Cross-Curricular Approaches Creatively: The Connecting Curriculum*. London: Routledge.

Barnes, J. (2015) *Cross-Curricular Learning 3–14 [Online]*, 3rd ed. London: Sage Publications.

Laurie, J. (2015) Planning and preparation for cross-curricular learning and teaching. In: Kerry, T., ed., *Cross-Curricular Teaching in the Primary School: Planning and Facilitating Imaginative Lessons [Online]*, 2nd ed. (pp. 126–127). London: Routledge.

Rowley, C., and Cooper, H. (2009) *Cross-Curricular Approaches to Teaching and Learning [Online]*. London: Sage Publications.

Appendix

Engineering Challenge   Name...

Igniting ideas

What is the problem you are being asked to solve?

Exploring ideas

What are three questions that you have about the problem (e.g., materials available, use of product, amount of time)?

1.

2.

3.

Things I need to think about when designing my solution.

Copyright material from Fay Lewis and Juliet Edmonds (2024), *Children as Engineers,* Routledge.

190 *Appendix*

 Developing ideas

When researching the challenge, here are some ideas I have found. Internet pictures, solutions sold in shops, fixing ideas.

Copyright material from Fay Lewis and Juliet Edmonds (2024), *Children as Engineers,* Routledge.

Designing ideas

Here are three of my ideas: Name..

Copyright material from Fay Lewis and Juliet Edmonds (2024), *Children as Engineers,* Routledge.

The one I like best is..

I think it is best because..

Making, testing, and improving ideas

Challenge Solution Evaluation Name..

What went well?

What parts of your design did not work so well?

What innovative ideas did other people produce?

Further research/findings

What would you tell someone else who was trying to solve the challenge problem?

Index

Pages in *italics* refer to figures and pages in **bold** refer to tables.

Aardema, V. 184
Abrahams, I. 34
activity: class to draw an engineer 12; engineering a cup of tea 9; perceptions of engineers 12; relevance of STEM subjects 13; working with engineers 15-16
agricultural engineering 41
Albrecht, B. 1
Aligiyah, G. 42
American Chemistry Society (ACS) 55
animal and humans: activities 71; aims of 57; design and technology content 61, **61**; EDP stages 61, **62-69**; engineering challenge 57; health and safety 70; heated wheat bags 58, *59*; misconceptions 71; potential solutions 58; resources 70-71; science content 59-60; science description 60; sustainable development goals 57-58; vocabulary 60
Armitage, D. 184
Armitage, R. 184
Ausubel, D. P. 2

Banks, F. 1
Barlex, D. 1
Beggs, J. 4
Burroway, J. 184

Cambridge English Dictionary 162
case studies: building a vacuum cleaner 3, *4*; engineering habits of mind 24-25; making a floating platform 5, *6*

Childrens' Engineering Challenge Sheet 31, 39, 41, 57, 73, 88, 108, 125, 146, 164
cross-curricular learning 186-187

Davies, B. 184
designing ideas, EDP 29, **49-50**, **100-101**, **139-140**, **154-155**, **176**
developing ideas, EDP 28, **48-49**, **64-66**, **99-100**, **138-139**, **153-154**, **175**
DeWitt, J. 12
Donaldson, J. 184

electricity: activities 181; aims of 164; batteries and circuits 170; cardboard pressure switch *165*, *166*; design and technology content 171, **171**; EDP stage 171, **172-179**; energy efficiency 167; engineering challenge 164, 181; health and safety 179-180; misconceptions 180; potential solutions 164-167, *165*, *166*; resources 180; science content 169; sustainable development goals 167, 169; switches 170-171; tilt switch *168*; vocabulary 169-170
engineering: cross-curricular learning 185-187; description 1, 7-8; engineered objects 8, *8*; impact of teaching science 14-15; importance of 12-14; picture selection 9; product and problems 182-184, *183*; public and children's perceptions 10-12, *11*; science learning 186-187; STEM; (see STEM (science, technology, engineering, and maths) subjects);

Index

sustainability inspiration 185; using fiction as inspiration 184-185; working with engineers 15

Engineering Design Process (EDP) 1, 20, *32*; designing ideas 29, **49-50, 100-101, 139-140, 154-155, 176**; design specification 20, 21; developing ideas 28, **48-49, 64-66, 99-100, 138-139, 153-154, 175**; down selection stage 22, *22*; EHoM 23, *24*; exploring ideas 27, 35-36, **46-47, 62-64, 97-98, 136-137, 151-152, 173-174**; igniting ideas 26, **45-46, 62, 96-97, 135-136, 150-151, 172**; incorporating ideation *21*; making, testing and improving ideas 30, 37-38, **50-53, 66-69, 101-105, 140-142, 155-159, 177-179**; opportunities for science 35; plans and drawings 22; primary classroom 25-26; school curriculum 37-38; science curricula 31-35; stages of *21*; technical knowledge 37-38; testing and improving ideas 36-37

engineering habits of mind (EHoM) 23-25, *24*

English, J. 1

EU Engineer project 14

everyday materials: absorbency/waterproofing 76; activities 88; aims of 73; design and technology content 77, **77**; EDP stage 77, **78-86**; engineering challenge 73; flexible/rigid 76; health and safety 86-87; misconceptions 87; opaque/translucent/transparent 76-77; potential solutions 74; resources 87; resources for activities 86; scientific content 74-75; sustainable development goals 73-74; thermal insulation and conductivity 76; vocabulary 75

exploring ideas, EDP 27, 35-36, **46-47, 62-64, 97-98, 136-137, 151-152, 173-174**

Fogg-Rogers, L. A. 12

food technology: activities 163; aims of 145-146; allergies and intolerances 162; avoid picking wild plants 162; design and technology content 149-150, **150**; diet and nutrition 162-163; EDP stages 150, **150-159**; engineering challenge 145; filtration and sieving 149; health and safety 160-162; hot water kettles and pans 161-162; hygiene 162; knives *160*, 160-161, *161*; misconceptions 162-163; potential solutions 147; resources 159-160, 163; scientific content 147-148; soluble and insoluble elements 148-149; sustainable development goals 146-147; vocabulary 148

forces: aims of 108; challenges 123; design and technology content *113*, 113-115, **114-115**; EDP stages 115, **115-122**; engineering challenge 108; gravity 112-113, 123; health and safety 123; levers 113-115; misconceptions 123; potential solutions 109-110; resources 124; scientific content 110-111; sustainable development goals 109; toys and waste 109; vocabulary 111-112

Fralick, B. 10

Gomez, A. 1

gravity: cars travelling down slopes 112; friction 112-113, 123; mass and weight 112; misconceptions 123

Guardian newspaper 146

igniting ideas, EDP 26, **45-46, 62, 96-97, 135-136, 150-151, 172**

Institute of Engineering technology 87, 163

International Food Policy Institute 42

Jeffers, O. 185

light and sound: aims of 125; design and technology content 133, **133-135**; EDP stages 135, **135-142**; engineering challenge 125; health and safety 142-143; misconceptions 143; opaque/translucent/transparent 132; potential solutions 127, **128-130**; resources 142, 143-144; scientific content 127-131; shadows 132-133, 143; sustainable development goals 126-127; vocabulary 131-132

living things and habitats: activities 107; adaptation 92-93; aims of 88; biodiversity 90-91; classification 93-94; design and technology content 94, **94-96**; EDP stages 96, **96-105**; engineering challenge 88; food chains, webs, and pyramids 91-92, *92*; habitats 90-91; health and safety 106-107; interdependence 93; microorganisms and decomposition 93; misconceptions 107; potential solutions 89;

resources 106; scientific content 89-90; sustainable development goals 88-89; vocabulary 90

making, testing and improving ideas, EDP 30, 37-38, **50-53**, **66-69**, **101-105**, **140-142**, **155-159**, **177-179**
Murphy, C. 4
Murphy, J. 185

National Science Standards 5
Natural Resources Defence Council 146

OECD 4

photocopiable Childrens' Engineering Challenge Sheet 39-40
Physicists in primary schools (PIPS) 124
plants/states of matter: activities 55-56; aims of 41; design and technology content 44-45; EDP stages 45, **45-54**; engineering challenge 41; evaporation 55; health and safety 54; misconceptions 55; resources 54, 55; science content 43; science description 43-44; sustainable development goals 41-43; vocabulary 43; water 43-44

Reiss, M. 34
Royal Academy of Engineering 12, 14, 25

Science and Plants for Schools (SAPS) 55
science curriculm: children's ideas and misconceptions 33-34; measurement 32; planning and carrying out investigations 32; raising scientific questions 31-32; recording and evaluating results 33; vocabulary 34-35
STEM (science, technology, engineering, and maths) subjects: engineering challenges 2, 182-184; learning 4-7, 7; multidisciplinary approach 1; in primary classroom 16; problems 16-17; real-world inquiry-based context 2-4
sustainable development goals (SDGs): electricity 167, 169; everyday materials 73-74; food technology 146-147; forces 109; light and sound 126-127; living things and habitats 88-89; plants/states of matter 41-43

UN Sustainable Development Goals 2, 41, 57, 167
U.S. Next Generation Science Standards 23

For Product Safety Concerns and Information please contact our EU
representative GPSR@taylorandfrancis.com
Taylor & Francis Verlag GmbH, Kaufingerstraße 24, 80331 München, Germany

www.ingramcontent.com/pod-product-compliance
Lightning Source LLC
Chambersburg PA
CBHW060300240426
43661CB00060B/2851